To the Rangers and Naturalists
of California's Desert Lands

Borrego Palm Canyon

The Anza-Borrego

Desert Region

Lowell and Diana Lindsay

Published in Cooperation with
the California Department of Parks and Recreation,
the Anza-Borrego Desert Natural History Association and
the U.S. Department of the Interior, Bureau of Land
Management, California Desert District

Wilderness Press
BERKELEY

FIRST EDITION October 1978
Second printing April 1979
Third printing April 1982
Fourth printing May 1983
Fifth printing March 1984
SECOND EDITION November 1985
Second printing August 1986
Third printing August 1988
THIRD EDITION July 1991

Cover photo by Lowell Lindsay
Maps by Lowell Lindsay
Design by Thomas Winnett
Library of Congress Catalog Number 91-20170
International Standard Book Number 0-89997-129-6
Printed in the United States of America

Published by   Wilderness Press
                2440 Bancroft Way
                Berkeley, CA 94704
                (415) 843-8080
Write for free catalog

Library of Congress Cataloging-in-Publication Data

Lindsay, Lowell.
    The Anza-Borrego Desert region / Lowell and Diana Lindsay.
    -- New ed.
        p.   cm.
    "Published in cooperation with the California Department of
Parks and Recreation, the Anza-Borrego Natural History Association ,
and the U.S. Department of the Interior, Bureau of Land Management, California Desert District."
    Includes bibliographical references and index.
    ISBN 0-89997-129-6
    1. Hiking--California--Anza-Borrego Desert State Park--Guide-
books. 2. Outdoor recreation--California--Anza-Borrego Desert State
Park--Guide-books. 3. Desert survival. 4. Anza-Borrego Desert State
Park (Calif.)--Guide-books. I. Lindsay, Diana, 1944- . II. Title
        GV199.42.C22A594   1991   91-20170
        917.94'98--dc20   CIP

Photo Credits

Patty Brown: 58

California Department of Parks and Recreation: 2, 15 (bottom), 27, 34, 47, 50, 60, 61, 74, 76, 80,
    97, 113 (right), 120 (top), 137, 139, 147 (left), 165

Ella Calvert: 113 (left)

Rita Dahl: 111

Mark Jorgensen: 15 (top), 145

Diana Lindsay: 13, 72, 123, 151

Lowell Lindsay: 11, 13, 19, 35, 44, 66, 70, 86, 93, 95, 100, 120 (bottom), 122, 124, 127, 128, 134,
    147 (right), 148, 150, 159, 164

Richard L. Thompson: 75

Fred Wood Collection: 51, 83

Preface and Acknowledgments
to the 3rd Edition

The most noticeable change to Anza-Borrego visitor services in recent years is the addition of the excellent Visitor Center near park headquarters. Of equal importance is the major role played by park volunteers and especially the Anza-Borrego Natural History Association which staffs the center. With budget cutbacks in Sacramento due to Proposition 13 and like measures, the state park system had to rely on park volunteers to fill in gaps. And that they have done. Volunteers have unselfishly offered assistance to park staff in such ways as developing the equestrian trail in Coyote Canyon, compiling research materials and newpaper clippings for the Visitor Center archives, becoming campground hosts, participating in scientific research, staffing the Visitor Center, becoming tour guides, and helping the park staff wherever needed. The ABDNHA has also taken on the responsibility of publishing some state park brochures, maps and interpretive materials. ABDNHA funds its expenses through donations and the sale of books in the Visitor Center. BLM's proposed desert center has not been as fortunate. With no driving force behind it, such as the state park has had with ABDNHA, plans for the proposed center have been shelved for the present.

Budget cuts have also resulted in the streamlining of park operations and ranger responsibilities. With less funds for park staffing, the park has had to cut back on some services previously offered. Visitors are now asked to pack out their own trash at several primitive camps where trash cans have been removed. All developed campsite and horse camp reservations are now on MISTIX, including group camps.

Nature has also played a role in streamlining. Some of the previously light auto roads have deteriorated and have become jeep trails or hiking trails only.

Mountain bicycling has achieved great popularity. Some jeep routes are now attractive bicycle routes. Popular downhill routes include Oriflamme, Grapevine and Coyote canyons. New hiking trails are being established also. The route of the Pacific Crest Trail is finalized in the Anza-Borrego region.

Scientific updating has caused some name changes of plants and Indian understanding and reinterpretation of the Yuha Man.

The authors wish to express their sincere appreciation to the following for assisting in the revision of this guidebook, thereby contributing substantially to a more accurate and useful body of knowledge for this valuable natural resource. First and foremost to Mark Jorgensen, Anza-Borrego Desert State Park naturalist, whose careful research, extensive and intensive knowledge of this desert, and detailed line by line review was crucial. To Art Morley, retired Anza-Borrego Desert State Park ranger, who carefully reviewed the first edition and provided numerous notes for revision in the test and in the foldout map. To the Visitor Center staff, park office staff, and state park rangers Patty Brown, Manfred Knaak, Fred Gee, Chris Smith, and Paul Remeika, who patiently answered questions and checked items in question. To state park ranger Jim Meier, who dedicated substantial time to verifying Coyote Canyon details. To Ken Smith, Anza-Borrego Desert State Park chief ranger, who readily and cheerfully offered assistance, encouragement and warm friendship through many years. To Dave Van Cleve, Anza-Borrego Desert State Park area manager, who offered the fullest and finest cooperation of his staff.

To Roger Zortman, area manager of the El Centro office of the Bureau of Land Management, and his staff for checking references to lands managed by BLM. To Anza-Borrego Foundation trustee and avid desert archeologist Bob Begole for his insights about paleo Indians and to Ken Hedges, curator of anthropology and ethnology at the San Diego Museum of Man in Balboa Park, for his input on the Indians of the Anza-Borrego Desert. To Geoff Levin, curator of botany at the San Diego Museum of Natural History, for his assistance as well as that of Ann Terry who checked park physical features for us.

To all of these and others who have offered encouragement and assistance, we are most grateful. You too, mom!

Lowell and Diana Lindsay
La Mesa, California
May 1991

Acknowledgments To 1st Edition

The authors wish to express sincere appreciation to the following for their invaluable assistance and encouragement, without which the *Guide to the Anza-Borrego Desert Region* would have remained an incomplete set of weathered notes buried variously in backpacks, jeep glove compartments and among mislaid letters.

To Maurice H. (Bud) Getty, manager of Anza-Borrego Desert State Park, for extensive, in-depth support of field work, review of text, encouragement and for many years of warmest friendship.

To Jack Welch, manager of San Diego Coast Area of the California State Park System, who provided highly detailed and extensive ranger patrol reports from the 1950s and who checked descriptions along the Anza trail.

To the many California State Park Rangers stationed at Anza-Borrego Desert State Park who have provided information and have taken us out on numerous patrols, including Gar Salzgeber, John McBride, Glenn Mincks, Terry Brann, Dan Tuttle, Ken Jones, Mark Jorgensen and naturalist Paul Johnson, with particular thanks to Ranger George Leetch, who has provided us years of cooperation and wisdom in our desert travels.

To the staff of the El Centro office of the Bureau of Land Management for their assistance and review of the text, especially former El Centro Resource Area Manager Cliff Yardley, current area manager David Mari and their staffs.

For official sanction of the book by the following agencies and organizations: California Department of Parks and Recreation; U.S. Dept. of the Interior, Bureau of Land Management, Riverside District Office; and the Anza-Borrego Desert Natural History Association.

To Dr. Robert Sawvell, professor of geography at West Texas State University, for extensive assistance and advice in the preparation of the maps for the text.

To William Knyvett, publisher of *Desert Magazine,* for permission to use Marshal South's "Tracks of the Overland Stage" in its entirety.

To Carl Bullock, associate director of the Santa Ana-Tustin YMCA, who has provided extensive field-work support and encouragement through the years.

To Thomas Winnett and Jeff Schaffer at Wilderness Press, who have carefully edited the text, provided invaluable technical assistance and developed an attractive format.

And to all the other friends and relatives who have helped to gather information.

Lowell and Diana Lindsay
Amarillo, Texas
January 5, 1978

Contents

List of Maps and Charts

AREA AND TRIP INDEX

6

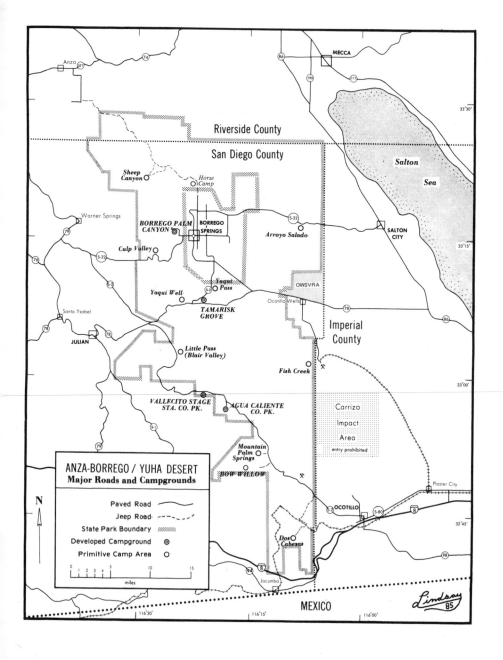

ANZA-BORREGO / YUHA DESERT
Major Roads and Campgrounds

N

Paved Road
Jeep Road
State Park Boundary
Developed Campground
Primitive Camp Area

0 1 2 3 4 5   10   15
miles

Introduction

The Anza-Borrego region is a vast and intriguing land covering much of San Diego County and parts of Riverside and Imperial counties from the Santa Rosa Mountains to the Mexican border. Its name captures the relationship of man and the land in the southwestern desert of California. Juan Bautista de Anza was the Spanish captain of the epic 1776 San Francisco colonial expedition. Borrego, Spanish word for bighorn sheep, is the very symbol of desert wilderness. The two names are paired in Anza-Borrego to highlight the intertwined human and natural history of this recreational preserve.

From prehistoric Indians through weekend vacationers, men have called this desert home, some for all their time, others for some of their time. From piney mountain crags to windy inland sea, a rich variety of desert plants and animals dwell, in terrain and landforms as different as their inhabitants. In its more than one million acres, about equally divided between Anza-Borrego Desert State Park and the federal Bureau of Land Management, the Anza-Borrego region appeals to a broad range of recreationists: off-highway vehicle drivers, backpackers, hikers, horsemen, mountain bicyclists, nature seekers and campers.

This guidebook is for all of those who come with a sense of care for a unique land and a desire to know and explore more of its secrets. It is likewise a reminder that the price of preserving the desert recreation experience for generations to come is responsible use of an irreplaceable and fragile resource. The park slogan, "Parks Are Forever, With Your Help," means just that.

Climate

Winters are generally mild, average daily temperatures ranging from 42° to 73°. Summer temperatures will rise above 100°, the hottest months being July, August and September, while December, January and February are the coolest. Daily temperatures and amount of yearly precipitation vary with elevation, the higher elevations being slightly cooler and having more precipitation. Average yearly precipitation has varied from five inches to as much as 14 inches in recent years.

Two distinct rainy seasons occur. Winter rains are of the Pacific marine type, which brings the steady rains needed to germinate spring flowers. Spectacular displays of wildflowers may occur from February through May if rainfall has been sufficient. The summer rains, on the other hand, are the Gulf marine type, and they are responsible for summer thunderstorms that cause fast water runoff and flash floods. These summer storms can be fierce and can cause considerable damage. Cloudbursts and the menace of floods almost always accompany a summer storm.

Running water, as in a flash flood, is the most effective agent of erosion. Wind, which can carry small sand particles that act as a cutting abrasive, is another eroder. Water and wind together have carved out the familiar desert landscape features, and these have been uplifted and shifted around by various movements along faults in the Anza-Borrego area. This desert landscape constantly undergoes change, as long as there continue to be running water, wind and earth movement.

Geologic History

But the Anza-Borrego area was not always a desert. It changed from part of an ocean to verdant grassland to the present desert largely because of dynamic forces along the great San Andreas fault system. The San Andreas is a gigantic fracture in the earth's crust running from the Gulf of California through the Salton Basin and San Gorgonio Pass and then along the Coast Ranges into the sea beyond San Francisco.

According to current geologic theory, much of present Baja and Southern California west of the San Andreas fault were once joined to the Mexican mainland several hundred miles south of their present positions. As the great continental and oceanic plates ground against each other, peninsular California sheared to the northwest, opening up the early Gulf of California, which extended as far north as San Gorgonio Pass. Through the eons the seas retreated and advanced as mountain building progressed. Thick Pliocene beds of oyster shells, coral reefs and other marine life exposed today along the eastern edge of the Anza-Borrego region tell the story of life in these ancient seas.

Meanwhile, the Colorado River was building its delta across the basin from near present-day Yuma west to the mountains. It is said that one can see the Grand Canyon of Arizona in the Yuha Desert in the sense that one can see sediments transported from the Grand Canyon into the Salton Basin by the Colorado River.

Once the ocean waters were effectively barred by the delta dam, conglomerates filled the basin, then grasslands, wooded areas and streams developed. A fresh-water lake formed in the area of today's Borrego Badlands. During the Pleistocene epoch, beginning some two million years ago, sabertooth cats, camels, turkeys, ducks, giant turtles and even an incredibly large condorlike vulture flourished.

Also during the Pleistocene epoch, vertical faulting became active, pushing the ridges that bordered the Salton trough to a higher elevation with each successive earthquake. It was this elevation of mountains which formed the geographic barrier between the Salton Trough and the coastal areas, preventing the cool, moist ocean breezes from reaching the trough.

The resulting "rainshadow" effect, coupled with drying of California climates in general, caused an arid climate to develop here, and a desert evolved about 15,000 years ago. Because of this change, grazing animals such as horses and camels moved out of the area to greener fields.

One last episode occurred perhaps a thousand years ago. Lake Cahuilla, a freshwater predecessor of the Salton Sea, was formed when the Colorado River temporarily shifted its course, filling the Salton Basin with 2000 square miles of lake. This lake became fringed with tule, arrowweed, willows, mesquite and palms, and was a haven for the Yuman Indians until it disappeared about 500 years ago. The fluctuations of the level of Lake Cahuilla are visible in the distinct terraces and tufa deposits left by this body of water. The high-water marker, 40 feet above sea level, can clearly be seen west of Highway 86 at Travertine Point. This 40-foot contour is higher than the cities of Indio, El Centro, Brawley, Calexico and Mexicali, as well as some of the richest farmland in the United States.

Today's Salton Sea was formed in 1905–07 when the Colorado River broke through irrigation floodgates near Yuma. Since then Hoover Dam and other dams have supposedly tamed the rampages of the Southwest's mightiest river. However, the ghosts of Lake Cahuilla and its ancestors born of the river still brood over the valley. Referring to these periodic inundations and man's control systems, a recent BLM report dryly remarks that "technology has merely introduced a temporary hiatus in the normal course of events."

Former monument at Travertine Rock

Desert Life

Although the topography and the climate have changed, the desert area still abounds with plant and animal life, including over 600 species of desert plants and over 350 kinds of vertebrate animals. Groups of these plants and animals are commonly associated with certain habitats, including desert wash, low desert and desert slope, chaparral, and pinyon juniper (see the table below).

Below are brief descriptions of the most commonly seen desert plants in the Anza-Borrego area. Scientific names are the latest that authorities have agreed upon.

Cresote bush (*Larrea tridentata*) is most common plant of the Colorado Desert and also one of the oldest. It is also know as "greasewood" because of its waxy leaf surface. This plant reaches a height of 15 feet. It has dark green leaves on a gray, black-ringed stem. Its yellow windmill-shaped bloom appears in April, followed by a white, fuzzy seed ball which is its fruit. The creosote's resiny sweet smell is particularly noticeable after a rain, which is the reason the Spanish called it *hediondilla*—"little stinker."

Burroweed (*Ambrosia dumosa*) appears most commonly in association with creosote. It is a low, rounded, white-barked shrub with ashy white foliage which is green only in the spring. Both desert bighorn sheep and wild burros use this plant as food. It is a member of the sunflower family, bearing yellow flowers in late fall and early spring.

Leafless during most of the year, the **ocotillo** (*Fouquieria splendens*) has thorny, whiplike cane branches which suddenly become green almost ovenight when the plant gets a little moisture. Its widespread, shallow root system gives these plants the unique ability to benefit from short periods of rainfall. This tall plant commonly grows on rocky soils, and it is conspicuous in Borrego Valley and especially in the mouth of Coyote Canyon. Its scarlet, flag-like bloom makes a striking show and is a favorite of photographers.

The **agave,** or century plant (*Agave deserti*), has thick, succulent leaves and grows in clusters from an underground root crown. In spring some of the older plants in a colony will send up 10-foot, asparaguslike stems on top of which short branches terminate in clusters of yellow blooms.

A member of the pea family, **mesquite** (*Prosopis glandulosa var. Torreyana*) will grow anywhere on the desert below 5000 feet elevation wherever ground water can be tapped by its root system, which may extend as deep as 150 feet. This depth is documented in a mine in Kansas. During the spring the thorny, 15–20-foot-tall tree has yellow blooms, which later bear the nutritious beans that are so important to the wildlife of the area and once were a staple of the local Indians.

Cat's-claw (*Acacia greggii*) is a deciduous shrub or small tree, a member of the pea family, that is found on rocky hillsides and in washes. It is extraordinarily spiny, and is also known as "wait-a-minute bush," "devil's-claw" and "tear-blanket." It has fragrant yellow flowers in spring, which give way to green seed pods that gradually turn reddish. The pods were gathered by Indians for food. The highest thorny branches are favorite nesting sites for the verdin.

The **indigo bush** (*Psorothamnus schottii*) is common in desert washes and on alluvial fans. Yet another member of the pea family, it gets its name from the deep

Agave

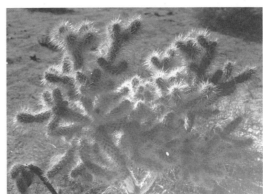

Jumping cholla

Silver cholla

Buckhorn cholla

Brittle-bush

purple-blue color of its blossoms. The bush has many slender stems and conspicuous blisterlike glands.

The **desert willow,** or catalpa (*Chilopsis linearis*), is a bushy tree that has long, narrow leaves and lavender or pink orchidlike blossoms that give way to narrow seed pods, which remain on the stems long afterward. It is a tree of desert watercourses.

Tamarisk, or salt cedar (*Tamarix spp.*), trees are usually seen in association with desert willows in watercourses. *Tamarix aphylla* is the large, treelike variety while *Tamarix chinensis* is the smaller variety, generally found in desert washes. The tamarisk is a native of Asia and Africa which was introduced to the California desert by early settlers as a shade tree and a windbreak. It has since spread throughout the desert wherever water is found. It is common in Borrego Valley, in the willows area of Coyote Canyon, at Tamarisk Grove Campground and at the site of the Carrizo stage station. The tamarisk is the subject of vigorous eradication programs in several southwest states because of its aggressiveness in crowding out native vegetation and using great amounts of water.

Brittle-bush (*Encelia farinosa*) is a common, low, rounded bush that appears to have had a dusting of flour, making it look a silvery green. A member of the sunflower family, it is a very showy plant with numerous yellow blooms on an almost leafless long stem that gives the shrub a bouquetlike appearance in spring. Its name refers to the dry, brittle stems, which may be all that is left after a drought when leaves are dropped to conserve water. The small drops of yellow sap that cling to the lower stems were used as incense by Spanish missionaries.

Chuparosa (*Justicia californica*) is a low, rounded bush, found at low altitudes along borders of sandy washes and rocky areas on the western edge of the Colorado Desert. In summer the leaves turn yellow and fall off, leaving the branches almost bare. The bright red tubular blooms are brushlike at the ends of the stems. Hummingbirds are frequent visitors seeking the nectar-filled blossoms.

Cheesebush (*Hymenoclea salsola*) is a rank-smelling shrub that attains a height of three feet. Early pioneers thought it had the smell of strong cheese. The plant is commonly found in sandy washes and rocky places below 6000 feet elevation widely spread throughout the desert. It is a bright green plant with light tan stems bearing creamy white flowers in the spring. It drops its leaves in summer and appears quite lifeless until the following spring.

Jumping cholla, or teddy-bear cholla (*Opuntia bigelovii*), is the spiniest of cacti, the barbed spines being so numerous that from a distance they give the plant a brilliant yellowish-white color. When older, the lower branches become black and disfigured. The upper joints are easily detached from the plant, a property that gives rise to the tale of the "jumping cactus." This cactus, which usually grows in extensive patches on alluvial fans and lower slopes generally under 3000 feet in elevation, has yellow blooms. The **silver cholla** (*Opuntia echinocarpa*) is quite similar to the jumping cholla but it is found at higher elevations.

The branches of **buckhorn cholla** (*Opuntia acanthocarpa*) are antler-shaped, and longer and narrower than those of jumping cholla. It also grows at a higher elevation. Its bloom is also yellow, but with a tint of red.

Beavertail cactus (*Opuntia basilaris*) is a low, spreading plant that does not have long spines like the cholla. Instead, it has tiny clusters of sharp bristles that can

Smoke Tree

Desert ironwood

penetrate the skin equally as well. Its name aptly describes the beavertail-like appendages. The blooms are a deep purple-red.

Barrel cactus, or bisnaga (*Echinocactus acanthodes*), is a cylindrical cactus that grows to heights of 9 feet, with yellow blooms that make a crown atop the cactus in spring. The plant has a tendency to lean toward the greatest light.

California fan palms, also called Washingtonia (*Washingtonia filifera*) are the only native palms in the western United States and are the largest of the true desert trees. They attain a height of 80 feet. They survive both in fresh and alkaline water areas where the water table is high, since the root system is very shallow. New leaves appear each year at the top of the trunk while the previous year's leaves die and bend down, forming a dense insulating mat around the base of the tree which protects it from extreme summer heat.

The **smoke tree** (*Psorothamnus spinosus*) was named for its gray-green color, which from a distance gives the impression of smoke. It is a spiny, almost leafless tree that attains a height of about 20 feet. In summer months it has a purple bloom. Smoke trees are found in and near washes.

The **palo verde tree** (*Cercidium floridum*) is a broad bush tree that attains a height of about 20 feet. Before the yellow blooms fully open, they look much like common garden sweet peas. The palo verde is able to drop all its leaves during the driest part of the year, leaving the production of chlorophyll to the smooth, light-green bark.

The **ironwood** tree (*Olneya tesota*) is a sandy wash plant, conspicuously found in the Borrego Mountain area. This tree grows to a height of 30 feet. It has a typical pea blossom, with the upper lip almost white and the lower part varying from white to purple. It blooms in June. The rest of the year the tree is bare and seemingly lifeless.

The best time to view wildflowers depends on elevation and location. At lower elevations, such as at Split Mountain, Carrizo Corridor, the base of the Superstition Mountains, Borrego Valley and Borrego Badlands, plants begin to bloom in February, with sand verbena, primrose, lupine and desert lilies the dominant species. The sand hills east of Split Mountain, often have vast displays of verbena, while the rock garden northwest of Split Mountain, near Elephant Trees, is a good area for cactus bloom.

At mid elevations, such as at Dos Cabezas, Coyote Canyon, Mescal Bajada, Blair Valley and Mason Valley, plants begin to bloom in March with beautiful displays of agave, cactus, brittle-bush, mallow, creosote and ocotillo.

At higher elevations, such as at Pinyon Ridge, Culp Valley, Wilson Trail, Jasper Trail and upper Oriflamme Canyon, plants bloom during April, May and June, including prickly poppy, chia, fishhook cactus, beavertail cactus, lupine, penstemons, buttercups, and other colorful plants.

For detailed information on desert plants see Philip A. Munz, *California Desert Wildflowers* and Edmund C. Jaeger, *Desert Wild Flowers.* Jaeger's *Denizens of the Desert* and Jim Cornett's *Wildlife of the Southwest Deserts* are two execellent guides to desert animals.

Desert Habitats

Habitat	Elev. Range	Plants	Animals
Desert Wash — found in dry water courses leading from canyons of desert mountains and in badlands washes. These washes support a greater diversity of plants and animals than does the surrounding desert because of the concentration of water received and carried at certain times of the year.	3000 to below sea level	Smoke tree, ironwood, palo verde, desert willow, cheesebush, creosote, burroweed, brittle-bush, mesquite, mistletoe, indigo bush, bunch grass, desert lavender, loco weed, trumpet flower, desert aster and various annual flowers including bladderpod, desert lily, verbena, dune and desert primrose, spectacle pod and sand lupine.	Jackrabbit, cottontail, desert woodrat, coyote, badger, kit fox, gray fox, antelope ground squirrel, phainopepla, verdin, zebra-tailed lizard, desert iguana and sidewinder. These animals are found in and adjacent to desert washes.
Low Desert and Desert Slope — found in desert valleys and on slopes. Topography is rough, steep and broken on the mountain slopes. Deep canyons and steep ridges are the rule. The slopes end rather abruptly at the desert floor.	3000 to sea level	Plants are generally sparse, but grow over wide areas. Common plants include creosote, burroweed, indigo bush, brittle-bush, ocotillo, cholla, barrel cactus and desert thorn.	Antelope ground squirrel, jackrabbit, white-throated woodrat, Merriam's kangaroo rat, little pocket mouse, road runner, cactus wren, raven, Say's phoebe, zebra-tailed lizard, desert iguana, sidewinder, red racer and, in dune areas, kit fox and desert kangaroo rat. On mountain slopes bighorn sheep, bobcats and a few deer are found.
Chaparral — found on higher desert slopes. A dense cover of shrubs, some reaching 15 feet in height, is characteristic. Water runoff courses often have thick stands of scrub oak.	3000-5500	Chamise, scrub oak, ceanothus, manzanitas, sumac and yuccas. On desert slopes these will grade into desert species such as brittle-bush and various cacti.	Mule deer, coyote, gray fox, bobcat, rabbit, mountain quail, scrub jay, poor-will, western fence lizard, western rattlesnake and numerous invertebrates.
Pinyon Juniper — found on desert slopes of the Santa Rosa, Laguna, In-Ko-Pah and Jacumba mountains and other localities. Consists of scattered trees 10-30 feet tall in open stands, mixed with shrubs and grading into a desert slope chaparral. Topography is gentle to very steep, with rocky areas common.	below 6000	Pinyon, juniper, scrub oak, sumac, cholla, California mountain joint fir, mountain mahogany, manzanita, Parry nolina, desert agave and buckwheat.	Coyote, jackrabbit, Beechey ground squirrel, piñon mouse, desert woodrat, California thrasher, poor-will, black-throated gray warbler, canyon and rock wrens, red-tailed hawk, king snake, gopher snake.

Man in the Desert

Archeologists have identified a succession of four distinct cultural types, or patterns, from the earliest Indians to occupy the Anza-Borrego region to the last, in historic times.

The earliest inhabitants are called paleo Indians. They lived more than 9000 years ago, when the climate was milder and lakes and streams were plentiful. Archeologists call the paleo Indians of the Anza-Borrego area San Dieguito Indians. They were primarily fishermen and hunters. They left rock-lined, cleared circles in the desert pavement, 6–8 feet in diameter, which may have outlined shelters that they used.

The age assigned to the earliest paleo Indians is highly contested among archeologists. One archeologist even believes that there was a cultural group of paleo Indians before the San Dieguito Indians, over 50,000 years ago, which he calls Malpi. Also highly contested are the remains of an early Indian known as the Yuha Man.

The Yuha Man was carbon-dated at 21,500 years from caliche (calcium-carbonate) deposits on bone fragments several years ago. Based on this dating, he was believed to have been the earliest known man in this region and possibly in the Western Hemisphere. However, in recent years, a new method of dating with an accelerator mass spectrometer has established a date of about 3000 years old. This new dating method would have Yuha Man possibly living during the second established succession of cultural types found in this desert. This second cultural phase is known as archaic, or desert archaic, and is said to have existed from 7000 to 3000 years ago in the Anza-Borrego Desert.

Pinto Basin Indians are examples of the desert archaic cultural type who lived in this desert. The Pinto Basin Indians were primarily seed gatherers who used various milling stones and hand stones such as metates (shallow holes) and manos, baskets, and darts for supplementary hunting. They lacked pottery and bows and arrows. Truckhaven Man also dates from this cultural period.

The third cultural sequence is known as prehistoric, or pottery archaic, and is dated roughly from 2000 to 1200 years ago. During this period Indians began using pottery, bedrock mortars (deep holes) and pestles, and small arrowheads, and began cremating their dead.

During the last cultural phase, the historic period, Yuman and Shoshonean (two distinct linguistic families) Indians were attracted to the Anza-Borrego region by freshwater Lake Cahuilla around 900 or 1000 A.D. Archeologists believe the Yumans preceded the Shoshoneans into the area, settling primarily south of what is today Highway S-22. Shoshonean groups occupied areas north of this.

These were true desert Indians who relied mainly on seed gathering for their livelihood. They used pottery and bows and arrows in addition to baskets and various implements for pounding and grinding seeds. They lived in small family groupings at semipermanent village sites where water was relatively abundant.

The Yuman-speaking Indians of the region are now known as Kumeyaay, the name the Indians have preferred. Until recently, ethnologists referred to them as Southern Diegueños. Several years ago there was controversy over what they should be called, and there is still not total agreement, but "Kumeyaay" receives the greatest acceptance.

The Shoshonean-speaking Indians of the area who lived generally north of Highway S-22 and east to Clark Valley and Rockhouse Canyon were known as Mountain Cahuillas, while those who lived north of S-22 and east of the Mountain Cahuillas were known as Desert Cahuillas.

The material existences and the environments of the Kumeyaay and the Cahuillas were much the same. Kumeyaay differed from Cahuillas primarily in social patterns, besides speaking a different language.

As primarily seed gatherers, these desert Indians made seasonal rounds within their territory to collect wild vegetable products. Mesquite beans and acorns were the main staples. The blooms, green pods and dried yellow pods of both the honey mesquite and the screwbean mesquite were all consumed. Mortars and pestles were used to extract juice from the green pods and to make flour from the dried pods. Bedrock mortars and heavy stone pestles were also used to grind acorn into meal in the oak groves before transporting it back to the villages.

The agave was one of the most usable plants. It was harvested in winter, the leaves, blooms and stalks all being edible. In addition, agave fibers were used to make sandals, skirts, nets, cordage, bowstrings, snares and mats, while the thorns were used as awls. Agave spines also provided needles for tattooing with ash or charcoal implants.

The yucca also had important uses. The fruit pods were eaten while the roots were used as soap and the fibers were used for making string, rope, sandals, nets and painting brushes.

Other plant resources included various cacti, fruits, berries, tubers, roots, succulents, seed pods and grass seeds.

Life for these desert Indians had remained essentially the same for hundreds of years. Events beginning in 1772 would bring change. Although there had been

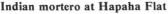
Indian mortero at Hapaha Flat

rumors among the desert Indians that "strange" men had settled along the coast and southeast of the Colorado River, none of these desert Indians had seen a white man before Lieutenant Pedro Fages of the San Diego Presidio entered the Anza-Borrego region in pursuit of some deserters. He trailed the deserters east to the desert floor on what would later become part of the famed Southern Emigrant Trail, and then northwest into Borrego Valley and Coyote Canyon and back into the interior valleys of Southern California.

Fages was followed two years later by trailblazer Juan Bautista de Anza, a commandant of Spain's most northern frontier outpost in Sonora, who was seeking an inland route from the Mexican mainland into Alta California that colonists and supplies could follow to the first small mission settlements along the coast. Anza's destination was Monterey, capital of Alta California.

Spain's hold on Alta California was tenuous. The struggling missions at San Diego, San Gabriel, San Luis Obispo and Carmel needed to have a dependable supply anu communication route. The arduous trail from La Paz north through the untamed wilds of Baja California's interior, from Loreto to San Diego, and the small and unreliable ships that plied the Pacific Coast, bringing supplies from San Blas, were not adequate. Moreover, possible encroachments by Russia and England made the need for a dependable route to California more imperative.

Anza set out from Tubac, Sonora, on January 9, 1774, with two priests, 21 soldiers and two Indians, one an interpreter and the other a guide. The latter, Sebastian Tarabal, had fled from San Gabriel Mission. He had made his way across the Colorado Desert to the land of the Yumas. The Yuma chief took Tarabal to Anza, whom the runaway agreed to serve as guide.

Tarabal proved to be a poor guide in recrossing the sand dunes. The party moved southwest some distance into what is today Baja California to avoid the dunes, made a premature venture westward which cost the lives of several animals, backtracked and went yet farther southwest to skirt the treacherous sand. Finally turning northwest, they crossed the present international border a few miles west of Signal Mountain in Imperial County. Anza's route (see the map on p. 21) then went north to Yuha Well and on to the Indian village of San Sebastian at the confluence of San Felipe and Carrizo creeks. The party then traveled northwest around Borrego Mountain to the Indian village of San Gregorio at Borrego Spring, across Borrego Valley and up into Coyote Canyon to the village of Santa Catarina at Lower Willows. The expedition then ascended Coyote Canyon to San Carlos Pass, descended to San Jacinto Valley and continued on to San Gabriel Mission, arriving on March 22, 1774. Thereafter Anza followed the existing road to Monterey, which struck out toward the coast, crossing San Fernando Valley and following the route of present-day Highway 101. At San Luis Obispo, he turned inland, going up through Cuesta Pass in the Santa Lucia Mountains to reach the Salinas River and Valley, which he followed to Monterey.

This first trip proved the feasibility of a road between Sonora and San Gabriel Mission. Anza reported the accomplishment to the viceroy of Mexico, who made plans to strengthen the hold on California by authorizing Anza to lead a group of settlers to colonize San Francisco. Anza recruited and outfitted a party of 240, which included many women and children and 800 animals. This group departed

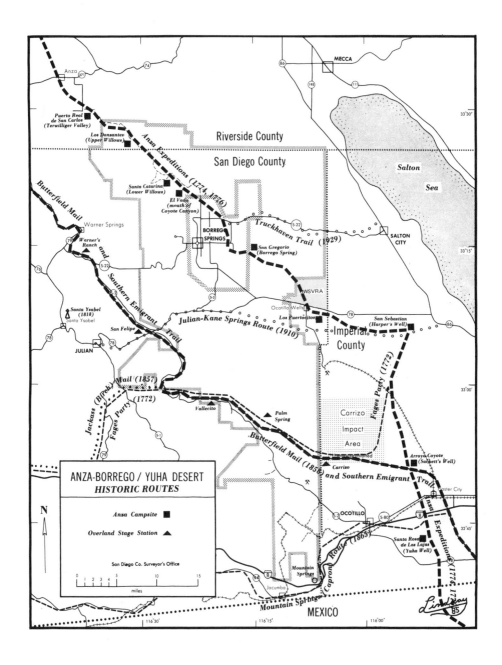

ANZA-BORREGO / YUHA DESERT
HISTORIC ROUTES

N

Anza Campsite ■

Overland Stage Station ▲

San Diego Co. Surveyor's Office

0 1 2 3 4 5   10   15
miles

Tubac on October 23, 1775, retracing the route of the first expedition. They arrived at San Francisco Bay on March 28, 1776. On that day Anza selected a site for the new settlement and fort and erected a cross, thus taking formal possession of the bay for Spain.

Anza, by delivering the colonists safely, had almost doubled the white population of Alta California and had established a land route that would be used by at least 300 colonists within the next five years. A Spanish census taken in 1790 showed that up to 50 per cent of colonists in Alta California at that time and almost all herds of horses and cattle had come by way of the Anza Trail.

However, as Indians became hostile to Hispanic civilizing and missionizing techniques, and as the War for Mexican Independence reduced emigration into California, use of this overland route diminished and then ceased.

Several years later, in 1824, interest in a land link between Mexico and California revived, and the Sonora Road was opened by Mexican explorers, supplanting the Anza Trail as the main route into California. This route, paralleling the Anza Trail 15-20 miles southwest of it, came up Carrizo Creek from the Yuha Desert to Vallecito and then went over San Felipe Pass to Warner's Ranch and on to Los Angeles. The road, however, received light traffic through the years by Mexican citizens and American trappers and explorers, and it was almost forgotten by the time the Mexican War broke out. Beginning with the war, however, the loneliness and isolation in Vallecito and Carrizo valleys was permanently broken.

Gen. Stephen Watts Kearny's Army of the West, the Mormon Battalion and emigrants rushing to the California gold fields made this route the main road into Southern California. The Southern Emigrant Trail, as this road was now called, became a part of the famed Butterfield Overland Mail route and was the path followed by Col. James H. Carleton's California Column during the Civil War and by cattlemen, prospectors and homesteaders in later years.

These early white men viewed the desert as merely a place to pass through as quickly as possible en route to more desirable lands. It was not until later generations, when the more hospitable coastal and inland valley areas became more crowded and hence less inviting, that the desert has been rediscovered and found to be not as barren, monotonous and repulsive as first perceived.

New generations of visitors saw with new eyes, disregarding preconceived notions of "desert," and viewed a land of contrast, startling changes and variety.

How-Tos and What-Nots of Desert Exploring

Pre-Trip Preparation

> For there are two deserts: One is a grim desolate wasteland. It is the home of venomous reptiles and stinging insects, of vicious thorn-covered plants and trees and unbearable heat. . . visualized by those children of luxury to whom any environment is intolerable which does not provide all the comforts and luxuries of a pampering civilization.
>
> The other desert—the real desert—is not for the eyes of the superficial observer or the fearful soul of the cynic. It is a land which reveals its true character only to those who come with courage, tolerance, and understanding. For those the desert holds rare gifts.
>
> —Randall Henderson, *On Desert Trails*

For those who would seek "the real desert" in the Anza-Borrego region, the following pages cover the basics of what to do and what not to do out there, by vehicle and afoot, in camp and on the trail. Of key importance is pre-trip preparation.

Desert explorers are well advised to heed an old military aviators' saying, "Pre-flight preparation precludes post-flight peril." Before your trip, you need to become familiar with your route and your destination and the supplies and equipment that will get you there and bring you back.

Telephone, write or personally visit with BLM or state-park personnel to determine current conditions in the area you will visit, including weather conditions, road and route conditions, latest entry regulations for vehicles, fire hazards, recommended camping areas and availability and potability of water.

Bureau of Land Management (BLM)
El Centro Resource Area Office
333 S. Waterman
El Centro CA 92243, tel. (619) 352-5842

Anza-Borrego Desert State Park
Park Headquarters
P.O. Box 299
Borrego Springs CA 92004, tel. (619) 767-5311

Let somebody know where you are going, what you are going to do there, and when you will return. Be sure it is someone who would notice that you were overdue and would notify the proper authorities. This is particularly true of backpacking trips.

NOTE: If you tell BLM or park rangers that you will check out with them at the end of your trip, be sure you do. If offices or contact stations are closed when you come out, leave a note, well anchored, in a prominent place nearby.

Good luck and happy adventuring in the Anza-Borrego!

Vehicle Care and Desert Driving

Unlike many mountain, forest and beach recreation areas, the desert allows the motorist to reach remote areas far from well-traveled roads and concentrations of people. The allure of the desert wilderness, however, can lead to a situation wherein a simple mechanical problem may be compounded into a serious, life-threatening emergency. It is essential, therefore, that the off-highway traveler be familiar with his machine, check and stock it well before his trip, be prepared to deal with the most common emergencies and breakdowns, and be experienced in sandy-wash, rocky-road and steep-slope driving.

Pre-trip preparation includes a thorough check of all systems (electrical, cooling, lubricating, fuel, brake and suspension) as well as main and spare tires. If maintenance work on anything is almost due, do it before the trip.

While on the trip, make a daily check of the following:

1. fluid levels in the battery, radiator, crankcase and automatic transmission;
2. condition of fan belts, coolant hoses, tires, oil pan, gas tank, springs, steering gear and engine mounts;
3. battery terminals (tight and free of corrosion);
4. mounting of accessories, including air cleaner, carburetor, generator, battery box, pumps;
5. no evidence of fresh oil, gas, coolant or transmission leaks.

Vehicle Equipment Checklist

The following checklist is adapted from the "What to take on the tour" section of the 1921 edition of the *Automobile Green Book*. Why not? The conditions of today's off-road travel are much the same as the conditions of yesterday's road touring. What grandpa knew about his horseless carriage is still good horse sense for grandson's off-roading.

Tool kit

Set of wrenches (open, box, socket, and adjustable)
Large and small screw drivers (including Phillips and slotted)
Punches and chisels
Files and hack saw
Pliers (clamp, needlenose, channel, locking vice grips)
Scissors and knife
Spotlight or trouble lamp, flashlight with spare bulb and batteries
Wirecutters and tinsnips
Hatchet or axe
Spade or collapsible shovel
Crowbar
Large hammer (when all else fails)

Tire and traction equipment

At least one extra mounted and inflated spare tire in good condition (two extras are even better—it's
    almost impossible for the average motorist to repair today's tires)
Spare lug nuts
Extra inner tube(s)—also can be cut to make large patches for tube or tire.
Patch kits for tubed and tubeless tires (maybe somebody else more skilled could repair that tube)
Extra valve cores and caps
Air-pressure gauge
Hand pump or engine pump

Jack (at least one, but two are better. One should be a bumperjack or "come along," which can substitute for a power winch)

Tow chain or cable or 1-inch manila rope and a two-hooked nylon spring line

Roll of 12-inch-wide chicken wire, flat boards, canvas strips, burlap rags, strip of carpet or any material to provide traction in soft sand

Snow chains (helpful in mud as well)

Tire air jumper or canned compressed filler

Fuel, oil, coolant equipment

2- to 5-gallon can of spare gas (correct octane)

5 quarts of spare oil

Minimum of 5 gallons of water for vehicle only (drinking and cooking water are in addition to this)

Funnel

Siphoning device

Extra fuel pump

Carburetor repair kit

Various cans of sealant, fuel treatment, oil conditioner, WD-40

Repair materials

Sheet of gasket material

Several sizes of soft iron wire

Bag of assorted nuts, bolts, lock washers, screws, cotter pins

Tape (electric and friction)

Assorted lengths and sizes of electrical wiring

Heavy string

Cake of soap (to plug pan punctures)

Assorted sizes of hose clamps

Fingernail polish (secures screws and nuts that tend to vibrate loose)

Ignition supplies and miscellaneous (make sure these fit your vehicle)

Assorted fuses and lamp bulbs

Distributor repair kit

Extra spark plugs and spark-plug wires

Spare ignition coil

Radiator hoses and hose clamps

Fan belt(s)

Spare set of keys

Spring clamps

Credit cards, checkbook, and spare cash (works when nothing else will)

Portable radio and extra batteries (for latest weather in emergencies)

Desert Driving

Beyond proper pre-trip planning, the single most important concern in desert off-roading is the possibility, even the probability, of getting stuck in sand, mud or soft dirt, or on high-centered ruts and rocks. If possible, it is wise to practice driving on such surfaces before the trip, with another vehicle standing by to tow as necessary.

If vehicle footing is at all uncertain, the minutes spent walking ahead to check it out may mean hours saved digging out. The same applies to turning around at a dead end or backing out a long stretch. When proceeding over a soft surface, gear down before entry, then maintain adequate forward momentum, without letting the wheels spin. So long as the wheels are not spinning, you're not going to dig in. Be aware, however, that the lower the gear, the greater the likelihood of spinning. The trick is to achieve a balance between sufficient power and speed to get through and not so much that you lose traction. Partly deflated tires can increase traction, but don't deflate them so far as to cause the tire to slip on the rim. Building up a questionable route with rocks or hard earth may be more minutes spent wisely against the possibility of having to dig out later on. Avoid sudden motions of starting, stopping and turning.

Beware of your particular vehicle's clearance. Just because a route looks well traveled doesn't mean that your particular vehicle can make it. High centers, sharp angles of descent and ascent in washes, and rocks can hang up vehicles with low clearance, long overhangs, or long wheel bases. The difference between a little bobtail rig and a long, heavy pickup camper or motor home becomes painfully obvious on many off-road pitches.

Here too the advantage of posi-traction or limited-slip differential becomes significant. With a conventional differential, one stuck drive wheel will cause the other to spin freely, leading to dig-in. The limited slip tends to keep the other wheel driving should its mate get stuck.

But then comes the inevitable time(s) when the road wins, and your vehicle loses. You're stuck. The first action is no action. Rather than immediately trying to fight your way through and getting even more hopelessly stuck, get out and survey the problem. Generally you will want to plan your exit out in reverse. Where you came from was clearly negotiable. Where you're going may not be. Dig away the sand or mud from in front of and behind the tires to form a ramp to harder ground. It will also be necessary to dig out for the differential, pans, and other low hangers underneath. If available, put rocks, blankets, carpets, chicken wire or whatever under the tires and on the exit route to improve traction. You may want to jack up the stuck wheels to get these materials beneath them. Brush may work too, as a last resort. First of all, it's illegal to destroy vegetation in any park or protected area, and second, that brush didn't grow there for the purpose of compensating for your lack of off-road expertise. Finally, nature may laugh last if the vegetation you use under wheel happens to have a thorny appetite for rubber.

Then, you can either decide to rock back and forth between low gear and reverse, or move directly out in the selected direction. Slowly apply the gas and/or slowly engage the clutch to see if there's sufficient traction for the wheels to take hold without slipping. If so, continue moving out decisively, but not so fast as to start slipping. Continue to gain momentum until you reach firm ground. Don't get overconfident before you reach firm footing, or you'll be starting the whole process all over again.

Should none of this work, you have two choices: continue engineering the road for traction, and perhaps also deflate tires to 12–15 pounds, or wait for an assisting vehicle with rope or chain. In the latter case there are three concerns: don't let the assist vehicle also get stuck during rescue; beware of possible parting of the line under tension and a vicious backlash; attach the line to firm structural points on both vehicles (which, for example, steering tie rods and VW bumpers are not). If you've deflated the tires, don't forget to reinflate them prior to hard-road or pavement travel.

Some final notes on off-roading:

1. Beware of side-slanting routes. A vehicle can easily negotiate a steep incline straight ahead, up or down, that would send it rolling should it get sideways. If you

start sliding sideways, attempt to turn downhill if at all possible. Better to get stuck into the side of a dugway facing downward than to roll to the bottom.

2. Travel with at least one other vehicle in company.

3. Don't push beyond the limits of your particular vehicle to display your macho.

4. Obey the rules and regulations of the park and the BLM, which are based on common sense and on a sense of responsibility on the part of every desert visitor, to protect our remaining parklands and natural preserves for future generations.

5. Respect dry washes if there is any possibility of rain, even in far distant mountains. Many true tales are told of campers, cars and even settlements being swept to their ruin in what appeared to be a dry wash. Flash floods are just that. They don't give warning.

6. Speed, promptness and precise scheduling are required attributes of our urban world. When off-road, however, the only real deadline you have is to get out, safely. Mañana is soon enough if it means just being a few hours late rather than leaving behind a broken hulk of metal and rubber. Today's excellent suspension systems and tires mask the terrific beating that vehicles take when speeding along dirt roads or trails. You may not feel the damage being done by high-speed off-road travel, but your vehicle certainly does. And sooner or later it will inform you in no uncertain terms.

7. Always stop and walk ahead to survey any hazardous condition. Then plan your route to negotiate the section carefully.

8. Be considerate of fellow campers and desert people and wandering children, especially around campsites. Motorcycles and many of today's OHVs are extremely

Damage by jeep cavalcade

loud and unnerving when revved up. Nothing can shatter the pleasure of desert recreation faster than the blast of a tailpipe. Both ear damage and accidents have been caused by such sound pollution. What may be music to the ears of the driver is madness to the minds of others. Fifteen miles per hour is the absolute maximum speed around campsites.

Weather, Water and Personal Equipment

The special conditions of desert camping and travel include unexpected climate extremes, great sun and wind exposure, and a greater water need despite the smaller natural supply. The common view of the desert is that of a hot and dry place. The wise desert visitor will temper this view. Daily temperature ranges of 50° from high to low are not uncommon. Both Yuma and Palm Springs have record daily ranges of 81°, from 120°F to 39°F in one 24-hour period!

Exposure to sun and wind during outdoor activities in the desert is due to a general lack of cloud cover and of natural vegetation. Low humidity, direct sun and high temperatures require a person to drink a lot of water at the very time that most of the desert's few streams, water holes and springs are drying up. Yet, by contrast, during August 1977, the hottest month of the year, 2.53 inches of rain were dumped on Borrego Springs in less than six hours, and 4.5 inches in two days, during the disastrous "50-year storm" of Hurricane Doreen. A station in Coyote Canyon recorded 5.25 inches one night during this storm! (This storm confounded the annual averages, which would lead one to expect less than five inches of rain in an entire year.) Severe sand and dust storms, especially in the spring, are other weather hazards. So the rule in the desert is to prepare for weather extremes, and enjoy anything less.

None of this is to say that the desert is not the place to vacation. On the contrary, over a million visitor-use days per year in the Anza-Borrego region prove just the opposite. The point is that the special environmental conditions of the desert require special planning and foresight to ensure a pleasant stay, especially in remote areas. The following 21-year averages in the Borrego Valley provide a guide to planning.

	January	April	August	November
High temperature (°F)	68	83	106	78
Low temperature (°F)	43	53	75	51
Rainfall (inches)	1.36	.28	.58	.71

Higher elevations will have lower temperatures overall, lower daily temperature ranges, greater rainfall and lower surface wind velocity. Wind velocity may, however, be significantly higher on mountain peaks and high plateaus, such as Ranchita or the Santa Rosas.

Wind, Water and You

As noted above, temperatures can drop as much as 50° from a hot day to a frigid, windy night. A pre-trip check with rangers or law-enforcement officials will give you a good idea of what to expect. The wind-chill factor can cause the effective temperature on exposed flesh to be far lower than the actual air temperature. For example, at an air temperature of 40°F with a wind speed of 20 miles per hour (not unusual on the desert), the flesh is experiencing an effective temperature of 16°F. An air temperature of 32°F with a 28-mile-per-hour wind results in an effective temperature of 0°F. Plan clothing and shelter accordingly.

At the other end of the temperature scale, the body copes with heat by sweating, which produces evaporation and subsequent cooling, all of which is beautifully designed to maintain normal body temperature of 98.6°F. At air temperatures above 92°F the body will absorb heat directly from the atmosphere, and at lower temperatures it will absorb heat from direct sunlight on the skin. Furthermore, the body produces its own heat as a result of activity, work, eating and exercise.

The implications of all this lead to . . .

The Water Maxims

Rule 1: **Store Water in Your Belly, Not Your Canteen.** Drink on demand and in sufficient quantities to amply satisfy thirst. Tank up like a camel before the trek and whenever you encounter natural water supplies. Treat the water if necessary.

Rule 2: **Conserve Sweat, Not Water.** Reduce sweating by rest and proper protective clothing. Travel during the cool of the day, before 10 a.m. or after 4 p.m., even at night (if light and terrain permit it), resting 10 minutes or more each hour. Rest often, in the shade, any available shade. Rest off the ground if possible. Temperatures may be 30–40° cooler one foot off the ground. Wear light-colored, light-weight, long-sleeved and long-legged, loose, layered clothing and a broad-brimmed hat. These will reduce sweat loss, reflect heat and permit circulative cooling between the layers, all of which reduce water needs.

Rule 3: **Keep Your Mouth Shut** when in trouble due to lack of water. Great things will happen. If you breathe through your nose, you won't smoke, talk, drink booze, gripe or eat. That way, you will reduce water loss from the large mucous membranes of the mouth and upper throat, and you will minimize the need for water to metabolize alcohol and food.

Not enough can be said about the need for an adequate water supply in arid areas. Parents who carefully guard the welfare of their children in the city may think nothing of letting junior jump on his minibike and ride miles and hours out into desolate desert badlands without a drop of water. The false security of the familiar family car, and no extra water supply, has led to many a sad end of a Search and Rescue operation, even on paved roads in the lonely out-there. Some seasoned hikers have tragically neglected the potential realities of a long trek—burning midday sun, dehydration and delirium. Lack of water is the single factor that makes the desert desert. Adequate water is therefore the single most important thing in wise desert travel.

All natural water supplies should be suspected. Any standard purification method is suitable.

1. Water-purification tablets—follow directions on container. Usually one tablet per quart of clear water or two tablets per quart of cloudy water are sufficient. Shake and let stand for 30 minutes.

2. Iodine or household bleach such as Clorox—2–6 drops per quart is sufficient, depending on purity. Shake and let stand for 30 minutes.

3. Boiling—5 minutes at a rapid boil will do the job.

NOTE: These three methods will treat biological impurities only. Chemical impurities cannot be removed except by distilling. Fortunately there are no known chemically hazardous natural water supplies in the Anza-Borrego area.

4. Sun still. This ingenious device, developed by the U.S. Department of Agriculture, produces up to 3 pints of water per day. Details are available in any survival book (see the bibliography). Practice the technique before you actually need the water. In a practice situation it can be an enjoyable and educational outdoor activity. Basically the technique begins with digging a hole about 18 inches deep at the center and 36 inches across. Place a collecting vessel at the center of the hole. Completely cover the hole with an impermeable (waterproof) plastic sheet (tube tent, rain coat, etc.), anchored around the edges with soil or sand, such that it's air-tight. Put a weighting object (rock, soil, etc.) in the center of the plastic sheet so that the sheet forms an inverted cone with the apex over the container. During the day, water will condense on the underside of the sheet, run down to the center, and drop into the container. Fleshy plants, cactus or impure water may be placed in the hole to accelerate the process.

Personal Equipment Checklist

This section is oriented toward light-weight, minimum-space, multipurpose equipment for an individual. Adapt as necessary to your particular needs. See the Vehicle Equipment Checklist above for automotive equipment and the bibliography for references on general camping and specialized activities, such as backpacking and outdoor survival skills.

Climate determines clothing. A basic rule for outdoor wear is "lightweight, light-colored, layered and loose." Light-colored outer layers minimize heat absorption and provide best visibility in most Southwest environments. Several layers of lightweight garments, such as a sweater, a sweatshirt, a light jacket and "fishnet" or thermal underwear are better than a single heavy coat. A person who starts a hike early in the cool of morning will soon be generating substantial body heat, and the air will be getting warmer. Then, into the afternoon and evening the temperature decreases, perhaps to a deep chill. Using the layered system enables one to adapt to successive changes rather than be limited to the all-or-nothing of a single heavy garment. Since insulation from heat or cold depends on the amount of dead air trapped in the small spaces of the material between the body and the outside air, layering also increases insulation.

The Ten Essentials

Credit the Sierra Club for widely popularizing this list as the very basic items that no one should ever be without while engaged in outdoor activities, whether in camp or on the trail.

Pathfinding

1. Map of area (study it and the guidebook before the trip)
2. Compass (practice using it)
3. Flashlight (with spare batteries and bulb)

Protection
4. Sunglasses (plus sunburn lotion, insect repellent and chapstick)
5. Spare food and water (carry a full canteen even for short desert walks and one gallon of water per person per day for extended travel)
6. Extra clothing (appropriate for expected low temperatures. Use "layered" system.)
Emergencies
7. Waterproofed matches
8. Candle for fire starting
9. Pocket knife
10. First-aid kit (antiseptic and assorted band-aids as a minimum)
"11." Toilet paper (also good for starting fires)

Clothing (includes what is worn)
1–2 pairs of trousers (one can be shorts or swimsuit)
2–3 shirts, sweaters, sweatshirts (one heavy and long-sleeved)
1 jacket or parka (windproof and water-repellent)
Socks (one change per day. Heavy socks for boots)
Visored or brimmed hat (for sun and rain protection)
Wool cap (unless parka has hood)
1 pair heavy shoes or boots, *well broken in*
1 pair light shoes (optional)
Bandanas or handkerchiefs (good for many uses)
Mittens or gloves
Raincoat or poncho (lightweight plastic or coated nylon)

Bedding and Shelter
Sleeping bag (goose-down filler best, but expensive. Inexpensive bag may be supplemented
 by extra blankets—don't sleep cold). Mummy or semi-mummy for backpacking.
Ground cloth (many things are suitable—plastic shower curtain, canvas, tube tent, extra
 poncho)
Plastic tube tent, pup tent or substitute
Air mattress or pad (ensolite, foam rubber, extra blanket—optional)

First Aid
Iodine (for first aid and water purification if necessary)
Moleskin (for foot blisters)
Adhesive tape
Gauze pads and bandages (several sizes)
Tweezers (for cactus thorns)
Toiletries

Miscellaneous
50 feet of ⅛" nylon cord
Duffle bag, backpack or knapsack
Spending money
Note pad and pencil
Sewing kit (needle, thread, buttons, safety pins)
Camera and film
Eating utensils (1 or 2 Sierra cups and a spoon are sufficient, but if car-camping you can take
 more).
Miscellaneous plastic bags
Group cooking gear and food supplies

Desert Rules and Common Sense

"You Are Responsible . . ." is the title of the State Park's excellent brochure detailing its regulations (included below). Within Park lands this is the law, and will be enforced. Anywhere on the desert, park or not, the reasons behind these rules make good sense, and they are recommended to visitors as guidelines for desert use.

On BLM lands there are quite specific regulations related to the use of off-road vehicles according to the type of area designation:

A. **Closed:** Vehicular travel is completely prohibited (e.g., San Sebastian Marsh, Fish Creek Mountains, Crucifixion Thorn Area).

B. **Open:** Vehicular travel is generally unrestricted, although equipment, safety and licensing provisions still apply (e.g., Plaster City area).

C. **Limited use:** Vehicle use is restricted to approved routes of travel. Existing roads are open unless posted otherwise. Closed routes are identified with red "Closed" markers. The maps in this book show the major and most popular approved roads and trails at the time of publication. Contact the Riverside or El Centro office of BLM for latest information. Most BLM lands in the Anza-Borrego/Yuha region fall under this designation (e.g., San Felipe Hills, Lower Borrego Valley, Yuha Basin and Davies Valley).

D. **Organized Events,** including competitive, commercial, or recreational gatherings of 50 or more off-road vehicles, require a permit from BLM.

Additional land-use regulations include:

A. **Private lands:** Under the control of the owner (e.g., Ocotillo Wells area, Coyote Wells area and Borrego Springs townsite). Violations generally are related to trespassing or flagrant disregard of common-sense courtesies.

B. **Naval Reservation:** (includes the Superstition Hills, Superstition Mountains, and the area west to approximately the Fish Creek Mountains and the Carrizo Impact Area.) Entry is prohibited except by permission. Contact BLM for details.

C. **Carrizo Impact Area:** Entry is absolutely prohibited at all times due to presence of unexploded shells left over from its use as a Naval practice bombing range.

D. **Ocotillo Wells State Vehicular Recreation Area:** Essentially the same as BLM "Open" designation. It surrounds Benson Dry Lake on the west, north and east, although travel on the airstrip on the lake bed is prohibited. The 14,000 acres of the OWSVRA were purchased for $2.2 million from the Off-Highway Vehicle fund, which receives part of the "green sticker" registration fees collected from OHV owners. The area is administered by the California Department of Parks and Recreation, and has its own administrative staff with headquarters off Highway 78, two miles west of Ocotillo Wells. Facilities in the OWSVRA are kept to a minimum, so that virtually the entire area is open to off-highway recreation. Camping is permitted throughout the area, but no water is available. Specific rules:

   1. All vehicles must be registered, either licensed or with green sticker.

   2. Speed limit is 15 mph within 50 feet of people or camps.

3. Headlights and taillights are required after dark.
4. Fires are permitted—bring your own wood.
5. The entire area is open to primitive camping—bring your own water.
6. Plant and animal life is protected.

For further information, call the OWSVRA office at (619) 767-5391.

E. **Horse Camp and Trail Riding:** Equestrians must observe the following rules.

Campsites and corral must be cleaned after use. Rake horse manure from your corral toward the center aisle of corrals. Move horse manure from saddle racks to center aisle. Park horse trailers on opposite side of campsites. Observe 15 mph speed limit in camp area. Ride single file on trails. Ride only on trails, on primitive roads and in washes. No horses are allowed in Sheep Canyon beyond the parking lot. No horses are allowed at the Sheep Canyon picnic tables.

Desert Hiking, Being Stranded, and Getting Unlost

In desert canyons, brush-covered hillsides, rocky outwash slopes and sandy washes, distances may be very deceiving. Here the hiker's normal 2-to-3-miles-per-hour pace on a trail may become ½-1 mile per hour. Dry waterfalls and precipitous mountainsides may cause lengthy and unexpected detours. Plan your trip and water supply accordingly.

If lost or stranded with a disabled vehicle, you should generally stay with it, even a motorcycle. It's a lot easier to spot than a lone walker on the desert. If lost afoot or with a functioning vehicle, stop, reflect, and make a plan. Know where you're going, and why. Should you decide to travel afoot in hot weather, walk only during the cool of the day, around dawn or dusk, and only if you have water. Rest at least 10 minutes out of every hour. Be prepared to signal searching aircraft or ground parties. Basically, you want to produce an unusual or unnatural effect in the terrain: smoke, fire, mirror flashes, flashes from mirror substitutes like glass or aluminum, noise, sudden movements, pieces of clothing waved, or whatever is available that contrasts with the natural terrain. Remember that most washes in the Anza-Borrego region lead east downstream to a paved road or habitation where help can be obtained. An exception is in the Carrizo Wash area between Highway S-2 and the Carrizo Impact Area. In this area travel upwash west to the highway. REFER TO A MAP and HAVE A PLAN!

An actual incident on a hot afternoon in May 1977 illustrates some of the points made above. An experienced desert motorcyclist, clad in riding leathers, felt faint and sent his party on ahead down the Arroyo Seco del Diablo (Dry Wash of the Devil) to seek help. He soon ran out of water, and he became dehydrated and delirious. Disregarding the plan to rest and await rescue, he proceeded down the arroyo to Carrizo Wash and turned east toward the Impact Area. Four hours after the cyclist had separated from his party, Ranger George Leetch found his body near the old Carrizo Stage Station.

The following activities are prohibited in the state park.

1. Driving any vehicle off a "designated route of travel," marked with upright brown 4″ x 4″ posts with yellow lettering. OWSRVA is the only area excepted.

2. Permitting anyone to operate a motor vehicle without a driver's license. Under-age drivers are o.k. under supervision in OWSRVA.

3. Driving a vehicle in an unsafe manner. The maximum speed limit on any dirt road is 25 mph; the limit on roads in camping areas, paved or dirt, is 15 mph.

4. Operating a motor vehicle that does not have a current license plate or off-highway vehicle registration (green sticker).

5. Possessing a loaded firearm or shooting any form of weapon.

6. Building a fire on bare ground, or collecting any form of vegetation, living or dead to burn. Dead wood helps to enrich the soil. A camp fire is o.k. in your own metal container. Carry out all your ashes.

7. Removing any natural object (plant, animal, rock, soil); in other words, you may not collect souvenirs or take anything out of the park.

8. Permitting a pet to be loose or off leash anywhere in the park. Pets must be under control at all times. A pet must be confined in a tent or RV at night. They are not allowed on any trail or in any wilderness area. They must have valid tags or rabies certificate. (Simpler rule—Leave dog or pet at home.)

Damage to vegetation occurs when not following designated or approved routes of travel

The Fish Creek anticline amazes park visitors

Motels and Camping in the Anza-Borrego Area

There are four types of camping or lodging available to Anza-Borrego's visitors: motels, developed family campgrounds, designated primitive campgrounds, and natural, or "do it yourself," campsites. This latter type of camping is now only rarely permitted in our parks and monuments, and the fact that you can do it here is a tribute to the Anza-Borrego State Park administration's continuing faith in the good outdoor citizenship of desert park visitors.

Camping at natural campsites may be done by vehicle-borne campers on any park or BLM land along roads and designated routes of travel, and backpackers are generally free to camp anywhere. For many, these natural campsites are the *only* way to camp in the desert. Such camping will remain available so long as visitors practice good habits of care and protection for their desert lands. Camping on private property is prohibited without the consent of the owner.

Motels are found in the towns listed below. During the tourist season, from November through May, it is necessary to make reservations. The respective chambers of commerce can provide a listing of lodgings, their facilities and their prices. Addresses and telephone numbers for the various chambers of commerce are:

Borrego Springs Chamber of Commerce
P.O. Box 66
Borrego Springs CA 92004
(619) 767-5555

Julian Chamber of Commerce
P.O. Box 413
Julian CA 92036
(619) 765-1857

Salton City Chamber of Commerce
North Marina Drive
Salton City CA 92274
(619) 394-4112

Indio Chamber of Commerce
P.O. Box TTT
Indio CA 92201
(619) 347-0676

Brawley Chamber of Commerce
P.O. Box 218
Brawley CA 92227
(619) 344-3160

El Centro Chamber of Commerce
P.O. Box 1141
El Centro CA 92243
(619) 352-3681

Developed Family Campgrounds

Developed family campgrounds are located near Borrego Springs at Borrego Palm Canyon (elevation 775', 65 tent sites) and at Tamarisk Grove (elevation 1400', 25 sites) at the intersection of Highways 78 and S-3. The sites at these campgrounds contain tables, wood stoves, shade ramadas, cupboards, piped water, and restrooms with solar-heated showers and handicap-accessible flush toilets. The sites at Tamarisk Grove can accommodate trailers and motor homes up to 21 feet long. There is also a 52-site pull-through RV area in Borrego Palm canyon suitable for motor homes, trailers and pickup campers. Each RV site offers full hookups. RV size limit is 35 feet. Reservations for these are available by writing MISTIX, P.O. Box 85705, San Diego, CA 92138-5705, or calling (800) 444-7275 if you wish to charge by VISA or MasterCard. Ask a park ranger for additional reservation information.

In addition there are five GROUP CAMP SITES that will accommodate up to 24 people each at Borrego Palm Canyon. All five can be reserved, to accommodate

120 people. Make reservations up to twelve weeks in advance through MISTIX. Youth groups must have one adult per 12 minors.

There is a private RV park in Borrego Springs called Overland Junction, located at 221 Palm Canyon Drive, about one mile from the park Visitor Center. The facility has 140 pull-through RV sites that can accommodate vehicles 43–86 feet long. Each space is 23 feet wide. Each site offers full hookups. The facility has two pools, two jacuzzis, a restaurant and a 44-room motel. For information, write: Overland Junction, 221 Palm Canyon Drive, Borrego Springs, CA 92004, or call (619) 767-5341.

There are also four developed campgrounds on Highway S-2 in the southern part of the park—three on Highway 78, at the east and west edges of the park, and one on Highway 86 east of the park.

Agua Caliente Springs County Park on S-2 has 56 full hookups for RVs, 48 partial hookups, 36 developed tent sites and 20 undeveloped tent sites. This park has flush toilets, showers, mineral baths and an outdoor wading pool. A store is nearby for supplies (619) 765-0218. Pets are *not* permitted at Agua Caliente. Four miles north from this campground on S-2 is Vallecito County Park, the site of a former Butterfield Stage Station. This park has a picnic area with tables, fireplaces, piped water, flush toilets, 50 undeveloped sites for RVs or tents, and a youth-group tent area (maximum capacity 45 youth). There are no showers. For reservations at either of these parks, write San Diego County Department of Parks and Recreation, 5201 Ruffin Road, San Diego, CA 92123, or call (619) 565-3600.

Butterfield Ranch, about 6 miles north of Vallecito County Park on Highway S-2 is privately owned but open to the public. It offers 189 full hookups, 44 partial hookups, 50 tent sites, and 4 improved tent sites. Facilities include swimming pools, jacuzzi, laundry, playground, cafe, general store and service station. For reservations write Butterfield Ranch, 14925 Gt. S. Overland, Julian, CA 92036, or call (619) 765-1463.

Desert Ironwoods RV Park and Motel is located on Highway 78 near Ocotillo Wells and the OWSVRA. Facilities include 106 pull-through full-hookup RV sites that can handle any size RV, tent sites, a motel, country store, laundry and pool. For reservations write Desert Ironwoods RV Park and Motel, 4875 Highway 78, Borrego Springs, CA 92004, or call (619) 767-5670. Banner Recreation Ranch is also located on Highway 78, but on the west side of the park on the Banner Grade. It is also privately owned but open to the public. The ranch has a few full-hookup RV sites and also primitive campsites for tents. For reservations and information write Banner Recreation Ranch, 36342 Highway 78, Julian, CA 92036, or call (619) 765-0813.

The Blu-In is located just east of Ocotillo Wells on Highway 78 across the Imperial County line. Facilities include 10 RV spaces with full hookups, a dump station, showers, including a handicapped shower, restaurant and a small store. For reservations or more information, write Blu-In, 2189 Hwy 78, P.O. Box 640, Borrego Springs, CA 92004. There is no telephone.

Salton City Spa & RV Park, on the east side of the state park on Highway 86, has 250 full-hookup RV sites but no tent sites. Facilities include a pool, jacuzzi, mineral spa, sauna, showers, laundry, tennis courts, playground, cable TV and store.

For reservations write Salton City Spa & RV Park, P.O. Box 5375, Salton City, CA 92275, or call (619) 394-4333. Salton City also has other RV campgrounds. For more information, contact the Salton City Chamber of Commerce, North Marina Drive, Salton City, CA 92274, (619) 394-4112.

Primitive Campgrounds

Primitive campgrounds are scattered throughout Anza-Borrego Desert State Park. Some have pit or chemical toilets and trash cans. Open fires are prohibited, and there is not water available. They are available on a first-come-first-served basis. Fees are charged at those primitive camps with toilet facilities and trash receptacles. Primitive campgrounds are included on the chart below and shown on the map in the back pocket.

Horse Camp

A campground designed especially for equestrians, at the entrance to Coyote Canyon, offers access to many miles of horse trails which traverse this stream-laced canyon. The Coyote Canyon trail system links the Horse Camp with the Pacific Crest Trail. The 10 campsites have tables, barbecue stoves or fire rings, drinking water and chemical toilets. A solar-heated shower is nearby. Electrical hookups are not available. There is parking for horse trailers and 40 corrals. The Horse Camp is located off Borrego Springs Road near the entrance to Indian Head Ranch. Sites can be reserved by writing MISTIX, P.O. Box 85705, San Diego, CA 92138-5705, or calling (800) 444-7275 to charge by VISA or MasterCard. For Horse Camp and equestrian regulations, see page 33.

State Park Campgrounds

	Elevation	Established Campsites	Tap Water	Shade Ramada	Toilets: Flush (F) Pit (P) Chemical (C) None (O)	Accessible by Family Car	Nearest Service Station (Miles)	Nearest Grocery Store (Miles)	Distance from Park Hdqrs. (Miles)	Map Coordinates	
Borrego Palm Canyon Campground	775	117	•	•	F	•	2	2	1	C-3	Also RV sit and group c
Tamarisk Grove Campground	1400	25	•	•	F	•	7	12	13	D-4	Also RV sit
Bow Willow Campground	950	15	•	•	C	•	10	10	55	G-5	
Sheep Canyon Primitive Camp Area	1500	4			P		13	13	14	C-3	
Fish Creek Primitive Camp Area	280	0			O	•	12	11	30	E-6	
Culp Valley Primitive Camp Area	3400	0			O	•	10	10	10	D-3	
Little Pass Primitive Camp Area	2500	0			C	•	11	26	29	E-3	
Yaqui Pass Primitive Camp Area	1730	0			O	•	3	8	13	D-4	
Yaqui Well Primitive Camp Area	1400	0			C	•	6	11	13	D-3	
Arroyo Salado Primitive Camp Area	880	0			C	•	16	16	19	C-5	
Mtn. Palm Springs Primitive Camp Area	760	0			C	•	9	9	54	G-5	
Dos Cabezas Primitive Camp Area	2000	0			O		10	10	65	H-5	
Vernon V. Whitaker Horse Camp	775	10	•		C	•	6	6	7	C-3	

USEFUL TELEPHONE NUMBERS AND ADDRESSES
(area code 619)

Anza-Borrego Desert State Park......................... Visitor Center 767-4205
P.O. Box 299   Administrative Office 767-5311
Borrego Springs, CA 92004   Recorded Info 767-4684

MISTIX Campground Reservations .... to charge (800) 444-PARK
P.O. Box 85705
San Diego, CA 92138-5705

Ocotillo Wells State Vehicular Recreation Area (OWSVRA)................ 767-5391
P.O. Box 360
Borrego Springs, CA 92004

Bureau of Land Management (BLM) 352-5842
El Centro Resource Area Office
333 S. Waterman
El Centro, CA 92243

San Diego County Dept. of Parks & Recreation 565-3600
(reservations for Agua Caliente Springs County Park and Vallecito County Park)
5201 Ruffin Road
San Diego, CA 92123

Private campgrounds and motels:

Banner Recreation Ranch... 765-0813
36342 Highway 78
Julian, CA 92036

Blu-In.. no phone
2189 Hwy 78 (P.O. Box 640)
Borrego Springs, CA 92004

Butterfield Ranch 765-1463
14925 Gt. S. Overland
Julian, CA 92036

La Casa del Zorro Resort.. 767-5323
Yaqui Pass & Borrego Springs Road   (800) 824-1884
P.O. Box 127
Borrego Springs, CA 92004

Desert Ironwoods RV Park & Motel 767-5670
4875 Highway 78   CB Channel 7
Borrego Springs, CA 92004

Hacienda del Sol 767-5442
610 Palm Canyon
P.O. Box 366
Borrego Springs, CA 92004

Oasis Motel... 767-5409
366 Palm Canyon
P.O. Box 221
Borrego Springs, CA 92004

Palm Canyon Resort (RV Park, Hotel, and Restaurant) 767-5341
221 Palm Canyon Drive   (800) 242-0044
P.O. Box 956
Borrego Springs, CA 92004

Salton City Spa & RV Park... 394-4333
P.O. Box 5375
Salton City, CA 92275

Stanlunds Resort Motel. 767-5501
2771 Borrego Springs Road
P.O. Box 278
Borrego Springs, CA 92004

Condominium Rentals:
Club Circle Resort Apartments 767-5944
  P.O. Box 338
  Borrego Springs, CA 92004
Rams Hill Patio Homes 767-5028
  P.O. Box "A"
  Borrego Springs, CA 92004
Villas Borrego Resort Apartments. 767-5371
  P.O. Box 1077
  Borrego Springs, CA 92004

Borrego Medical Center. 767-5051
  (24 hour emergency medical service)
  Rams Hill Road
  P.O. Box 938
  Borrego Springs, CA 92004

Pioneers' Memorial Hospital 344-2120
  (24 hour emergency medical service)
  207 W. Legion Road
  Brawley, CA 92227

Borrego Springs Chamber of Commerce 767-5555
  P.O. Box 66
  Borrego Springs, CA 92004

Northeast Rural Bus Service 765-0145

Automobile Club of Southern California. . . . . (800) 458-5972
  (emergency roadside service for Anza-Borrego)

Highway condition information 293-3484

Weather forecast 289-1212

Forest Service, Cleveland National Forest 232-3769

All emergencies requiring police/ambulance assistance 911

California Highway Patrol (non-emergency) 296-6661

San Diego County Sheriff (non-emergency) Borrego Springs. 767-5656

San Diego County Sheriff (non-emergency) Jacumba 766-4585

Imperial County Sheriff (non-emergency). . . . . (800) 452-2051

CB Communication—Park Rangers & Anza-Borrego
  REACT Monitor . . . . Citizens' Band Channel 9
  Burro Bend REACT (Ocotillo Wells) . . . . Citizens' Band Channel 20
  Desert Ironwoods REACT . . . . Citizens' Band Channel 7

Cuyamaca State Park. 765-0755

Los Coyotes Indian Reservation (Banning Taylor). 782-3269
  P.O. Box 249
  Warner Springs, CA 92086

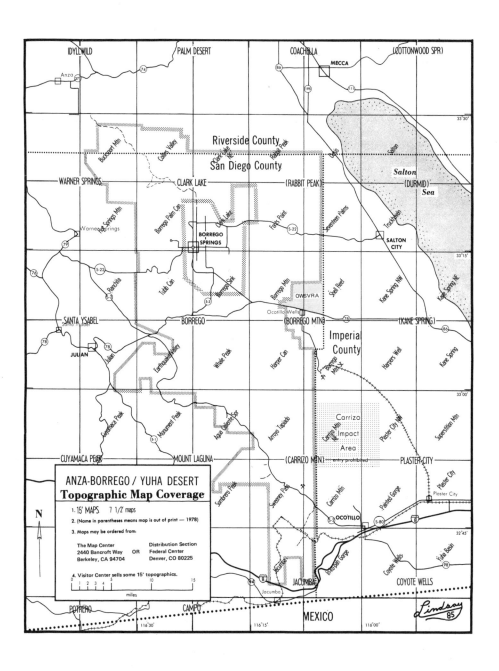

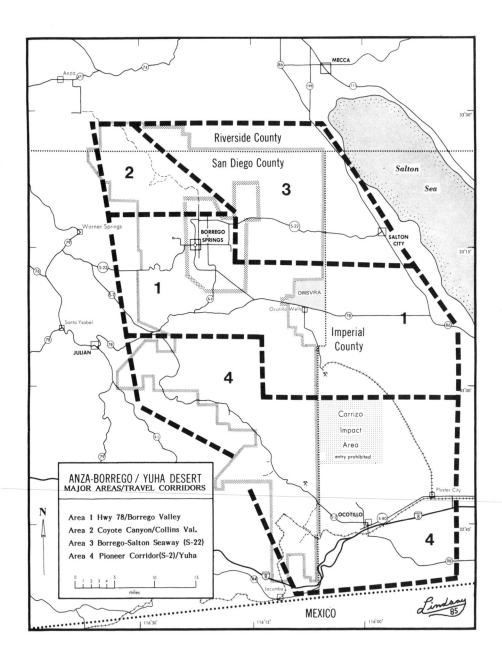

ANZA-BORREGO / YUHA DESERT
MAJOR AREAS/TRAVEL CORRIDORS

N

Area 1 Hwy 78/Borrego Valley
Area 2 Coyote Canyon/Collins Val.
Area 3 Borrego-Salton Seaway (S-22)
Area 4 Pioneer Corridor(S-2)/Yuha

The Trips

Trip Descriptions and Route Conditions

This guidebook to the Anza-Borrego/Yuha region describes four areas, each of which is aligned along a major corridor of travel through the area. The trip descriptions, which are the heart of the book, are classified as follows.

Basic Trip: The basic corridor route through an area, numbered the same as the area. For example, Trip 4 is Highway S-2 through Area 4, The Pioneer Corridor.

Alternate Trip: A major route which departs from the basic trip, numbered the same as the basic trip plus a letter. For example, Trip 4A is Pinyon Mountain Road, which departs from Trip 4, Highway S-2.

Side Trip: A shorter route off a basic or an alternate route, having no number.

The route condition for a trip is classified according to the most difficult portion of the road or trail along that route. THESE ARE APPROXIMATIONS ONLY, because conditions on desert routes change constantly due to flash floods, mud and rock slides, changes in vegetation patterns, road work by jeep clubs, etc. What is passable by family car today may be jeep-only tomorrow. The route conditions are:

Paved or dirt road—generally passable by conventional auto and heavy recreation vehicles.

Light auto road—generally passable by unladen pickup truck or small, high-clearance auto.

Jeep road or route—generally passable by off-highway vehicle, such as four-wheel drive, dune buggy or motorcycle.

Hike—foot travel. Some hiking trails are maintained and signed; some are simply cross-country routes.

REMINDER:—Throughout the state park and in most BLM areas, vehicle travel is permitted only on designated routes of travel, such as dirt roads. Washes may or may not be so designated. Watch for signs or route-of-travel posts. Violators will be fined. The trend in park-road management is to eliminate duplicating routes to the same point.

As in any off-road guidebook, stated mileages may vary somewhat from those actually noted by the user due to variance in odometer accuracy, wheel slippage in sand or rough spots, and variations in route conditions. In this guide stated mileages have been carefully calculated on the basis of several sources, including topographic, BLM, state-park and auto-club maps, as well as several vehicle or foot transits of each route by the authors. However, travelers should continually cross-check map, guidebook, odometer, and compass references with the terrain. Be sure to reverse left-right designations when proceeding in the opposite direction from that logged. [Bracketed M numbers] represent Mile Markers on Hwys S-2, S-3, S-22.

Much of this guidebook describes roads and trails remote from service facilities, and anyone who follows one of them should be an experienced desert traveler and seasoned camper.

Monument at Scissors Crossing—start of Trip 1

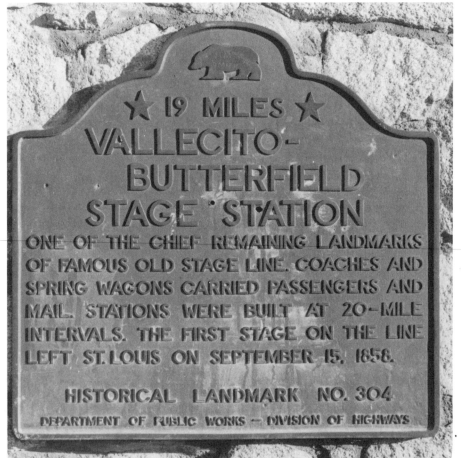

★ 19 MILES ★
VALLECITO-
BUTTERFIELD
STAGE STATION
ONE OF THE CHIEF REMAINING LANDMARKS
OF FAMOUS OLD STAGE LINE. COACHES AND
SPRING WAGONS CARRIED PASSENGERS AND
MAIL. STATIONS WERE BUILT AT 20-MILE
INTERVALS. THE FIRST STAGE ON THE LINE
LEFT ST. LOUIS ON SEPTEMBER 15, 1858.

HISTORICAL LANDMARK NO. 304
DEPARTMENT OF PUBLIC WORKS — DIVISION OF HIGHWAYS

AREA 1: The San Felipe Corridor and Borrego Valley

(Highways 78, S-3 and S-22 west)

Overview and Access

The San Felipe Corridor and the Borrego Valley form the broad midriff of the Anza-Borrego region, extending eastward from pine-covered uplands and mile-high peaks to palm-filled canyons and below-sea-level desert plains. This area, although the most inhabited and best-known area of the Anza-Borrego, still calls the desert explorer to little-visited retreats which may be found atop high mountain ridges, in deep desert canyons or in sandy washes.

Highway 78 from Julian toward the Salton Sea, traversing the drainage system of San Felipe Wash and its tributaries, has been a major corridor of travel since the late 1800s. As early as 1772 Pedro Fages opened the eastern part of this corridor from San Sebastian/Harpers Well through the Borrego Badlands and Borrego Valley en route to Coyote Canyon. Along this same route the visitor can retrace the steps of Juan Bautista de Anza and hundreds of colonists and pioneers who followed the original Sonora-to-San Francisco overland trail.

Borrego Valley, the recreational focal point of the northern Anza-Borrego region, encompasses the town of Borrego Springs and the park headquarters/main campground/visitor center complex. Highway S-22 traverses the valley east-west, generally parallel to Highway 78 and the San Felipe corridor. S-22 and 78 are joined by various historic and scenic routes which are major recreational thoroughfares today. These routes include Grapevine Canyon and the Jasper Trail, Highway S-3 over Yaqui Pass, the Borrego Springs Road, and San Felipe Wash through the Borrego Badlands.

Ocotillo Wells, in Lower Borrego Valley, is another popular recreational focal point, with Borrego Mountain to the northwest, the Ocotillo Wells State Vehicular Recreation Area to the north and the Split Mountain/Fish Creek area to the south. Farther east the R9/R10 poleline road offers access to the San Felipe Hills and the San Sebastian/Harpers Well areas. Highway 86 forms the eastern boundary of the region, connecting S-22 and 78.

As is true throughout the State Park and most BLM areas, vehicle travel is restricted to designated roads. The only exception in this area is the 38,000-acre Ocotillo Wells State Vehicular Recreation Area. Private property, including most of Borrego Valley, is subject to the control of the property owners.

Trip 1: San Felipe Corridor (Highway 78)

From: Scissors Crossing in San Felipe Valley

To: Highway 86 junction (38.8 miles one way; all paved road with jeep routes in side canyons and washes)

Via: Sentenac Canyon, Highway S-3/Tamarisk Grove Campground junction, Mescal Bajada, The Narrows, Borrego Mountain, Benson Dry Lake/Ocotillo Wells/Split Mountain Road junction

With Side trips To: Yaqui Pass and Borrego Valley, old Kane Springs Road, Borrego Springs Road, West Butte of Borrego Mountain, Blow Sand Canyon, Squaw Peak, Shell Reef and Salton City

Mileage From:

Scissors Crossing	Hiway 86	Checkpoint Description
0.0	38.8	The trip begins at Scissors Crossing, the junction of Highway 78 and S-2 at a monument marking the route of the Butterfield Overland Mail. On a flat about ½ mile northwest, Warren F. Hall built and operated the San Felipe station of the Butterfield Overland Mail, which operated from 1858 to 1861. This old station was one of the major stops on the Butterfield line, situated halfway between Vallecito and Warner's Ranch. The station was later used by Banning stages and by the military during the Civil War. The station was built on a former Indian village site; only the vague outlines of the station walls remain today. The San Felipe Valley was part of an ancient trade route of Cahuilla, Kumeyaay, Kamia and Luiseño Indians well before it became part of the Butterfield route. It was also traversed by explorers, trappers, soldiers and emigrants.
0.3	38.5	Junction with Highway S-2 northwest (left) and San Felipe Creek.
1.0	37.8	Enter Sentenac Cienega (marsh) and Sentenac Canyon. Narrow Sentenac Canyon forms a partial barrier to water flowing from San Felipe Valley. The water that is held back forms Sentenac Cienega. The overflow of water continues on through the canyon but goes underground 2.5 miles farther. The abundance of water supports a lush plant growth, with many mesquite trees rimming the canyon and the cienega. In the canyon are cottonwoods, willows, a dense growth of carrizo grass and a great variety of other plants. The cienega and canyon have long been a favorite haunt of students of botany. In 1832 English botanist Thomas Coulter collected screwbean mesquite and noted a variety of plants in and near the cienega. The bird life in Sentenac Cienega and Sentenac Canyon is outstanding in spring and fall due to its location on the migration flyway. Deer, coyotes, foxes and bobcats are also often seen in the area. The cienega and canyon were named for Paul Sentenac, a Frenchman who in the 1880s homesteaded 160 acres east of Scissors Crossing and built a stone cabin atop the rocky little hill at the mouth of Sentenac Canyon. Sentenac raised cattle, goats and sheep, pasturing them in and around the cienega or down on the desert near Yaqui Well in San Felipe Wash. The Sentenac Canyon road was begun in 1917 and completed in 1932. Before the completion of this route, the old road wound over the hills south of Sentenac Mountain and emerged into San Felipe Wash on the desert through Plum Canyon.

Scissors Crossing	Hiway 86	Checkpoint Description
2.9	35.9	San Felipe Creek bridge (elevation 2000). Several years ago the US Border Patrol maintained a camp here, and the officers constructed a crude swimming pool under the old bridge. The pool has since washed out. After leaving the bridge area, note the first heavy stands of *Agave deserti* on the hillsides to the right of the grade. The young flower stalk, roasted in a rock-lined pit, was one of the staple foods of desert Indians. It is said to taste like a cross between baked squash and sweet potato.
4.1	34.7	To the north (left), at the confluence of San Felipe Creek and Grapevine Canyon, is an Indian area of some distinction. Surface evidence includes pottery fragments and flaking and grinding tools. A flood in 1961 exposed part of a sand bank in which 5 fire hearths were discovered at different levels, the lowest being 32 feet below the present surface. Archeologists used carbon samples from the fire in which an arrowhead was found to date the fire as 5000 years old. The 4 other embedded fires and surface evidence indicate continuous use for 5000 years.
4.3	34.5	Entrance to Plum Canyon on the south (right). The entrance to Grapevine Canyon (see Trip 1B) is on the north (left). Plum Canyon is negotiable by light auto for 1.5 miles. The Grapevine Canyon

Looking west over the narrows of San Felipe Wash

Scissors Crossing	Hiway 86	Checkpoint Description
		route is an even older road to the desert than the Plum Canyon route.
5.4	33.4	Kenyon Cove is on the south (right). The cove area was named for former Park Superintendent William Kenyon, who established the ranger patrol system and guided the development of this state park for many years.
6.1	32.7	Lizard Canyon is to the south (right). This rough, sandy, rocky wash is negotiable by jeep for about 1½ miles.
7.0	31.8	Junction of Highway 78 and Yaqui Pass Road (S-3).

Side Trip Via S-3 to Yaqui Pass and Borrego Valley

0.0   Junction.

0.1   Cross San Felipe Creek. Turn west (left) for Yaqui Well and Grapevine Canyon (see Trip 1B).

0.3   Tamarisk Grove Campground has 25 sites, each with parking spur, picnic table, shade ramada, food locker and barbecue. Drinking water and restrooms with flush toilets and showers are available. A park ranger is in attendance. Opposite the entrance station across the highway is the 1-mile Cactus Loop Trail.

1.6   Remnants of the old Yaqui Pass roadbed, constructed during World War II for use by Gen. George Patton's vehicles, are visible just downhill.

1.9   Kenyon Overlook Foot Trail. It is ¼ mile to an excellent view (on a clear day) of Mescal Bajada, Pinyon Mountains, and the Salton Sea.

2.1   Yaqui Pass Primitive Campground (elevation 1730) has no toilets, no trash cans and no water.

2.8   As the road drops down from Yaqui Pass, a sweeping panorama of Borrego Valley comes into view. This view focuses on the heart and the most-visited parts of the Anza-Borrego region: the resort town of Borrego Springs and, to the northwest, the Park Visitors Center, Park Headquarters, the main campground, and Hellhole, Borrego Palm and Henderson canyons, which drain the San Ysidro Mountains. To the north is the entrance to Coyote Canyon, with its year-round running creek, and Coyote Mountain, which separates Coyote Canyon from Clark Dry Lake and Clark Valley. Beyond these are the Santa Rosa Mountains and Toro Peak. Font's Point, the high point of the badlands, and Borrego Mountain can be seen in the east.

6.8   La Casa del Zorro was the first and is the finest resort lodge in the valley. In 1936 Noel Crickmer purchased the original ranch at this location, and then turned it into the Desert Lodge the following year. This quiet desert hotel was purchased in 1960 by James S. Copley, owner of a newspaper chain.

  2½ miles northwest of La Casa del Zorro via Borrego Valley Road is the original center of the townsite at the now defunct "Borego" store, gas station and post office, which was opened in 1924 by Elsie A. Wynn and sold to homesteader Ed Duvall in 1927. The "Borego" store retained the original spelling of the valley despite the official

Scissors Crossing	Hiway 86	Checkpoint Description
		change to the Spanish spelling of Borrego in the 1950s. The store is on private property.
	9.0	The Glorietta Canyon turnoff is 2.2 miles west of La Casa del Zorro via Borrego Springs Road. The dirt road turnoff south climbs up into Yaqui Meadows and swings west (right) into Glorietta Canyon after 2 miles. From the dead end, hikers may continue up canyon and eventually onto Pinyon Ridge, near Desert Viewpoint. (See Trip 1A—Old Culp Valley, Wilson Trail.)
	12.1	Christmas Circle in Borrego Springs. From this valley hub, the mountains and State Park lands which enclose Borrego Valley may be seen in every direction.

End of Side Trip

Scissors Crossing	Hiway 86	Checkpoint Description
7.9	30.9	Stag Cove on the south (right) may be traveled for 0.4 mile. The wash is sandy but negotiable by conventional cars with care.
		Mescal Bajada is the piedmont lying at the north base of the Vallecito Mountains. It is about 4 square miles in area, extending from Stag Cove on the west to The Narrows along Highway 78 on the east. Three major washes—Chuckwalla, Mine and Pinyon—drain from the Pinyon Mountains across the area. The latter two serve as routes of travel. The flooding in these washes can be violent during summer storms. This flooding has carried down loose gravel and sand from the surrounding mountains, which has been deposited on the piedmont as alluvium. It is from the resulting alluvial fans (*bajadas* in Spanish) that the area derives its name. A heavy stand of desert agave (*mescal*) covers a large part of Mescal Bajada. The dissected, underlying piedmont formation can be clearly seen at The Narrows rest area. Six varieties of cacti that grow in the Anza-Borrego area are represented on Mescal Bajada. Ocotillos are especially thick on the sandy surfaces, with many smoke trees and desert lavenders in the washes. After adequate winter rains, the spring flower display here is outstanding.
9.0	29.8	Chuckwalla Wash to the south (right) is open to foot traffic only. It offers a hiking route which penetrates deep into the North Pinyon Mountains.
9.8	29.0	Mine Canyon on the south (right) may be negotiated by jeeps for 4.6 miles. An Indian area known as Rocky Point is 1.5 miles from Highway 78. Grinding stones, slicks and morteros can be found on the left at the base of an outcropping. Much of the surface evidence of Indian use has been flooded away, but the number and size of the morteros are indications of heavy use for a long time. A better indication of the extent of Indian use are the hundreds of agave-roasting pits scattered across the flat and on the mountainside. Well-defined trails cross the area in the direction of Yaqui Well, The Narrows and Harper Flat. The mine, for which the canyon was named, was an unsuccessful gold mine which has since been blasted shut.
11.2	27.6	Pinyon Wash on the south (right) is jeep-only for 4.9 miles. At mile 1.6 is the junction with Nolina Wash, to the right (south). Nolina Wash is negotiable for another 1.6 miles. From the road's end in Pinyon Wash, it is roughly a 2-mile hike south over boulders into

The Narrows service station (1933)—now gone

Scissors Crossing	Hiway 86	Checkpoint Description
		Harper Flat. Harper Flat was the site of one of the largest Indian camps in the Anza-Borrego area. Bedrock morteros and metates, shards, flaking and rough hand tools testify to the heavy use it had years ago. A complex of Indian trails radiates from the area. Harper Flat has an abundance of vegetation typical of a desert area of this elevation (2600 feet average elevation)—Mojave yucca, nolina, ocotillo, agave, desert willow, California juniper, desert lavender, indigo and cassia.
11.7	27.1	Parking area for Narrows Earth Trail is to the south (right). The trail is ⅓ mile long. A park brochure, which may be obtained from the visitor center or from any ranger, describes the geology of the area.
11.8	27.0	Quartz Vein Wash on the south (right) is a sandy road negotiable by jeep for 0.4 mile.
12.3	26.5	The old Borrego Valley Road is on the north (left, signed) nearly opposite a substation. The dead end road may be followed through Cactus Valley up the ridge. The old road passes through one of the last remaining areas of tall barrel cacti. Years ago, according to old timers, the wide alluvial fan sloping down the north side of Yaqui Pass supported a fine growth of these barrel cacti, many of them 5 and 6 feet tall. But commercial interests have hauled away the tallest barrels to decorate lawns and gardens in the cities.
12.7	26.1	Nude Wash, on the right, is negotiable for 0.4 mile.
13.9	24.9	The old Kane Springs Road junction is straight ahead to the east.

Side Trip Along the Kane Springs Road (dirt road)

0.0	Junction.
2.5	Harper Canyon jeep road is to the south (right). It may be followed about 2.1 miles to the roadhead at elevation 1200. The foot route from there up the narrow, rocky canyon

Scissors Crossing	Hiway 86	Checkpoint Description
		emerges onto Harper Flat at elevation 2230, in the heart of the Vallecito Mountains.
	3.0	A dirt road joins from the north (left). It is 1.6 miles to Highway 78 on this very sandy road.
	3.3	Cactus Garden area. This area was so named because of its profusion of cacti. Six of the 12 varieties of cacti indigenous to this part of the Colorado Desert are found here. Also in abundance are other desert plants that grow in rocky terrain and dry washes, such as ocotillo, ironwood tree, smoke tree, desert lavender and indigo bush.
	8.5	Junction with the paved Split Mountain Road near the abandoned townsite of Little Borrego and the Miracle Hotel (large concrete slab southeast of the junction). It is 2.5 miles north (left) to Highway 78 in Ocotillo Wells.

End of Side Trip

| 15.7 | 23.1 | Junction with Borrego Springs Road (paved) to the north (left). |

Side Trip Along Borrego Springs Road

	0.0	Junction.
	0.8	The road drops steeply into and crosses the mile-wide San Felipe Wash at Texas Dip. Jeeps may proceed down-wash north (right) 4.7 miles to the Borrego Sink Wash junction (see Trip 1C).
	6.3	Junction with Yaqui Pass Road (S-3) at La Casa del Zorro.

End of Side Trip

| 17.2 | 21.6 | Turnoff north (left) to Borrego Mountain (signed). Borrego Mountain is composed of two buttes. The West Butte is mainly an area of colorful clays and sandstones uplifted and tilted during the raising of the granite mountain. Deep erosion has exposed the strata of colored clays and sandstones. The East Butte is covered with a dark desert varnish. A striking feature on the east end of East Butte is a huge flow of blow-sand. |

Miracle Hotel in Little Borrego—now gone

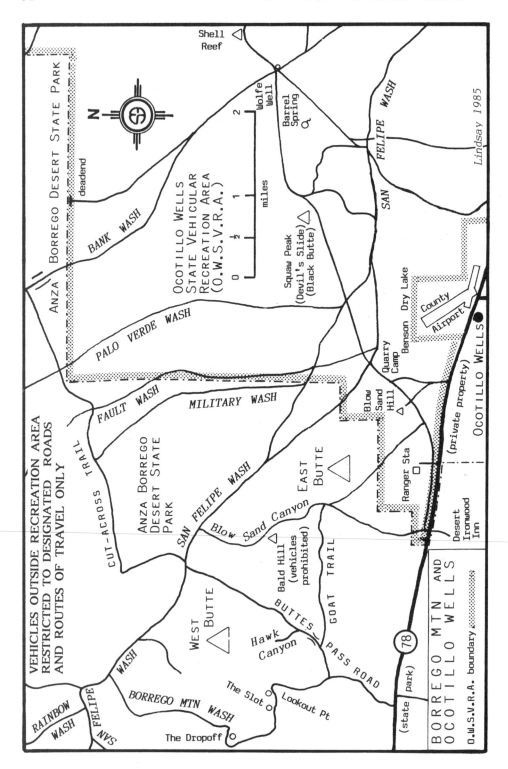

Scissors Crossing	Hiway 86	Checkpoint Description

Side Trip into West Butte Section of Borrego Mountain

0.0 Turnoff on Highway 78, 1.5 miles east of Borrego Springs Road and 5.2 miles west of Split Mountain Road in Ocotillo Wells. Proceed north on the dirt road.

1.0 Desert Lookout fork (signed). One may travel two directions here—northwest (left) to Desert Lookout or east (right) to Buttes Pass/Goat Trail.

To Desert Lookout and Borrego Mountain Wash

1.0 Desert Lookout fork. Turn northwest (left) to . . .

2.1 Desert Lookout. A short scramble down leads the hiker into the Slot, a superb example of badlands erosion. In the shadowy defile, yellow sandstone walls rise 50 feet or more on either side. At each turn down-wash there are new surprises as the passageway narrows until a large person might have difficulty squeezing through. The hiker may continue west and north about 0.7 mile to rejoin the vehicle trail at the bottom of . . .

2.9 The Dropoff. Conventional vehicles must backtrack from the top of the Dropoff to Highway 78. OHVs can negotiate the sandy pitch down into Borrego Mountain Wash. From the bottom the route is ONE WAY ONLY north.

3.1 The Wind Caves are visible about 0.3 mile east of the wash. Here the sandstone hills have been dramatically pierced like swiss cheese by wind and water erosion. The route now traverses a difficult drop over sandstone ledges where the route again becomes two-way. Cautious driving is mandatory through the narrow sandstone palisades.

5.6 Junction with San Felipe Wash route (see Trip 1C).

To Buttes Pass/Goat Trail

1.0 Desert Lookout fork. Turn east (right) to . . .

1.5 Buttes Pass/Goat Trail fork. One may travel two directions here. North (left) leads into Buttes Canyon. East (right) leads 1.9 miles along Goat Trail to Blow Sand Canyon (jeep only). (See below for Side Trip to Blow Sand Canyon from Highway 78.)

1.5 Buttes Pass/Goat Trail fork. To enter Buttes Canyon, turn north (left) over Buttes Pass and into the canyon to . . .

1.9 Hawk Canyon turnoff northwest (left). One-half mile up this turnoff is a popular and excellent camping area in a salmon-tinted cliff bowl, offering the greatest variety of colors of any canyon walls in the Anza-Borrego region. Golden eagles have been sighted here.

Continuing north down Buttes Pass Road, there are three excellent walk-in campsites in coves west (left) of the road.

3.6 Join San Felipe Wash route (see Trip 1C)

End of Side Trip

17.2	21.6	Continue the basic trip eastbound along Highway 78.
17.4	21.4	Turnoff south (right) leads 1.6 miles over a dirt road to join the old Kane Springs Road at the Cactus Garden.
19.5	19.3	Turnoff south (right) leads to the Desert Ironwoods Inn. Turnoff north (left) is a . . .

Scissors Crossing	Hiway 86	Checkpoint Description

Side Trip to Blow Sand Canyon

0.0   Turnoff north and climb (jeep only).

1.5   Continue north (straight). Fork to southeast (right) goes 2.5 miles back to Highway 78.

1.7   Fork. West (left) fork is Goat Trail, which leads 1.9 miles to Buttes Pass. North (right) fork drops into Blow Sand Canyon, an impressive high-walled wash.

2.5   Bald Hill is the large sand dune to the west (left), the only such formation within the huge state park. The fragile slope is absolutely closed to vehicles.

3.5   Junction with San Felipe Wash route (see Trip 1C).

End of Side Trip to Blow Sand Canyon

| 20.4 | 18.4 | Turnoff north (left) to OWSVRA Ranger Station. |
| 22.4 | 16.4 | Split Mountain Road junction in Ocotillo Wells (gas, restaurants and supplies). This self-styled "Dune Buggy Capital of the World" is strategically located near the southern border of the Ocotillo Wells State Vehicular Recreation Area. In this area OHV travel is unrestricted. The recreation area is bounded generally by Borrego Mountain and Fault Wash on the west, Cut-Across Trail and Bank Wash on the north, the county line on the east, and Benson Dry Lake and Highway 78 on the south. Travel beyond these boundaries is restricted to designated routes of travel. For information about the OWSVRA, refer to page 32. |

The route northwest up San Felipe Wash is Trip 1C.

The route south to Fish Creek and Split Mountain is Trip 1D.

| 23.6 | 15.2 | Turnoff north (left) for . . . |

Side Trip to Squaw Peak (Devil's Slide, Black Butte) and Shell Reef (jeep road)

0.0   Wolfe Well Road turns off 1.2 miles east of Split Mountain Road. (House in the tamarisk trees at 23.1 was the Toner turkey ranch, which was forced to close by noise pollution created by military aircraft using Benson Dry Lake during the late 1930s.) Proceed northeast over low hills to . . .

2.3   Cross the San Felipe Wash to the north bank. A jeep road forks north (left) 1.5 miles to Devil's Slide, an isolated island of gneiss and schist about ½ mile long rising some 200 feet above the surrounding flat desert. The dark desert varnish covering the exposed rock of Devil's Slide makes it appear as an almost black island in contrast to the light-colored sand of the surrounding desert. There are several old mine shafts and tunnels along the south flank of this small mountain. Miners used the area around Barrel Spring, lying in a large mesquite sand dune about one mile east of the mountain, as a base camp while working these mines. Supposedly, ghostly apparitions can be seen near these mines. These apparitions, described as flickering lights, have usually been sighted soon after rain has fallen in the desert. Other lights appearing in the sky, known as Borrego fireballs, have also been reported. Devil's Slide is in the center of the OWSVRA. It is a popular hill with good climbs for OHVs.

Scissors Crossing	Hiway 86	Checkpoint Description
		The main route continues northeast to . . .
	3.9	Wolfe Well, a former oil-test site marked by pipe and rubble. The route forks here.
		The east (right) route leads 4.5 miles to Tarantula Wash. Beyond the wash are the San Felipe Hills, with gas domes, old oil-test sites and Indian village archeological sites (see Trip 1F).
		The northeast (straight) route leads to Shell Reef, 1.0 mile from Wolfe Well. Shell Reef is a 4-million-year-old oyster-shell reef that appears to be a mountain that has slid apart, leaving a long trough through which vehicles may drive. The five-foot-thick layer of fossil shells on the reef shows that this area was once a sea bottom. OHV traffic on Shell Reef itself is prohibited due to its significant but fragile prehistoric fossil beds.
		The northwest (left) route leads 4.3 miles to Cut-Across Trail via Bank Wash.

End of Side Trip

Scissors Crossing	Hiway 86	Checkpoint Description
24.1	14.7	Los Puertocitos Historical Monument, on the south side (right) of the road, designates this Anza expedition campsite on the edge of the Ocotillo Badlands in the waterless flat just east. The badlands here are an isolated hump of wrinkled folds and rolling sand. Through these hills is the gap from which Anza derived the name of Los Puertocitos. The notch in the mountains on the northwest horizon marks San Carlos Pass, in Coyote Canyon, which was Anza's exit route from the desert.
25.5	13.3	County Line.
27.6	11.2	San Felipe Wash crossing the Blu-In store (gas, food and supplies). Jeeps may proceed either way in this OHV-populated wash.
28.4	10.4	Cahuilla Road turnoff north (left). Just beyond Tarantula Wash, 5.3 miles north, is the abandoned Standard Oil test site for which the road was originally named. The road then swings east, providing access to the San Felipe Hills.
30.5	8.3	Tarantula Wash crossing.
31.7	7.1	The R9/R10 poleline road (Texaco Oil Well Road) crossing is marked by an electrical substation on the south (right) side of the road.
		The route south to Kane Springs Road, San Sebastian Marsh and Harpers Well is Trip 1E.
		The route north into the San Felipe Hills is Trip 1F.
38.8	0.0	Junction with Highway 86.

Side Trip on Highway 86, Between Highway 78 and Highway S-22

Mileage From:

78	S-22	Checkpoint Description
0.0	12.4	The junction of Highway 86 and Highway 78 is called "Trifolium" for the Trifolium Extension Canal, which is the northwest terminus of the Imperial Valley irrigation system. A US Border Patrol inspection station is here.
		It is 1.7 miles southeast (right) to Kane Springs.
		Proceed northwest (left).
4.1	8.3	Turnoff east (right) to Salton Sea Test Base (US Navy). No

78	S-22	Checkpoint Description

trespassing. The beach line of ancient Lake Cahuilla is between the road and the base of the San Felipe Hills to the west (left). The hills here would have been the east edge of a long peninsula jutting out into the lake, probably attracting a substantial Indian fishing operation with village sites nearby on the peninsula.

8.5   3.9 Campbell Wash crossing at Bridge no. 58-15. This wash is the drainage for the northern San Felipe Hills.

9.7   2.7 Tule Wash crossing at Bridge no. 58-14.

Side Trip to San Diego County Line
0.0 Tule Wash junction with Highway 86. Proceed west.
2.4 South Fork of Tule Wash. Bear west (right).
2.5 Tule Spring is alkaline
3.8 Giant Sand Dune, an unfortunate misnomer as it's dwindling away rapidly.
9.5 Pumpkin Patch turnoff south (left).
10.4 County line and boundary of Anza-Borrego Desert State Park (see Trip 3B for mileages up Tule Wash within the Park).
End of Side Trip

9.8   2.6 County dump turnoff west (left). The road joins the old military jeep road, which proceeds west and was the preferred access to Pumpkin Patch in earlier years. The dump is 3 miles west. Beyond, the road is difficult to follow due to flash flooding.

10.2   2.2 Air Park Drive. It is 1.0 mile west (left) to the Salton City Airport.

10.9   1.5 The foundation of the old Squeaky Springs Service Station is on the west (left) side of the road. This was also called Winona on older maps. It was mentioned in early logs as a tow-out and repair facility for travelers stuck in the arroyos to the west.

11.2   1.2 Arroyo Salado crossing at Bridge no. 58-13.

Side Trip to San Diego County Line
0.0 Arroyo Salado junction with Highway 86.
2.5 Fork to first north wash. Salt and Soda Springs is 0.5 mile up this wash on the northeast bank. Continue west, bearing left up Arroyo Salado.
3.9 Fork. The North Fork of Arroyo Salado joins here at the Lone Palm tree. Bear left up Arroyo Salado.
4.4 Fork. This is another junction with the North Fork of Arroyo Salado. Bear left up Arroyo Salado.
10.0 San Diego county line and the boundary of Anza-Borrego Desert State Park (see Trip 3B for a description of Arroyo Salado within the Park.)
End of Side Trip

12.4   0.0 Junction with Highway S-22 in Salton City. It is 28.3 miles to Borrego Springs along S-22 from here.

Borrego Valley

Borrego Springs

The town of Borrego Springs sits snugly on the floor of Borrego Valley surrounded by the park's imposing mountain ranges. It is a quiet community offering a welcome slower pace for those seeking tranquility, clear air and sunshine. With its many luxury developments, it is worlds apart from that cold, snowy day in December 1775 when the second Anza expedition crossed Borrego Valley to its encampment at the mouth of Coyote Canyon.

For those who prefer non-camping accommodations, Borrego Springs offers eight motels and apartment houses, almost all with pools and some with kitchen facilities, the prices ranging from $40 to $80 per day. There are also trailer parks available, but in a peak tourist season all accommodations fill up quickly.

Grocery stores, pharmacies, service stations, post office, small novelty and gift shops, art galleries, restaurants, sheriff's office and the chamber of commerce are found near Christmas Circle. No bus or taxi service operates in town. However, the Northeast Rural Bus System, operated by the County Transit Authority, offers bus service to El Cajon (near San Diego) several times per week. The 14-passenger bus will carry bicycles with advance notification. Call (619) 765-0145 for schedules and more information. Three community golf courses and tennis courts are open to the public. Night life is quiet, centering around the few restaurants and cocktail lounges in the valley. For further information about the town and accommodations, contact the Chamber of Commerce, P.O. Box 66, Borrego Springs CA 92004, tel. (619) 767-5555.

Camping areas in the Borrego Valley vicinity include the developed campground at Borrego Palm Canyon, and primitive, nonfacility camps in Coyote Canyon, at Pegleg Smith Monument and around Borrego Sink. The latter two areas are privately owned but have been open to public camping. Backpack-only camping is permitted in the west-side canyons.

A 140-space RV park, called Overland Junction, is located at the junction of Palm Canyon Drive and the Montezuma Grade (S-22), about one mile from the Visitor Center. This facility has full hookups, two jacuzzis, two pools, and restaurant facilities in addition to a 44-room hotel, known as Palm Canyon Resort. Call (619) 767-5341 for information and reservations.

Borrego Palm Canyon campground entrance

Visitor Center

NOTICE: Most of Borrego Valley is private property, requiring compliance with regulatory signs, fences, etc. Camp and travel only where obviously permitted or designated.

Christmas Circle is the hub of the valley's road network. Selected local mileages from this point, one way over paved roads, are as follows:

West to Visitor Center 1.7
West to Highway 79 near Warner Springs, via S-22 .... 23.3
North to Coyote Canyon (at pavement's end) 5.3
East to Pegleg Smith Monument via the airport 7.0
East to Salton City via S-22 .... 28.3
Southeast to Ocotillo Wells via Highway 78 .... 18.3
Southeast to Highway 86 via Highway 78 .... 34.7
South to Tamarisk Grove Campground via Highway S-3 .... 11.8
South to Ocotillo and I-8 via Highways S-3, 78, S-2 .... 67.1
Southwest to Julian via Highways S-3, 78 .... 29.2

Visitor Center, Park Headquarters and Main Campground

The park Visitor Center is 1.7 miles west of Christmas Circle on Palm Canyon Drive, just past the Anza-Borrego Park Headquarters. The Visitor Center was literally built right into the hillside. Natural vegetation was carefully removed for construction of the center and then replaced, and it is now part of the center's roof and observation viewpoint. The Visitor Center has an excellent slide program and exhibits on desert geology, plant and wildlife. Interpretive literature and information about the park and the desert in general are available 9–5 daily, except from June through October 1, when the center is open 10–3 on Saturdays and Sundays only. The center sells maps, guidebooks, wildlife posters and illustrated publications. The center is operated by the Anza-Borrego Desert Natural History Association, a volunteer group that raised much of the money needed to build it.

Park headquarters is the administrative center and control point for the park. All ranger patrols are coordinated here by radio transmission. All nature walks, hikes, tours and campfire programs conducted during the main visitor season, from November to May, are also planned and coordinated at the park headquarters. This is a business office. For general information and park orientation, go to the Visitor Center, not park headquarters.

The main full-facility campground is located 1.2 miles north of the Visitor Center, at the mouth of Borrego Palm Canyon at the base of the distinct Indianhead, or "old rain-in-the-face," formation on the San Ysidro Mountain skyline. Visitors will find varied accommodations at the main campground. Trailer sites, with sewer, water and electrical hook-ups, have showers laundry tubs and flush toilets nearby, as do the tent sites, which have shade ramadas, tables and some fireplaces. Day-use picnic areas have shade ramadas, tables, water, gas stoves and flush toilets. Modest fees are charged according to the extent of services desired, with limits on the number of vehicles and people per site and on length of stay. Make reservations with Ticketron, (800) 952-5580. A 24-120-person group overnight site is also available. Check with rangers for reservations or telephone (619) 767-5311.

Hiking Routes in Borrego Valley's Westside Canyons

The Borrego Palm Canyon Trail

The trail is accessible from the west end of the main campground near the campfire circle. This canyon, known as "Tala" by the Indians, was the first site sought for a desert state park, in the late 1920s. It receives more annual visitors than any other single section of the park. The reasons become obvious as the walker proceeds up-canyon along the easy 1½-mile self-guiding nature trail. What at first appears to be a dry, lifeless canyon turns out to have a variety of plant life, palm grottos and a seasonal stream. Before your trek, obtain the descriptive trail leaflet from a ranger or at the Visitor Center.

0.0   Elevation 840. Beginning at the pupfish pond, the trail winds past towering rock walls and through a natural botanical garden where ocotillo, brittle-bush, chuparosa, desert lavender, ironwood tree, cholla, beavertail, mesquite, desert willow and cresote are the major plants. In spring a patchwork blanket of colorful blooms surrounds the nature trail. The canyon also has signs of former Indian habitation—mortero holes and broken bits of pottery. If one is lucky, one may even see a bighorn sheep along the rocky crags of the canyon walls.

1.5   A seasonal cascade of water falls over large boulders within a sheltered palm grove (elevation 1440), making it a popular picnic and rest area. The hiker may take an alternate trail back to the campground from here which parallels the creek trail but is higher on the dry south side of the canyon, so that one obtains a different perspective of the desert biotic community.

          Hiking is much more difficult up-canyon beyond this first palm grove, with dense undergrowth and huge boulders to scramble over and around. Twists and turns in the canyon prevent seeing more than ¼ mile ahead. However, the effort is well worth it, as this is the most colorful section of the canyon. Most of the 800 or

First grove of palms in Borrego Palm Canyon

Swimming pool at Palm Canyon Campgrounds in 1940s (now gone)

more palms that are found in the canyon are in these upper reaches. In one bright-hued sector above the falls, the canyon walls close in and the stream tumbles over a rocky cataract of tan-colored schist rock.

3.2   Elevation 2200. The main (middle) fork trends west (right) while the south fork trends southwest (straight ahead), leading toward the summit of the San Ysidro Mountains. A waterfall is about 0.7 mile up the south fork.

4.3   Elevation 2680. The north fork branches up a fairly prominent side canyon marked by a light-colored triangular peak at its head. The north fork can be followed, keeping to the left at major branches, about 3 more miles to a saddle at 4680 feet which overlooks Indian Canyon. Indian Canyon can be descended carefully over rock faces and ledges (see the Indian Canyon hike in Area 2). This descent should be attempted by experienced climbers only.

    The middle fork of Palm Canyon continues from mile 4.3 for about another 2.5 miles to the boundary of Los Coyotes Indian Reservation, and eventually leads to the old Indian village of San Ignacio, or "Pachewal." Permission of the tribal council is required to cross this boundary. Contact the tribal spokesman for the Los Coyotes Indian Reservation at Warner Springs.

Hellhole Canyon

This long, deep canyon curves southwest-west-northwest in a large arc to Hellhole Flat and features superb stands of palms, sycamores and cottonwoods. There is no vehicular access into Hellhole Canyon. The easier hike is to descend Hellhole from Culp Valley (see mile 3.7 below).

0.0   Elevation 760. The trail leads southwest toward Hellhole Canyon from park headquarters near the Visitor Center.

0.2   A short climb leads right, up to Panorama Outlook, for a good view of the campground and Borrego Valley. Continue south across the steep gully that joins from the west (right) to round the next ridge, then trend southwest (right) along the

	base of the ridgeline, ascending the alluvial fan into Hellhole Canyon. The mouth of the canyon is covered with boulders and the route becomes very difficult to negotiate.
2.7	Elevation 1500. The lower grove of California fan palms and remains of sycamores and cottonwoods are sandwiched between the steep canyon walls. Beyond the grove there is no apparent route, and the hiker has a choice of fighting underbrush in the streambed or detouring higher up along the steep, rocky slopes. Both ways are rugged, but the higher route avoids the mesquite's sharp thorns.
3.0	Elevation 1760, 30-foot waterfall called Maidenhair Fall. The face of the fall and its neighboring grotto are covered by a lacy curtain of maidenhair fern, a rare sight in a desert canyon. The falling water, rich luxurious growth, and the sunlight dappling through the tree tops create a very soothing setting.
3.7	Elevation 2280. Hellhole Canyon forks. The south fork climbs southwest 1.2 miles to Pena Spring (elevation 3440). An easy ½ mile southeast of Pena Spring is Culp Valley Primitive Campground. From here the hiker can return to the valley floor via the California Riding and Hiking Trail, 5.5 miles down the ridge between Hellhole and Dry canyons. Here also at the campground, the hiker may be met by prearranged automobile for a return down Montezuma grade to the valley. The main Hellhole Canyon continues on from the mile 3.7 fork.
4.6	Elevation 2730. The north fork branches right, climbing northwest 1.3 miles past Hellhole Flat on the right and on up the southeast flank of San Ysidro Mountain. The main Hellhole Canyon continues on about another 2 miles west toward the Thimble, a symmetrical peak (elevation 5775) at the head of the canyon.

Henderson Canyon

This canyon is reached 3.5 miles north of Christmas Circle on Borrego Springs Road. From the sharp turn east onto Henderson Canyon Road, a dirt road leads west approximately 1½ miles across Galleta Meadows to the beginning of the hiking route. This canyon, unlike most west-side canyons, contains no palm trees. It is a steep, rough, dry scramble, rising rapidly to the summit.

The luxury homes around De Anza Desert Country Club, built on the flood plain of Henderson Canyon, sufffered extensive damage from flash flooding during Hurricane Doreen in August 1977. This was termed a "50-year flood," meaning that the volume of water (resulting from 3 inches of rain in one day on the valley) has a two percent probability of occurring in any given year. Such statistics provide little comfort to the homeowner, however, when one recalls that less than one year earlier (September 1976) Hurricane Kathleen dumped almost that much rain on Borrego Springs in one day, and the 1980 hurricane repeated the same "50-year" flood story.

Trip 1A: Culp Valley and Vicinity

From: Borrego Springs

To: Ranchita (12.6 miles one way); paved all the way

Via: S-22 and the Montezuma Grade

With Side Trips to: old Culp Valley Road and Jasper Trail (jeep)

Mileage From:

Park HQ	Ranchita Store	Checkpoint Description
0.0	12.6	Proceed south and west up S-22 and the Montezuma Grade.
1.6 [M 16]	11.5	End of desert section of the California Riding and Hiking Trail. It is

Park HQ	Ranchita Store	Checkpoint Description
		about 5.5 miles to Culp Valley Campground via the trail along the ridge, with a climb from 1200 to 3400 feet.
4.1 [M 13.5]	8.5	Road crosses Dry Canyon, a large, dry, deep arroyo between Culp
[M 12.5]		and Hellhole canyons.
5.2	7.4	Crawford turnoff overlooks Culp Canyon and a spectacular view of
[M 12]		Borrego Valley below and Borrego Badlands beyond. On a clear day one can see the Salton Sea, backdropped by the Chocolate Mountains.
		Tubb Canyon is the next canyon south. There is an old trail in Tubb Canyon that was used by Mrs. "Doc" Beaty in the early days to carry mail by foot or muleback from Borrego Valley to Culp Valley. Access to Tubb Canyon from Borrego Valley is over private property. The canyon has an abundance of water. Big Spring is located near the head of Tubb Canyon, tucked away in the corner of the mountain and heavily overgrown with seepwillow, catclaw, mesquite and cottonwood. The spring is one of the largest water producers in the Anza-Borrego area, flowing on the surface for ¼
[M 10.5]		mile, then going underground. The spring is a main watering hole for bighorn sheep.
7.1	5.5	Turnoff west (left) at the 3000-foot-elevation sign is the old Culp
[M 10]		Valley Road.

Side Trip Along the Old Culp Valley Road

0.0   Turnoff.

1.3   Cottonwood Spring. Large, old cottonwoods in this beautiful glade shelter the cement tank that holds water piped from the year-round spring.

3.0   Turnoff south (left) was formally known as the Wilson Trail, which may be followed on foot some 6 winding miles east along Pinyon Ridge to Desert View Point. Hikers may descend another 5 miles from this point to Tamarisk Grove Campground for a prearranged pickup. The Wilson Trail was named for Alfred Wilson, an early-day cattleman of Ranchita. He ran cattle in Borrego Valley before the turn of the century, driving them down the Tub Canyon Trail as well as what he called the "Pam" (Palm) Creek Trail. This latter trail descended through the South Fork of Hellhole Canyon from near Pena Spring into main Hellhole and on over to Palm Canyon Creek.

3.5   Turnoff south (left) to the Slab, the foundation of an old house that was made of white granite rocks and cement. It rests on a brushy knoll overlooking Culp Valley. According to Ralph Jasper of Montezuma Valley, who once owned this property, the house was built by Bert Jones in the 1930s. The old homestead has a beautiful view of the Borrego Badlands, the eastern end of the Santa Rosas and the Salton Sea.

4.5   Jasper Trail crossing. Continue to . . .

5.0   Junction with W-W (Walt and Wanda Phillips) Ranch road. Turn north (right) to . . .

5.7   S-22 just east of Ranchita.

End of Side Trip

Park HQ	Ranchita Store	Checkpoint Description

Highway S-22 continues through Culp Valley, which is an area of about 15 square miles, reaching considerably beyond Culp Valley proper. The elevation varies from 3000 to 4500. The plant zone is Upper Sonoran, tending toward chaparral. California juniper, sumac, scrub oak, mountain mahogany and silk-tassel bush are common. The mountains of the Culp Valley area are composed of old granite. Decomposed material fills the valley and swales between. The exposed peaks and hills have eroded into huge piles of granite boulders, quite suitable for rock-climbing practice. Several springs furnish surface water, the main one being Pena Spring.

[M 9.5]

8.3   4.3   Culp Valley Primitive Campground (elevation 3400) turnoff to the north (right, signed).

[M 9]

A 0.6 walk northwest leads to Pena Spring. The California Riding and Hiking Trail crosses the Pena Spring Trail at 0.4 mile. Pena Spring is a year-round spring located at the head of the South Fork of Hellhole Canyon. Coyotes, gray foxes and bobcats are attracted by the small animals and birds that inhabit the area.

The campground area is nestled in a boulder-strewn valley. The camp area has no toilets, no trash cans, no water and no camping fee. About ½ mile east is Lookout Point, which overlooks Hellhole Canyon. From the campground the California Riding and Hiking Trail may be followed 400 yards east to Vista Point for a scenic view of Hellhole Canyon and the Borrego Desert. The San Ysidro Mountains are to the north and west. The huge, conical monolith of granite is the Thimble, a guide to travelers crossing the Borrego Desert from the east for many years. When viewed from the valley below, the Thimble looms on the horizon as a perfect cone, distinc-

[M 7]

tive, easily remembered and visible on clear days for long distances. This monolith stands just south of San Ysidro Peak.

10.8   1.8   Jasper Trail turnoff south (left, signed).

Side Trip Down Jasper Trail to Grapevine Canyon (jeep only)

0.0   Turnoff south on S-22 opposite the site of the old Culp Valley Ranger Station (elevation 3910). The road and the California Riding and Hiking Trail, which is on or near it in this stretch, wind through heavy chaparral growth of mountain lilac, juniper, silk-tassel and sugarberry sumac. Bear west (right) to . . .

1.4   Cross the old Culp Valley Road. Extreme caution required from here on!

1.7   Fork. Bear south (left) then east to . . .

2.4   A summit. Stop for an excellent view of surrounding mountains and desert canyons. Then the road drops steeply through a canyon, climbs up the west bank to traverse a knife-edge ridge, and descends steeply back into the same canyon. Vegetation has sharply modified from chaparral to desert-canyon plants.

4.8   The road departs the canyon west over a small ridge. The W-W Ranch may be seen west and below in Grapevine Canyon. The road drops into a small ravine and turns south to . . .

5.4   Grapevine Canyon junction (elevation 2900). Tamarisk Grove Campground is 8.7 miles east, S-22 at Ranchita is 4.5 miles northwest (see Trip 1B).

End of Side Trip

Park HQ	Ranchita Store	Checkpoint Description
10.8	1.8	S-22 proceeds west to . . .
11.1 [M 6]	1.5	Summit of the Montezuma Grade and the approximate park boundary.
11.8	0.8	W-W Ranch turnoff is south (left). This is the Trip 1B route into Grapevine Canyon (see below). The turnoff is readily identifiable by two parallel dirt roads proceeding south.
12.6 [M 5]	0.0	Ranchita store, post office and gas station.
17.6 [M 0]	5.0	S-22/S-2 junction. 5 miles west to Hwy 78.

Trip 1B: Grapevine Canyon

From: Highway S-3 at Tamarisk Grove Campground

To: Highway S-22 near Culp Valley Campground (13.2 miles one way; light auto but occasionally jeep only; a mountain bicycle route)

Via: Yaqui Well, Angelina Spring, Stewart Spring and W-W Ranch Road
Mileage From:

Tamarisk Grove	S-22	Checkpoint Description
0.0	13.2	Tamarisk Grove Campground. Proceed west down S-3 to . . .
0.2	13.0	San Felipe Wash crossing. Turn west (right) up-wash. Sand may impede travel here.
0.8	12.4	Yaqui Well and wildlife area to the north (right). The primitive camp area starts here and extends about 1 mile west. Many lost-gold-mine stories and legends of desert ghosts center on this area. One of these stories involves the Indian for whom the area was named. A Yaqui Indian of Sonora who married a Kumeyaay woman from Grapevine Canyon lived in the well area in the 1880s. The Indian later moved to Warner's Ranch and worked in the vicinity. Reportedly this Yaqui Indian made periodic trips to the desert whenever he needed money, always returning with black nuggets. After he was killed in a brawl, $4000 worth of gold was found in his bunk.
		Yaqui Well, a famous old seep in San Felipe Wash, produces water year-round, which is retained in a pool scooped out of the sand. The well was heavily used by Indians, cattlemen, prospectors and travelers in earlier years. The area has been set aside to allow wildlife undisturbed use of the water. Magnificent stands of desert ironwood trees and mesquite trees grow in the area. Bedrock metates and house rings on the rocky rise near the spring indicate that the seeds of ironwoods and mesquite beans were harvested by the Indians. Yaqui Well has long been a favorite bird-watching location. Desert mistletoe grows profusely on the ironwoods and mesquite, attracting phainopeplas, mourning doves, flycatchers and seed-eating birds.
2.5	10.7	Fork, bear right. The left fork is a poleline access road from Highway 78, 0.4 mile away. The route here passes through a beautiful cactus garden, said to contain one of the largest, densest and most varied display of succulents anywhere in the Park.
4.5	8.7	The California Riding and Hiking Trail joins with a dirt road from the southeast (left). It is 2.0 miles southeast down this road to Highway 78, opposite Plum Canyon. Continue northwest up-wash.
4.6	8.6	Bitter Creek Canyon to the left. Hikers may go 1.3 miles southwest to Bitter Creek Spring. The spring is located about 150 feet up the side of a hill and is carried to a trough at the bottom by a pipe. The

Tamarisk Grove	S-22	Checkpoint Description
		use by birds and animals is heavy, but it has never gained as much use as Stewart and Angelina springs.
6.5	6.7	Site of Richter Springs. Just south of the wash is a large rock with clearly visible morteros.
7.0	6.2	Angelina Spring (signed). During summer the water may be a foot or so beneath the surface, requiring digging. A small stream generally flows in the wash for some distance before disappearing into the porous sands. This waterhole is shaded by cottonwoods, willows, arrowweed and tanglebrush. The plant growth is dense, giving good cover for California quail and many other birds. A flat area adjacent to Angelina Spring had a greater amount of Indian use than did the other several locations along Grapevine Canyon, as indicated by the many bedrock morteros and metates, the amount of shards and flaking, and the hearth areas.
8.3	4.9	Stewart (also spelled "Stuart" on the topo map) Spring is located on the north hillside in a tangle of underbrush about 20 feet above the wash bed. Water piped down from the spring into a trough is available year-round. The bird life is always good—exceptional during migrations. California quail are in the vicinity at all times, as well as a few mountain quail. The quail, small birds and rodents attract Cooper hawks, red-tailed hawks and owls.
8.7	4.5	The Jasper Trail turnoff is north (right, signed). The California Riding and Hiking Trail also departs Grapevine Canyon at this point. It is 5.4 miles to S-22 up this very rugged but scenic jeep route

Stewart Spring

Tamarisk Grove	S-22	Checkpoint Description
		(see Trip 1A). The Grapevine route continues west up-wash.
9.3	3.9	Fork, bear northwest (right). The ranch west (left) of the road is the W-W (Walt and Wanda Philips) Ranch. Tungsten-mine works are farther north along the road.
10.3	2.9	Fork, turn north (right). An old cabin is on the northwest corner here. Climb northeast out of Grapevine Canyon past the Alfred Wilson ranch on the west (left). (See Alternate below.)
12.5	0.7	The turnoff east (right) is the old Culp Valley Road. Five miles east is its junction with paved S-22. Continue north to . . .
13.2	0.0	Junction with S-22, 0.8 mile east of Ranchita store and 0.7 mile west of the Park boundary. This junction is posted "W-W Ranch" and is readily identified by the two parallel dirt roads leading south toward the old Culp Valley Road. It is 11.8 miles east down Montezuma Grade to park headquarters.

Alternate Exit from Grapevine Canyon

10.3 Fork marked by old cabin on northwest corner (see above). Proceed straight northwest, hugging the north side of Grapevine Canyon.

11.7 Turnoff north is another route direct to S-22. Continue straight to cross, at mile 12.1, a saddle marking the watershed between the Anza-Borrego Desert to the east and the Pacific slope to the west.

Now traveling down Hoover Canyon through pastures and oak meadows, take care to shut gates that cross the road.

13.8 Pavement at Highway S-22, marked by a metal gate with a sign prohibiting hunting and fishing and another sign, VISTA IRRIGATION DISTRICT. This point is 2.5 miles east of the S-2/S-22 junction and 2.6 miles west of the Ranchita store and post office.

Trip 1C: San Felipe Wash and Southern Borrego Badlands

From: Highway 78 at Ocotillo Wells

To: Highway S-22 near county dump (15.6 miles one way; light auto with care, only jeeps in side washes)

Via: San Gregorio and Borrego Sink

With Side Trip to: Cut-Across Trail, Ant Hill or Inspiration Point

Mileage From:

Ocotillo Wells	S-22	Checkpoint Description
0.0	15.6	A dirt road proceeds northwest along the west edge of Benson Dry Lake (elevation 155). Travel on the lake bed is prohibited, since it is a county airport.
1.1	14.5	Turnoff west (left) leads 0.5 mile to the Quarry, a popular OHV campsite for those who enjoy the challenges of the huge sand dune on the southeast buttress of Borrego Mountain. This dune is used for buggy and motorcycle competition. The headlights from OHVs maneuvering on this dune at night can be seen for miles around. The maze of roads in the vicinity of this dune can be confusing. There is no travel restriction, since this is in the Ocotillo Wells State

Ocotillo Wells	S-22	Checkpoint Description
		Vehicular Recreation Area. Continue generally north-northwest to . . .
2.2	13.4	Fault Wash and San Felipe Wash junction (signed). The Cut-Across Trail is 4 miles north along Fault Wash. This and Military Wash, slightly to the west, were the site of much World War II training activity by Gen. George Patton's armored troops. Concrete bunkers and other military debris have been found in the area as well as many kinds of ammunition shells. BEWARE of any unusual looking debris, and report its presence to park rangers or the county sheriff. The route continues northwest (left) to . . .
2.7	12.9	The Cove turnoff to the southwest (left). This is a small, primitive campsite in a little valley dotted with ironwood trees and nestled next to the pastel-shaded bluffs of Borrego Mountain. There are no water sources or trash containers. Carry out all refuse. The ironwood trees and all vegetation are protected. DO NOT USE ironwood trees for firewood. Campers have thoughtlessly destroyed many of these trees. Ironwood trees appear to be bare and seemingly lifeless most of the year, but they bloom in June with a typical pea blossom. The trees can grow to a height of 30 feet. The route proceeds northwest along the edge of Borrego Mountain.
4.9	10.7	Turnoff southwest (left, signed) leads into Blow Sand Canyon.
5.9	9.7	This is a signed intersection of the Cut-Across Trail to the north and east (right) and Buttes Canyon road to the southwest (left).

Side Trip Along the Cut-Across Trail

0.0	Intersection on south bank, San Felipe Wash. Proceed north across the wash to . . .
0.9	The north bank at Third Wash. Turn east (right) to cross . . .
2.4	Military Wash (closed north).
3.1	Fault Wash. (It is 4.4 miles north via Fault Wash to the Short Wash Trail.)
3.8	Palo Verde Wash. (It is 6.4 miles north via Palo Verde Wash to Highway S-22.)
4.9	Bank Wash (closed north). (It is 4.3 miles southeast to Wolfe Well.) The route now passes through the mud hills to . . .
6.1	Basin Wash. Down-wash 2.3 miles is a junction with Tule Wash. Proceed up Basin Wash, leave the wash at mile 6.3 and climb over a low divide north into . . .
6.5	Tule Wash. Up-wash 0.2 mile west is Una Palma (One Palm). Proceed downwash east to . . .
7.9	A signed junction with Five Palms Spring Trail. Five Palms Spring (only two palms left) is at mile 8.8 northwest (left) up this trail and a junction in Arroyo Salado is at mile 9.2. The park boundary is at mile 9.1 east (straight) down Tule Wash (see Trip 3B).

End of Side Trip

Ocotillo Wells	S-22	
5.9	9.7	The main route continues west up San Felipe Wash beside the West Butte of Borrego Mountain.
7.0	8.6	A small wash that joins from the southwest (left) is passable a short way to a deadend near an old gold or tourmaline mine at the base of West Butte.

Ocotillo Wells	S-22	Checkpoint Description
7.6	8.0	Junction with Borrego Mountain Wash trail from the southwest (left). This road dissects an extensive and colorful badlands region just west of Borrego Mountain. Borrego Mountain Wash is wide at first but soon narrows as it runs between exposed, tilted and twisted strata of dark red sandstone. One mile from San Felipe Wash is a fork. The east (left) fork goes a short way and ends abruptly at deeply eroded sandstone falls. The south (right) fork is negotiable for another 1.3 miles to a signed turnaround point near the Wind Caves, where the road becomes ONE WAY ONLY, *from* the opposite direction down from the Borrego Mountain Dropoff and the Slot. You must backtrack to San Felipe Wash (see Trip 1).
7.9	7.7	Junction with Hills of the Moon Wash joining from the north (right, signed). The wash can be explored for about 5 miles up from San Felipe Wash, to where it narrows. This distance may be shortened by falling chunks of clay from the banks until subsequent rains cause water runoff that clears the channel. Hills of the Moon Wash is virtually devoid of vegetation.
8.2	7.4	Junction with Rainbow Wash, which joins from the north (right). The vehicle trail goes about 2.8 miles up this colorful wash, winding between conical, banded, multicolored mud hills. The wash narrows until vehicle traffic is stopped. A hiker may continue up the wash and then climb the ridge to the northwest (left) about 1.5 miles to Font's Point.
8.5	7.1	A post marks the junction where San Felipe Wash turns southwest and leaves our route and the Anza Trail. San Felipe Wash crosses the paved Borrego Springs Road at Texas Dip, 4.7 miles southwest. The main route continues due west into Borrego Sink Wash.
11.3	4.3	A jeep trail joins the main route from the northeast (right). This trail follows the north bank of San Felipe Wash for about 2.5 miles to the east, where it joins Rainbow Wash. About 0.3 mile up this trail are the ruins of a cabin. Karl Bennis reported that this cabin once belonged to the Borrego Valley "schoolmarm."
11.5	4.1	The route enters dense vegetation marking the general area of Borrego Spring and what was once the San Gregorio Indian village at the narrowest point of the Borrego Sink drainage. The route forks here. The southwest (left) fork leads about 0.1 mile to the Anza San Gregorio Monument atop a hill on the south side of the wash. The monument is near the old McCain cabin site, a cattle-camp outpost near the turn of the century. The original "Borrego Spring" site, Anza's spring of San Gregorio, is also here on the south bank of Borrego Sink Wash.
		About 0.2 mile southwest of the monument a route forks northwest and then quickly turns southwest on a heavily cross-rutted trail to run along the southern edge of Borrego Sink Wash and Borrego Sink west about 3.5 miles to La Casa del Zorro. At the east end of Borrego Sink, this route passes Metate Hill, named for the many stone mortars (*metates*) and pestles (*manos*) formerly found here. The main route continues west (straight ahead) from mile 11.5.
11.6	4.0	The site of "Borrego Spring II," 0.2 mile north of the route at the base of some low gray hills, is marked by a dugout depression in the north bank of the wash. Faulting activity probably accounts for the

Ocotillo Wells	S-22	Checkpoint Description
		shifting location of Borrego Spring, although no surface water is currently found at the Borrego Spring II site.
13.1	2.5	Four-way junction just north of Borrego Sink. Borregó Sink is the low point of the Borrego Valley, receiving runoff from Coyote Canyon. It can be very miry during and after wet weather. The vegetation on the salt flats around Borrego Sink and the old Borrego Spring is a typical example of desert growth in alkaline soil. It is mainly mesquite, which can have a tap root as deep as 150 feet. Besides mesquite, other examples of flora include arrowweed, desert thorn, pickleweed, galleta (bunch grass) and various members of the saltbush genus. The main route turns north (right) from the four-way junction.
13.5	2.1	The tamarisk windbreak to the west (left) is a good campsite.
15.1	0.5	The route is paved from the county refuse site.
15.2	0.4	**Side Trip to Ant Hill or Inspiration Point**
		The gully just north of the dump provides access east (right) into the Borrego Badlands. For small off-highway vehicles only. The basic route forks about 1½ miles east of the dump. The east (right) fork leads another 2 miles to dead end at Ant Hill below Font's Point. The northeast (left) fork leads 2½ miles through a tight, winding wash up onto Inspiration Point. From there, Inspiration Point Wash may be negotiated 3 miles north to S-22. Total through-distance from the dump to S-22 via Inspiration Point is about 7 miles.
		CAUTION: Route is very sandy. Vehicles must remain on designated routes or drivers will be cited.
		End of Side Trip
15.6	0.0	Junction with Highway S-22 at the intersection of Pegleg Road and Palm Canyon Drive.

Former Park Manager (1972–1981) Maurice ("Bud") Getty on the Jasper Trail

Trip 1D: Split Mountain, Fish Creek and Northern Carrizo Badlands

From: Ocotillo Wells

To: Olla Wash (21.3 miles one way; paved to Gypsum mine, dirt through Split Mountain, jeep thereafter)

Via: Little Borrego townsite, Elephant Trees, and Fish Creek Primitive Camp-ground

With Side Trips To: Gypsum Railway and Carrizo Wash

Note: As is true in all park badlands areas, OHV traffic is absolutely prohibited on mud hills and slopes out of wash bottoms. Even footprints on the fragile mud walls quickly start the erosion and rutting process, which disfigures and eventually destroys the formations.

Mileage From:

Ocotillo Wells	Checkpoint Description
0.0	Ocotillo Wells. Proceed south on Split Mountain Road.
2.6	A poleline road which generally follows the route of the old Kane Springs Road joins from the west (right) as the paved road swings left.
3.1	Little Borrego Townsite is just south (right) of the road along "Main Street." The only visible sign left today of this "boom town," which was an early victim of the 1930s depression, are several concrete slabs which attract desert campers looking for a level place to park their vans and trailers. The large slab was the base of the 14-room Miracle Hotel which was a boarding house rather than a hostel. The old Kane Springs Road, here named "Broadway," ran east and west through the center of town.

The old Kane Springs Road joins from the west.

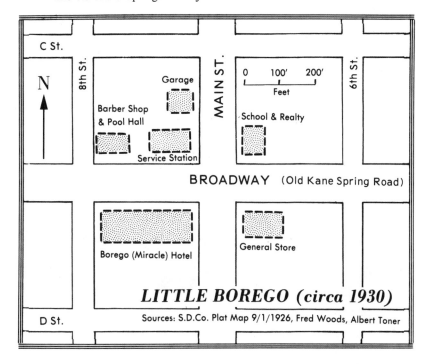

LITTLE BOREGO (circa 1930)

Sources: S.D.Co. Plat Map 9/1/1926, Fred Woods, Albert Toner

Ocotillo Wells	Checkpoint Description
4.0	The old Kane Springs Road continues to the east (left), 0.3 mile south of a substation. You can follow this sandy, rutted track by jeep some 19 miles to Highway 86 at Kane Springs, reliving an early-day desert travel experience.
5.7	Elephant Trees Ranger Station and park boundary.
5.9	Elephant tree turnoff west (right, signed). A conventional car may proceed one mile up this dirt road to a parking area and a turnaround. A 1½-mile trail from the parking area leads to a rocky hillside on this alluvial fan where several stands of elephant trees can be seen, or the visitor can follow the 1½-mile nature trail which has been laid out by park personnel. The plants described along this trail are representative of the area. The Elephant Trees Discovery Trail brochure can be picked up at the Visitor Center, the trailhead or from any ranger. The elephant trees themselves are a rarity. Some 500 specimens have been counted in this area of the park. Although commonly found farther south in Baja California and Sonora, in the United States the elephant tree, *Bursera microphylla,* is found only along this western edge of the Colorado Desert and in the Gila Range of Arizona. The tree can be recognized by its swollen trunk, tentacled branches, blood-like sap within the bark, and unique color combination of yellow-green papery bark, reddish-brown twigs, dark green foliage and blue berries. Visitors are urged to remember that these and all plants within the state park are protected.
8.1	Turnoff west (right, signed) leads to Fish Creek Primitive Campground and the Split Mountain area.

Side Trip to Old Kane Springs Road Via Gypsum Railway Road and Carrizo Wash

0.0	Split Mountain Road at turnoff to Fish Creek Primitive Campground. Follow the paved road south toward the U.S. Gypsum Company properties, one of the nation's largest gypsum strip mines.

Elephant tree near Split Mountain (co-author Lowell Lindsay)

Ocotillo
Wells   Checkpoint Description

0.1   Turn east (left) along a good dirt road paralleling the narrow-gauge railroad. This railroad freights gypsum ore some 25 miles southeast to the processing plant at Plaster City.

3.1   The Fish Creek Mountains to the south and east have been proposed by BLM for designation as a wilderness area, in recognition of their significant and diverse geological and archeological features. The area is closed to all vehicular travel and is the most roadless, least impacted area in the Yuha Desert. These very rugged and scenic mountains contain Indian rock rings, campsites and trails, and habitats for prairie falcons. The canyons and cliffs offer excellent opportunities for day hikes.

4.4   The road crosses the old beach line of freshwater Lake Cahuilla, where scattered fields of shells tell of life in these waters. Farther along the road, beach terraces and the water line may be seen against the mountainside across the railroad.

7.4   A small wash crosses the road. Use jeep only from here. You must jog northeast from here to intercept the road along the poleline visible a little over a mile away. Take the jeep road northeast from here to . . .

8.9   Intercept the poleline road. Turn southeast (right) to enter . . .

10.4 Carrizo Wash, the major drainage system for the entire southern Anza-Borrego area. (NOTE: If you miss the jog to the poleline at mile 7.4 and continue down the road, you enter the Naval Reservation—prior permission required. The large railroad trestle at mile 9.4 crosses Carrizo Wash. Turn northeast—left—down-wash to exit the Naval Reservation and cross under the poleline.)

Tamarisk groves, mesquite thickets and shifting sand drifts make Carrizo Wash exceptionally attractive but also difficult to travel. Select the route carefully and stay in the wash to . . .

17.1 Intersect the old Kane Springs Road. This may be difficult to identify. If you encounter thickets with water, you've gone too far and have entered the San Sebastian Marsh, which is closed to vehicles. Backtrack to old Kane Springs Road. It is 8.5 miles east (right) to Highway 86 and 5.3 miles west (left) and north via a poleline road to Highway 78 (see Trip 1E).

End of Side Trip

8.1   Split Mountain turnoff to the west (right, signed). A former strontium mine is on a low hill to the right. Conventional autos may proceed up the wash with care. Fish Creek Primitive Campground is located here (no toilets, no trash cans, no camping fee.

10.1 The road enters Split Mountain. For the next 2.5 miles cliff walls, towering several hundred feet above, enclose the road on both sides. This "split" separates the Vallecito Mountains on the west from the Fish Creek Mountains on the east, with Fish Creek Wash running through the split. Split Mountain features a variety of unusual phenomena, beginning with the split itself, and including other features such as anticlinal folds, narrow chasms, expansive lifeless hills of soft clay, fossilized oyster-shell reefs, Pliocene fossils, perpendicular canyon walls rising more than 600 feet in places, mud palisades, and peculiar concretion holes which were once thought to be dinosaur tracks. It is no wonder that this area rivals Coyote Canyon as a favorite of park visitors. The gorge forming Split Mountain is, geologically speaking, an antecedent stream canyon: early in the history of these mountains, a stream flowed through this area, and as the mountains rose, the stream continued on its same course, cutting into the slowly rising land. This process has continued to the present.

12.1 An anticline is on the west (right) bank.

**Split
Mountain**

Ocotillo Wells	Checkpoint Description
12.4	Exit Split Mountain into Carrizo Badlands. Conventional autos should proceed no farther. Exploration afoot beckons to the desert adventurer.
12.6	Turnoff west (right) is the north fork of Fish Creek Wash (signed). Jeeps may proceed up-wash about 4 miles, exploring several more tributary washes: Oyster Shell, Lycium and North Fork. Stone Wash and Mollusk Wash, tributaries to Lycium and North Fork, respectively, may be explored afoot for an even more rewarding desert experience. The clay hills surrounding these washes are highly fossiliferous, containing masses of sea shells from an ancient sea bottom that existed 3–5 million years ago. Main wash continues southwest. Bear left.
12.9	Small wash enters from the southeast. It is an interesting hike up this wash to a set of wind caves and the so-called dinosaur tracks, with an excellent view of the Carrizo Badlands to the west. Bear left about ¼ mile up this arroyo, following a well-marked trail on desert pavement that resembles a cobblestone path. Atop the lower windcave formation is a two-eyed "phantom" which turns into a three-eyed "phantom" at a different angle. Above this first group of wind caves is another group. All wind caves face into the prevailing wind. The peculiar erosional patterns here were for many years thought to be tracks of ancient dinosaurs, but have since been proved to be otherwise. A trail leads to the top of the hill overlooking the wind caves, which affords the visitor a spectacular view

Ocotillo Wells	Checkpoint Description
	of the folded and wrinkled Carrizo Badlands. The view to the southwest presents the image of a choppy sea, with undulating, crashing waves frozen in motion. From atop this hill a trail leads down a ridge to the west to emerge near Split Mountain exit.
13.0	Mud Hills Wash enters from the south (closed to vehicles). This old route to Carrizo Springs now is blocked by the Carrizo Impact area, a no-loner-used Navy bombing range which is still extremely dangerous due to numerous unexploded shells. Mud Hills Wash may be hiked. One-half mile south is the "Elephant Knees" formation.
15.3	Loop Wash turnoff to the north (right). It rejoins the main wash 2 miles up.
15.8	Camel's Head Wash, joining from the south (left), is for foot travel only.
18.0	Dropoff Wash (one way down only) joins from the southwest (left). It provides hiking access to the Arroyo Seco del Diablo Dropoff, about ½ mile up-wash, accessible by jeep from the southern part of the park (see Trip 4D).
20.6	Sandstone Wash turnoff (signed) to the west (left). This wash can be driven about 3 miles to a vehicle deadend. The wash is characterized by vertical sandstone walls which are seamed and cracked in many places giving the appearance that loose chunks are ready to fall. The passage is relatively narrow. The canyon wall is light brown in color, with the darker, chocolate brown of desert varnish in many places. The floor of the wash contains light-bluish-gray granite sand, cobbles and boulders which have washed down from the mountains. At the end of the jeep passage, the canyon forks. A 1-mile hike up the west (left) branch to the saddle of the mountain achieves a fine vista of the surrounding badlands. Sandstone Canyon has long been considered one of the most impressive canyons of the park.
21.3	Olla Wash turnoff (signed to the west (left). This wash can be driven about 2 miles to a deadend at the Mud Palisades. Interesting geological formations and oddities of erosion are everywhere. Vegetation is sparse, mostly desert willow,

Carrizo Badlands

Sandstone Canyon

mesquite, catclaw, desert agave and miscellaneous desert shrubs. Huge monoliths of clay and rock, known as the Mud Palisades, at the upper end of Olla Wash presents a formidable barrier against any farther travel either by jeep or on foot. Located at the base of Whale Peak in the Vallecito Mountains, these weird products of erosion offer considerable interest to the adventurer. Beyond here the route becomes ONE WAY ONLY, *from* the opposite direction, with access from the Earthquake Valley area of the Park off Highway S-2 (see Trip 4A). Vehicles must turn around and proceed down-wash back to Split Mountain.

Mud Palisades

Trip 1E: Harpers Well and San Sebastian Marsh Area

From: Highway 78, San Felipe Substation

To: Highway 86, Kane Springs (13.8 miles one way; jeep only—very sandy and rutted)

Via: Poleline road and the old Kane Springs Road

San Felipe, Fish and Carrizo creeks are dry washes except when occasional flash floods bring torrents of water rushing down their winding courses. But beneath the sandy surfaces of these washes, underground rivers flow out east toward the desert floor, and they surface about 80 feet below sea level to form small streams and ponds. The muddy but verdant San Sebastian Marsh, with a unique desert riparian-aquatic habitat, is formed at the confluence of these three creeks, five miles west of Highway 86 and two miles south of Highway 78 near an area called Harpers Well. It is a permanent and dependable source of water used by the wildlife that abounds in the area, by migratory birds that must have a dependable watering stop in their annual flights, and by men since ancient times.

Huricanes Kathleen (1976) and Doreen (1977) eradicated many dirt roads and trails in the area and severely impacted the marsh habitat with sand and silt. But given time, no vehicle intrusion and minimal human disturbance, the marsh should restore itself.

NO VEHICLE TRAFFIC IS PERMITTED WITHIN THE MARSH AREA (see foldout map). All roads have been adequately signed, so visitors should have no difficulty determining when they have reached the boundaries. The marsh covers about 6 square miles around the confluence of Fish, Carrizo and San Felipe washes. Such a fragile and unique ecosystem deserves the best of care from its visitors. This marsh area has been designated a National Landmark by the National Park Service.

REMINDER: All driving in this area must be on approved routes of travel. For maps and latest information, contact the BLM office, 333 S. Waterman, El Centro CA 92243 or call (619) 352-5842.

Mileage From:

Substation	Kane Springs	Checkpoint Description
0.0	13.8	The substation is on Highway 78 (elevation sea level) 7.1 miles west of Highway 86 and 9.3 miles east of Ocotillo Wells. Proceed south along the poleline road. Beware of sand traps.
1.6	12.2	Tarantula Wash is a good camping area for heavy trailers and campers.
2.3	11.5	Cross San Felipe Wash.
3.3	10.5	Cross Fish Creek.
3.7	10.1	The poleline jogs east (left) 50 yards.
3.9	9.9	Junction with the old Kane Springs road. Turn east (left). The route was originally marked with posts stamped with the letter K. Some of these posts as well as old culverts may still be found. The poleline road may be followed south about 5 miles to the Gypsum Railroad road.
5.3	8.5	Cross Carrizo Wash. Hikers may proceed 2.9 miles northeast (left) down-wash to view the marsh. Giant reeds and cattails are found on

Substation	Kane Springs	Checkpoint Description
		this western end of the marsh, where San Felipe Creek merges with Carrizo Creek. This is the most impressive viewpoint for the marsh. The route continues straight ahead.
6.0	7.8	Salk Survey Marker. Remains of a windmill are found on the site of San Felipe City, an early-day desert settlement that was abandoned after a few years.
8.2	5.6	Mesquite Drill Hole (yellow pipe south of road) was an oil-test site of the early 1900s.
9.2	4.6	Harpers Well (elevation minus 120) was an old oil-test well of the 1900s and a watering hole used by pioneers and prospectors alike, formerly surrounded by palm trees.

The road drops steeply into Mark Wash and climbs out the other side. Storms will modify one's exact route through here. This site is the best departure point to hike into San Sebastian Marsh, 1.3 miles west. This east end of the marsh has a thick tamarisk growth. The water flows faster at this end, providing a better area for desert pupfish and leopard frogs. There is also more inkweed found at this east end, while pickleweed is found all around the marsh. Other plants found on the periphery of the marsh include salt grass, mesquite and quail brush. The marsh is home for a large variety of birds, reptiles and mammals.

San Sebastian Marsh was named by Juan Bautista de Anza during his first trail-blazing expedition in 1774 in honor of his Indian guide Sebastian Tarabal. Here Anza found an Indian village with more than 400 persons. Anza reported there was plenty of water and pasturage, although he said both were quite salty except for one spring.

There are many legends connected with this locale. One of the most interesting is the "Abominable Sandman of Borrego." Victor Stoyanow, an ex-military officer and freelance writer, reported evidence of it in the Harpers Well area and along Carrizo Wash in 1964. The tracks were described as bearlike, with five blunt digits terminating in tiny depressions as if made by claws, long toenails or spikes. The sets of prints that were found were 7 feet apart in some places. There were alleged indications that the creature had climbed a tamarisk tree and had broken branches to a height of 6 feet. No human footprints were in the area besides those of Stoyanow. Two friends, an archeologist and a hunter, accompanied him on a second visit to the area, but after viewing the prints neither could guess what made the splay-toed tracks.

A better-known story is that of the lost ship of the desert that sailed up the Gulf of California and the Colorado River and into the flooded Salton basin only to become stranded in an inland sea after the water receded. The ship has been variously described as a Viking ship, a Spanish pearl ship and an English pirate ship loaded with Spanish treasure. Sightings have likewise been variously reported in the Yuha Desert, the Carrizo Badlands and the Fish Creek-Split Mountain area, and near San Sebastian Marsh. Some shreds of historical data support the lost-ship story. The periodic flooding of the Salton basin is certainly historic fact. It isn't difficult to surmise that a ship could have entered over the Colorado River delta during a particular combination of high tides, favorable winds and basin flooding.

Substation	Kane Springs	Checkpoint Description
13.8	0.0	Junction with Highway 86 atop the Kane Springs mesquite dune hill (elevation minus 150). If you are going west along Kane Springs road from Highway 86 toward Harpers Well, take care to select the route that goes around the *north* side of the low hills west of the Kane Springs dune hill. It is 1.7 miles northwest to the Highway 86/78 junction.

Trip 1F: San Felipe Hills

From: Substation on Highway 78

To: Highway 86 at Tule Wash (13.6 miles one way; jeep only)

Via: Artesian Well, Gas Domes, McCain Spring and Giant Sand Dune

Mileage From:

Substation	Hiway 86	Checkpoint Description
0.0	13.6	The trip begins at the electrical substation on Highway 78, 7.1 miles west of the Highway 86 junction. Proceed north along the poleline road.
2.5	11.1	Concretion area.
3.2	10.4	Crossroads. Ocotillo Wells is about 11 miles west via Wolfe Well. The poleline road continues north (straight).
		Turn east (right) for entry into San Felipe Hills over a rugged dirt road. The San Felipe Hills are spring-formed dunes which have developed in sandy areas where rising seep water allows growth of vegetation, which in turn traps blowing sand so that it accumulates. The sand may pile up so high that water cannot rise up through it to the surface, and the spring or seep is then completely sealed. The core of the dune is a black, mucky mass of soil and decayed vegetation. Such dunes also appear on the flats west of US 86 between Arroyo Salado and Tule Wash. The small, remote, lonely valley that is the heart of the San Felipe Hills may be seen from atop a ridgeline. The road descends, occasionally through heavy sand, to . . .
5.2	8.4	The Artesian Well in the center of the valley. The Artesian Well (Department of the Interior Water Reserve) began in the 1920s as an oil-test well drilled by Frank Beal. The litter from the operation is still lying about the landscape. According to A.C. Routhe, the first man to conduct oil exploration in the Borrego area and a witness to the actual drilling of this well, all went well with the drillers until they discovered they were in the wrong section, instead of the adjoining section as called for in their lease. The simplest expedient was to move some survey markers, moving the line east and thus causing the well to appear to be in the leased section. This they first did. Then they negotiated a lease with Southern Pacific, owners of the adjoining section. At 4000 feet they struck hot water, which ended the operation. It was abandoned, and it ran wild and hot until about 1935, when the government capped it off and designated it as a water reserve. The Imperial Valley Petroleum Corporation test wells are several hundred yards southeast of here.
		Proceed north through the valley, bearing west (left) of the wash and turn northwest over a low ridge of red mud formations.
6.3	7.3	The Gas Domes are located here atop a fairly flat hill covered with Bermudalike salt grass. The ground is whitened with alkali and is

Substation	Hiway 86	Checkpoint Description
		damp in many places. At the very top of the hill is a small dome, perhaps 4 feet tall, conical and composed of hard gray clay. By putting one's ear close to the vent on the top of one of these dunes, one can hear the petroleum gases bubbling through water deep within the hill. There is one other dome on this hill. They erupt water periodically.
		Continue northwest and west, past sand dunes south (left) of the road to . . .
8.2	5.4	Rejoin the poleline road. The steep bluff several hundred yards southeast of this junction marks McCain Spring, undoubtedly a favored Indian camp area in earlier days.
		One mile southwest of this junction, at the head of the South Fork of Tule Wash, is the remains of the Diamond Bar test well, or Routhe Well, named for A.C. Routhe, the owner of the well. Routhe owned the well jointly with the Salton Basin Land Co. The old Diamond Bar was never a producer, even though oil-bearing sands 125 feet thick were encountered in the process of drilling down to 3600 feet. Routhe blamed a poor drilling crew for the failure of this well, which supposedly cost him and his backers $210,000. Drilling at the well began in 1919 and continued until late 1922.
		Turn north along the poleline road to . . .
9.8	3.8	The former Giant Sand Dune at Tule Wash. Enter Tule Wash and proceed northeast (right) to . . .
13.6	0.0	Highway 86/Tule Wash junction at Bridge no. 58-14.

Vertical sandstone cliffs at entrance to Split Mountain

Natural Features

Most historic routes of travel in the Anza-Borrego region have followed earthquake faults through canyons and below cliffs called fault scarps. One of the most spectacular scarps in the United States occurs nearby on the east and northeast sides of the San Jacinto Mountains near Palm Springs. Similar scarps in the Borrego Desert occur in the Santa Rosa Mountains and along the west side of Borrego Valley, and there are less imposing faces on Coyote Mountain and the Fish Creek Mountains.

All fault zones in the Anza-Borrego region are associated with the famous San Andreas Fault, which runs from the ocean northwest of San Francisco, south along the Coast and Transverse Ranges, and through San Gorgonio Pass and the Salton Sea basin into the Gulf of California. The two most important fault systems paralleling the San Andreas to the west in the Borrego area are the San Jacinto and the Elsinore fault systems.

Branches of the San Jacinto Fault run through Coyote Canyon and Clark Valley, across the edge of Borrego Valley and past the northeast side of Borrego Mountain to the Fish Creek Mountains. The Anza expeditions followed the natural route formed by this fault system. A branch of the Elsinore Fault forms the Overland Trail route from Warner Springs into San Felipe Valley/Earthquake Valley along Highway S-2. Minor parallel faults account for the Grapevine Canyon route, the Split Mountain route and the middle portion of the old Kane Springs Road.

In the Borrego area major mountain masses and their intervening valleys have been formed by the upshifting of some blocks bounded by faults and the subsidence of others. From northeast to southwest, these blocks include the Santa Rosa Mountains, Clark Valley, Coyote Mountain, Borrego Valley, San Ysidro Mountain/Pinyon Ridge/Yaqui Ridge, Grapevine Canyon, Grapevine Mountain, San Felipe/Earthquake Valley and the Volcan/Granite Mountains.

A notable exception to the fault-zone routes-of-travel rule is the Banner Creek/San Felipe Creek route between Banner and Borrego Mountain, a distance of some 35 miles along the San Felipe corridor. This route crosses valleys and mountains in a northeast-trending course across the fault lines, past Scissors Crossing, through Sentenac Canyon, Mescal Bajada and The Narrows to old Borrego Spring at San Gregorio, northwest of Borrego Mountain. Geologist Norman Hinds surmised that Banner and San Felipe creeks were antecedent streams, present before faulting, and that subsequent uplift was slow enough to permit the flowing waters to cut downward about as fast as the rock barriers rose.

Some of the oldest exposed rocks in this area include those found in Quartz Vein Wash and along The Narrows Earth Trail. These are seen as bands of light and dark material. These pre-Cretaceous metasedimentary rocks were laid down perhaps 500 million years ago as alternating layers of sand and mud in an ancient seabed at least 500 miles to the southeast. They were metamorphosed before and during granitic intrusions; then subsequent northward movement along the highly active San Andreas Fault brought this seabed to its present location. Other outcroppings of old rock in this area are found in the San Ysidro and Santa Rosa mountains.

Another object of geological interest is Borrego Mountain. Like many mountains in California, it is composed of granitic rock. Long before this area was uplifted to form Borrego Mountain, it was an area of thick sediments. One granitic body—a pluton—intruded into these sediments from below. Later, a second pluton intruded into the first, which cracked under the strain of this intrusion. The large cracks which formed filled with pegmatite minerals from the second pluton—feldspar, quartz and mica. These cracks are readily seen today as varicolored dikes and veins in the mountain.

The sand dune on the east slope of Borrego Mountain is growing because as new sand particles are blown in from the desert, they are dropped in the eddy currents that form here due to the shape of the mountain and its orientation with respect to the strong winds.

The geology of the Fish Creek Mountain area, south of Borrego Mountain, is also interesting. It might seem absurd to the desert visitor when he learns that if he looks up to the mountains, he will see material from ancient sea bottoms or dry-lake deposits, whereas if he looks out at flat lands, he will see sediments which are the remains of ancient mountains. Nevertheless, the brownish mica schist of today's mountaintops in this area is muddy ocean sediment from the floor of an ancient sea, and the salmon-tinted mass of gypsum high up on a mountainside east of Split Mountain is the remains of a dry-lake mineral deposit, while the desert flats consist of material eroded and carried down from ancient mountains.

Father Pedro Font of Anza's expedition in 1775 and William Blake of the Southern Pacific Railway Survey in 1853 both noted the numerous shells found in the soil in the area southeast of the Fish Creek Mountains and the area surrounding San Sebastian Marsh. Some of the shells date back to the Pliocene Epoch, some 3–5 million years ago. The oyster shells and pectens in the Split Mountain/Fish Creek area are these older Pliocene sea deposits. At a lower elevation, superimposed on the folded, much older marine deposits, are freshwater Lake Cahuilla fossils from as recently as 500 years ago. These bivalves and gastropods are easily seen all around the San Sebastian Marsh area.

Cultural Features

There has been more activity and development in the Borrego Valley area of the desert than in any other area described in this guidebook. Whereas much of the modern history of other areas in the park involves people who passed through on their way to elsewhere or who sojourned briefly, the story of Borrego Valley involves those who settled upon the land and, with varying degrees of success, developed it. Some attempts, like those at San Felipe City and Little Borrego, failed, and the townsites have been reclaimed by the desert. Borrego Springs, on the other hand, has successfully flourished, becoming a quiet desert community surrounded by recreational land.

Cattlemen were the first to come and settle the land, followed later by farmers and developers. One of the earliest cattlemen of the Borrego Desert was John McCain. Sometime after 1875 he homesteaded the area around Borrego Spring and used it as his base of operations. Frank and Fred Clark used the Clark's Dry Lake area as their main cattle camp, while Julius and Amby Harper wintered their cattle on Pinyon Mountain. Paul Sentenac built a cabin in Sentenac Canyon and used the Scissors Crossing and Yaqui Well areas for his cattle.

Borego schoolhouse

Dr. Woillard at Broadway and Main

Upstairs at the Miracle Hotel

Grocery store at Borego

Farmers began entering the area after 1910, soon after the completion of the old Kane Springs Road, and "townsites" began developing in the next several years.

In 1918 San Felipe City, between the Fish Creek Mountains and Harpers Well near San Felipe Wash, consisted of a derrick, a house, an old shed and a couple of enterprising men. Although other hopeful settlers, especially veterans after World War I, homesteaded land in the San Felipe City area, the heat, flash floods, high winds and drifting sand soon caused them to give up the struggle.

Little Borrego, to the west of San Felipe City near the Split Mountain Road, had a similar story. Tom Hawn, an Alhambra realtor, developed the townsite. In 1924 the 14-room Miracle Hotel was built. The town also boasted a general store, a school, a service station, a barber shop and a pool hall. But the light traffic on the Kane Springs Road during the Depression years and the difficulty of keeping the road in good repair made this enterprise unprofitable, and the town was soon abandoned.

The last resident of the Miracle Hotel was an old Frenchman, Eugene P. Woillard. When Woillard first came to the United States, he settled in Florida and tried to grow pineapples. When this venture failed, he moved to the Imperial Valley and tried, again unsuccessfully, to raise ostriches for their plumes, which he had intended to send to Paris to have them designed for hats by his uncle, a Parisian lace manufacturer. Woillard also claimed to have named the avocado.

In later years Woillard moved to Little Borrego and used the abandoned Miracle Hotel for his "healing" operations with "radium water" and electricity. "Doc" Woillard also had a Model T sedan, which he called the "Princess Radium Health Car," that he used for house calls. During one of his excursions in his car in the late 1930s, he drove off the Yaqui Pass Road and was killed.

Others, including Albert and Anna Toner and a man named Benson, homesteaded in what is now called Ocotillo Wells. Benson, for whom the dry lake is named, owned a quarter section next to Toner and operated a store and gas station on the spot where the Burro Bend Cafe now stands. Unfortunately for Benson, his water well was located in the path of the proposed new Highway 78, and he was forced to sell out.

When Benson Dry Lake became a Navy air field during the mid-1930s, noise and disturbance from the air field put an end to what had been successful turkey ranch operations for Toner and a neighbor to the east of him.

Settlement of Borrego Valley proved more successful. In 1913 permanent residents numbered five. In 1924 Elsie A. Wynn opened up a small store and auto-repair shop and became Borrego Springs' first postmaster. In 1926 O.H. Ensign and sons Paul and Roy sank the first good well in the valley, making large-scale irrigated farming possible. The Ensign Ranch gradually grew to 1160 acres and became well-known for its date trees.

Valley growth remained slow during the Depression years, and this lag in growth allowed the state to begin purchasing land for the Park. However, the opposing interests of land developers caused Park land purchases to drag out for several years, resulting in many private land holdings existing within the ultimate Park boundaries.

The next step in the valley's growth came in 1945 when Joseph DiGiorgio purchased 2000 acres of land and brought electricity to the valley. Two years later A.A. Burnand Jr. began subdividing 1800 acres and disclosed his plans for turning the valley into a resort community. Development of the De Anza Country Club and surrounding estates followed several years later. Valley development has continued throughout the years, but growth has remained slow to moderate. The seasonal population of Borrego Springs is 2000–3000.

AREA 2: Coyote Canyon Corridor and Collins Valley Hikes

Overview and Access

Coyote Canyon and its extensive tributary canyons are among the most attractive areas of the Anza-Borrego region for off-road explorers, equestrians, hikers and backpackers. These areas offer genuine wilderness retreats, a wealth of animal and plant life, unique riparian habitats, and extensive archeological, cultural and historical features. Trips here are always interesting, no matter how many times one travels the rocky road or hikes the palm-studded, boulder-strewn canyons.

Three clusters of desert willows, known as Lower, Middle and Upper Willows, are found along Coyote Creek, a year-round stream and hence a rarity in the California desert. Smoke trees, tamarisk trees, mesquite bushes, wild grapes and wild apricots dot the creekside. Virgin groves of California fan palms and numerous springs are found in the many tributary canyons. Most types of plants and animals found elsewhere in the Anza-Borrego area can also be found in Coyote Canyon.

CAUTION: Most of this route is not available to conventional automobiles. Dangerous rocks, sand traps, and high road centers await the careless driver. Oil, fuel and grease stains along the route attest to numerous smashed pans, hoses, tanks, pumps and various other parts.

NOTE: The CANYON IS CLOSED to vehicles from June 15 to September 15 to protect bighorn-sheep watering areas. The reopening each year often reveals a "new" canyon, for summer floods can dramatically alter the shape and route of the road through Coyote Canyon, especially near Lower Willows and over the rugged jeep trail into Collins Valley. Mileages listed for Coyote Canyon may vary somewhat from year to year because of the flooding. Inquire at the Visitor Center for latest route conditions.

Northbound mileages are from Christmas Circle in Borrego Springs; southbound mileages are from Highway 371 near Anza in Riverside County. The wide southern entrance to the canyon from Borrego Springs ascends and narrows until the arduous Lower Willows bypass into Collins Valley, the latter named for an early homesteader there. From Collins Valley the canyon swings northwest to the narrow, difficult route through Middle Willows, widens again near the Riverside County line, squeezes into a deep, cleftlike gorge in the Upper Willows area, and emerges in a wide area at the mouth of Alder Canyon called Fig Tree Valley. From Fig Tree Valley the road leads to the Turkey Track, where Tule, Nance and Horse canyons branch off the end of Coyote Canyon in such a way that a giant turkey's footprint can be imagined. From here an old Civilian Conservation Corps road climbs "Anza Ridge" in a series of steep switchbacks, runs west along the ridgetop, drops through a pleasant little valley at the head of Nance Canyon, and then climbs another ridge near San Carlos Pass and leads on to Highway 371, a paved road, at the settlement of Anza. Total distance from the Highway 371 junction to Borrego Springs is about 36 miles. Highway 371 leads east to Highway 74 and down into the Coachella Valley/Palm Springs area. Highway 371 west leads to Highway 395 and on to Corona and the Riverside Freeway into Orange County.

To traverse the whole length of Coyote Canyon requires an off-road vehicle, although light trucks and autos may reach Lower Willows from Borrego Springs. The middle and upper reaches of the tributary canyons are accessible to hikers only. Backpacking groups frequently park near Lower Willows and hike through en route to the canyons along the west side of Collins Valley.

NOTE: Hiking and backpacking routes in the popular Collins Valley westside canyons are described in a separate section after Trip 2.

Middle Willows in Coyote Canyon

Trip 2: Coyote Canyon

From: Christmas Circle

To: Highway 371 (36.2 miles one way)

Via: DiGiorgio Road, Desert Gardens (dirt road, occasionally jeep only), Ocotillo Flat to Lower Willows (light auto route), Collins Valley (jeep route), Middle Willows, Fig Tree Valley, Turkey Track, San Carlos Pass (jeep only) and Terwilliger Valley. Entire route suitable for mountain bicycles. Rugged and wet in the Willows.

Mileage From:

Christmas Circle	Hiway 371	Checkpoint Description
0.0	36.2	Proceed east ½ mile to DiGiorgio Road. Turn north (left) to . . .
3.5	32.7	Intersection with Henderson Canyon Road. Pegleg Smith Monument is 4.1 miles east (right) on Henderson Canyon Road. Continue north (straight).
5.2	31.0	End of pavement. Cross Coyote Canyon creek bed to edge of valley and proceed northwest along the foot of Coyote Mountain. To the northeast is a natural scar on the mountainside that can be imagined to be an angel, complete with a story: when Anza's second expediton labored through Borrego Valley during one of the bitterest winters on record, the angel appeared and pointed the way to Coyote Canyon and eventually to San Gabriel Mission.
6.0	30.2	A mudhole may be here in wet seasons. This can become impassible to all but 4-wheel drive. Check at the Visitor Center for latest information.
8.0	28.2	Alcoholic Pass is the break northeast (right) of here in the long ridge lying between Coyote Canyon and Clark Valley. Elevation of the pass is some 1600 feet, or about 700 feet above the stream bed of Coyote Creek.

Side Trip Over Alcoholic Pass

The hiking trail to the pass, part of an old Indian trail from Los Coyotes Indian Reservation to Clark Lake, begins at the end of a small spur ridge and ascends its backbone to the pass. Early settlers in Clark Valley used this trail as a short-cut to Coyote Canyon rather than go 5 or 6 miles farther southeast around the end of Coyote Mountain. The climb into the pass is not difficult. The north side slopes gently down into Clark Valley, where the trail joins the Rockhouse Canyon Road. The extensive ocotillo forest on the Coyote Canyon side grows on the rubble fan that has washed down from the flanks of the ridge. Coyote Mountain is composed of complex crystalline rocks and Tertiary sediments that have been uplifted between two faults of the San Jacinto fault system. An extensive deposit of clay overlaps the granite of Coyote Mountain, containing petrified bones of prehistoric land animals.

End of Side Trip

8.5	27.7	Desert Gardens (signed). The Anza-Borrego Committee of the Desert Protective Council established this Desert Garden as an example of what private donations can purchase for the park. The committee, which since has become an independent, nonprofit foundation, seeks donations to buy private landholdings within the

Christmas Circle	Hiway 371	Checkpoint Description

ultimate Anza-Borrego Desert State Park boundaries. It is the goal of the Anza-Borrego Foundation to eliminate private inholdings within the park that have been identified as having scientific, cultural or scenic value worthy of protection. The foundation sponsors an annual Desert Walk each spring, led by an expert guide in the field of geology, archeology, botany, zoology or history. Check with the Visitor Center for the exact date each year. A signpost at Desert Gardens reads: FOR THE INSPIRATION AND ENJOYMENT OF ALL MANKIND AND TO HONOR THOSE FOR WHOM THE DESERT GARDENS ARE ACQUIRED, MARCH 28, 1971. A path from the sign leads to two stone-and-slab tables, a peaceful and relaxing place for a picnic. Overlooking these tables is a trail to a low hill where a stone bench is found, and one can sit and enjoy the view of the ocotillo forest that surrounds this slope of Coyote Mountain. A new addition to the Desert Gardens area is an interpretive panel which shows plant and animal adaptations to the desert. Also seen are buckhorn and teddy-bear cholla, creosote bush, and beavertail and barrel cactus.

9.1   27.1   First Crossing. Motorhomes and trailers must not proceed beyond here. The main route is just across the creek on the southwest side.

El Vado, Anza's camp in the mouth of Coyote Canyon, is located 1.2 miles south (left) of First Crossing on the Horse Camp road.

Recommended Route to Horse Camp (suitable for horse trailers and motor homes). Vehicles with reservations at the Horse Camp should enter by way of Borrego Springs Road or Henderson Canyon Road. From the junction of Borrego Springs Road and Henderson Canyon Road, proceed north on the Horse Camp dirt road just east of Indian Head Ranch Road.

0.0   Junction of Henderson Canyon Road and Borrego Springs Road, 3½ miles north of Christmas Circle. Proceed north on a good dirt road just east of Indian Head Ranch Road and west of an attractive lemon grove.

2.4   Park boundary (signed).

3.2   El Vado Monument. El Vado is Spanish for the creek "ford," which provided a campsite for the Anza expedition in 1775.

3.5   Fork. The Horse Camp is 0.3 mile straight ahead to a deadend. The northwest (right) fork leads 1 mile to join the main Coyote Canyon route at First Crossing.

The Horse Camp has 10 campsites with a total of about 40 corrals. Reservations for the camp must be made through MISTIX, P.O. Box 85705, San Diego, CA 92138-5705. Campers must supply their own feed and clean their corrals. Campsites include water, barbecue stove or fire ring, chemical toilets and nearby solar-heated showers. The park maintains an office at the site. A leaflet entitled "Riding Trails of Coyote Canyon" details the more than 30 miles of signed horse trails in the canyon. The trail system was developed by park volunteer Vern Whitaker. See page 33 for specific rules for equestrians and Horse Camp use.

End of Recommended Route to Horse Camp

Coyote Creek in Lower Coyote Canyon. Trees are desert willows.

Christmas Circle	Hiway 371	Checkpoint Description
9.1	27.1	The main route proceeds northwest (right) up a road on the southwest bank of the creek. Ocotillo Flat horse trail forks northwest (right) from First Crossing, then rejoins the main route at Second Crossing after a 2-mile loop.

This is Ocotillo Flat, which is populated by tall ocotillos, encelias, agaves, and a variety of cacti including fishhook, cholla and beavertail. This area and Desert Gardens contain two of the most outstanding and healthy stands of ocotillo in all of California. Here, close up against some of the larger shrubs, are also found some huge fishhook cacti, many of them growing in clumps up to 2 feet across. This area and Lower Willows are the best birding spots in the northern half of the park. Luzuli buntings, blue grosbeaks, flycatchers, hawks and eagles are seen regularly. The sandstone formations on the north side of Ocotillo Flat are called the Coyote Canyon Badlands.

Scattered at intervals over the flat are spots of black dirt indicative of ancient fires, and at the base of the confining north ridge, the badlands, one may see mortar holes and the chips of arrow makers. This area and the vicinity of Lower Willows were heavily populated by Indians because of the presence of water, agave and mesquite.

10.2	26.0	Second Crossing. A new, automated gaging station is located here on the southwest side of the creek. On the north side of the creek, after the second stream crossing, is a long, straight row of 15-foot-high ocotillos about 75 yards long. At the west end of the row another line of ocotillos runs south for about 50 yards. The south and east sides are not so well defined, but one can readily see that this was a man-made enclosure and a very effective living corral.

Christmas Circle	Hiway 371	Checkpoint Description

The ocotillos could not have grown to their present size in just a few years. Consequently, they are believed by some to have been placed by members of the Anza expedition while encamped at El Vado to corral the many head of cattle they had. A more plausible explanation is that the fence was built by early-day cattlemen or possibly even the native Indians of the area. It was a common practice in the west to use armed ocotillo staves as fencing. Given a little water, a living plant usually results.

A popular area, known as Tractor Camp because of the half-buried tractor in the sand, is about one-quarter mile west of Second Crossing via the left fork. The main route continues northwest (right) up-canyon.

This is also the site of the Coyote Canyon LOWER CLOSURE in summer, June 15–September 15. The canyon is closed during this time period to protect bighorn-sheep watering holes.

10.9   25.3   Third Crossing and Lower Willows Bypass route to southwest (left) across creek. Route in creekbed beyond this point is hiking and horseback only. The bypass was completed in 1988 to protect the sensitive and invaluable desert treasure of Lower Willows from adverse vehicular impact. This habitat of rare and endangered species and summer watering holes for Bighorn Sheep is unmatched in the vast expanses of the Colorado Desert.

Side Hiking Trip Through Lower Willows

0.0   Third Crossing parking area. Continue northwest along creek.

0.2   Box Canyon joins Coyote Canyon from the north (right). See below for a description of this side hiking trip.

0.3   An old gaging station, elevation 1189, marks the entrance to Lower Willows and Anza's Santa Catarina campsite. A new hiking/horseback trail on the north side skirts this unique wild and jungly growth of willows, vines and tamarisks. A fire early in 1988 destroyed much of the vegetation, but given the ample water supply and excellent growing conditions, the area should soon renew itself.

1.7   Exit the dense willow growth. Water from Indian Canyon and Salvador Canyon joins the main creek here from the west, although the joining creekbed is impassable even afoot. The main route proceeds northwest (right) up the main canyon through a final dense willow grove.

1.8   New Spring and pool on the southwest (left) side of the creek. This high-volume spring erupted unexpectedly in the winter of 1983–84. Water from it is crystal clear, in striking contrast to the somewhat muddy water of the main creek. Visitors have captured the waters of the spring in a rock pool.

From New Spring the route continues northwest up-canyon into the broad, open expanse of Collins Valley. Middle Willows, always a guaranteed water supply, is about a four-mile hike.

End of Side Trip

Christmas Circle	Hiway 371	Checkpoint Description

Side Hiking Trip up Box Canyon

0.0   Third Crossing parking area. Continue northwest along creek.

0.2   Box Canyon joins Coyote Canyon from the north (right). Enter Box Canyon, which forks about 1.5 miles north of Coyote Creek, the main branch going north (right) through a deep, narrow gorge. This fork of Box Canyon can be followed on foot about 5 more miles to Jackass Flat and on to Hidden Spring in Rockhouse Canyon. The northwest (left) fork rises gradually for another mile through a low saddle, from the top of which can be seen the entrance to Salvador Canyon on the other (west) side of Coyote Creek. From this saddle the top of the ridge can be followed southeast (right) to a small dry pond, or playa, lying between two peaks. The playa is approximately 5 acres in extent and it has one outlet, a steep gulch coming out of its south side and ending in Coyote Creek at Lower Willows. The gravelly bottom of the playa contains cresote, ocotillo, burroweed, wild buckwheat, and buckhorn and barrel cacti. A round-trip hike from Box Canyon to the dry lake, down the drainage to Coyote Creek and back down to the entrance of Box Canyon is about 6.5 miles.

End of Side Trip

10.9   25.3   Third Crossing and Lower Willows Bypass route to southwest (left) across creek. The route parallels the old Collins Valley cattle trail, which is still visible and is used by hikers and horsemen. The challenging vehicle route is absolutely four-wheel-drive/jeep only for a one-mile pitch AND requires a highly skilled and experienced driver. Whether climbing or descending, a scout should be deployed afoot to restrain opposing traffic from the gully until clear. There may be more brutal jeep traverses somewhere out in that great desert, but the authors know of none.

12.2   24.0   SANTA CATARINA HISTORICAL MONUMENT is located at the divide. The monument was placed in 1967 by Squibob (San Diego-Imperial County) Chapter of E Clampus Vitus, a historical fraternity which flourished in mid-19th century gold camps of California's Mother Lode country. The group now perpetuates the rich trove of Pacific Southwest folklore and legend. The monument commemorates the Anza party's stay at the spring during Christmas 1775. A lone eucalyptus tree in the valley below marks the site of an early-day homestead, and some palms are also visible.

12.7   23.5   Fork to the east (right) goes a short distance to deadend in an impassable bog which is Santa Catarina Spring. This is a major source of Coyote Canyon's permanent water supply, which is of prime importance to Borrego Valley. Coupled with the other waters flowing underground into Borrego Valley, it maintains a surprisingly stable water level despite heavy use for agricultural and domestic purposes. Santa Catarina Spring covers an area of several acres and is the largest single natural emergence of water in San Diego County. This contributes to Coyote Creek's being the longest perennial stream in the county. The great amount of water and the resultant growth of vegetation make Santa Catarina Spring very

Christmas Circle	Hiway 371	Checkpoint Description
		attractive to wildlife. Small animals and their predators abound, and the area has a year-round population of a variety of birds. A wild growth of willows, young palms, vines and tamarisks enmeshes the spring area. The largest Indian site in the northern half of the Park is found at the spring. A heavy deposit of middens overlays a large area. Indians inhabited this area until about four generations ago.
12.9	23.3	Junction at elevation 1345 feet. North (right) is the main route up-canyon. West (left) is the loop trip to Sheep Canyon.

Loop Trip to Sheep Canyon Campground

0.0   Junction at elevation 1345 feet. West (left) is the loop trip to Sheep Canyon to rejoin the main route up-canyon at "Wash" survey marker. This loop trip is an alternate route clockwise around the higher southern and western rim of Collins Valley, yielding superb sunset views of the Santa Rosa Mountain massif to the east.

1.7   Fork (signed). Southwest (left) turn leads in 0.5 mile to Sheep Canyon Primitive Campground. There are pit toilets but no water, although the stream may run as far as the campground in the winter and spring. Some conspicuous lone palms growing on the western mountain slope above the bajada guard the canyon's entrance. Visitors are reminded that all vegetation, both growing and down, is protected. No ground fires are permitted here or anywhere in the park. Sheep Canyon provides an excellent base from which to explore afoot the canyon treasures beyond. See below for detailed hiking descriptions of Sheep, Cougar, Indian and Salvador Canyons.   .

3.1   Main route junction at survey marker "Wash".

End of Loop Trip

14.1	22.1	Sheep Canyon junction (signed) at survey marker "Wash", 1402 feet. Southwest (left) leads 1.9 miles into Sheep Canyon campground (see loop trip above.) The main route continues northwest up-wash toward Salvador Canyon.
15.3	20.9	Junction (signed). The main route turns northeast (right). Vehicles may travel another ½ mile up-wash from this junction to deadend in the mouth of Salvador Canyon. This canyon, known to the Cahuilla Indians as "Mowal," is named for the youngest member of the second Anza expedition, Salvador Ygnacio Linares, who was born just west of here. Salvador Canyon is not a conspicuous canyon; there are neither palm trees nor other landmarks near the entrance to distinguish it from a score of other side canyons. But within its steep, narrow, verdant gorge are the many palms that once earned it the name of Thousand Palms Canyon, so referenced by Randall Henderson, desert explorer and founder of *Desert Magazine*. Henderson once counted 360 palms within the main canyon and its forks. See below for a hiker's route description up this canyon.

An almost pure stand of desert agave covers this north Collins Valley area.

Christmas Circle	Hiway 371	Checkpoint Description
16.3	19.9	Monkey Hill, possibly named by local Indians for its resemblance to a hill near Lake Henshaw where a circus monkey was found and caught, is the outcropping just east (right) of the route. Another version says Coyote Canyon's Monkey Hill refers to a feature in the book *Swiss Family Robinson.*
17.9	18.3	Survey Marker 1837, just beyond which is Middle Willows. The area around these willows is the most likely place in the Park accessible to vehicles to see bighorn sheep. It is also the most difficult part of Coyote Canyon to navigate because of its many twists and turns. Two clusters of palm trees are found here, and a flat area for camping is near one of the clusters, at the northwest end of Middle Willows.
		Yucca Valley, another pleasant little valley known for its thick cover of stubby Mojave yucca, extends south from the west side of Middle Willows. For hikers only, it may be entered from the upstream edge of the willows. For about 1.6 miles and a 400-foot ascent through creosote, juniper, yucca and joint fir, the hiker is following bighorn sheep trails via their descent route from the mountains into Middle Willows. A saddle at the head (south end) of Yucca Valley provides the best view of Salvador Canyon's numerous palm trees and enticing side canyons. Known as Canyon View, this saddle is 500 feet above the floor of Salvador Canyon.
19.6	16.6	Partial fence line marking Riverside/San Diego County line.
20.2	16.0	UPPER CLOSURE of Coyote Canyon. Vehicles may not proceed southeast down canyon past this point during summer closure months of June 15 through September 15. This is to protect bighorn-sheep water holes.

Cooling off in Coyote Creek

Christmas Circle	Hiway 371	Checkpoint Description
20.4	15.8	Cleveland Gorge, so named for the rare Cleveland penstemon (*Penstemon clevelandii,* subspecies *connatus*), which grows in the rocky clefts of the gorge. The red blossoms on long stems make this plant easy to recognize when in bloom.
20.6	15.6	Anza (White Child) Monument at Survey Marker 2207 and an old corral just west (left) of route. This monument commemorates the birth on Christmas Eve 1775 of Salvador Ygnacio Linares, one of the first non-Indian children born in California. Thereafter the route passes through Upper Willows and swings southwest around the edge of Fig Tree Valley. Hikers proceeding up or down Coyote Canyon should follow the steam bed through Fig Tree Valley, avoiding the longer jeep route around the edge of the valley.
		The main village of the Los Coyotes Indians, which they called Wiliya, was located in this wide valley. The clan chief lived there. Four other villages in Coyote Canyon were "colonies" of Wiliya. One to the north was an extension of it, while the others were located in Tule Canyon and Collins Valley. Anza's camp on Christmas Eve 1775 was made at or near Wiliya. He called the Indians at the village Los Danzantes (The Dancers) because of these Indians' peculiar mannerisms of jumping, slapping their thighs and jerking while communicating with the Spaniards.
20.9	15.3	Fork. Northwest (right) route proceeds straight up the main canyon about 1 mile to rejoin main route near bench mark 2415.
		West (left) fork enters the dense growth of Upper Willows. This is a very short but very rugged passage.
21.1	15.1	Sharp turn south (left) out of the creek bed.
21.3	14.9	Bailey's Cabin, an old line shack, corral and water tank just east (left) of the road. The shack, a former cattle outpost belonging to early cattleman Howard Bailey, offers storm shelter to hikers, while the corral is available for equestrians' use.
22.1	14.1	Turnoff to the southwest (left) leads into Alder Canyon.

Side Trip Up Alder Canyon

0.0   Turnoff. Gaping wounds on a small ridge just west of here bear mute testimony to the irresponsibility of a small minority of off-road drivers.

0.9   Hiking-trail turnoff left leads east and south around the hillside to Mangalar Spring. The spring lies on the east slope of the bottom of a small canyon a few feet above the wash. The sumacs by the spring, known by their Cahuilla Indian name of Mangalar, are not tall but very old, gnarled, crabbed and heavily-trunked. Mangalar Flats, which slopes gently down from the spring toward Coyote Creek, is covered with creosote bush, Mojave yucca, buckhorn cactus, catclaw, cheese bush and burro weed. On the hillsides above the spring are found desert apricot, sumac and beavertail.

1.9   Deadend near ruins of an old cabin. Seasonal streams ripple down both forks of Alder to join in the tree-shaded grove where old cottonwood trees are found. Alders may be found upstream of these old cottonwoods. The diameters of some of these trees are about 3½ feet. Vegetation in this canyon is indicative of higher elevation and changing life zone. Juniper, scrub oak, white sage, Mojave yucca, and mangalar sumac

New Spring in Coyote Canyon

Christmas Circle	Hiway 371	Checkpoint Description

are found in addition to buckhorn cholla, desert apricot, goatnut and catclaw. From the grove there is an excellent view of Toro Peak to the northeast. The Santa Rosa Mountains east and northeast show red, orange and brown in places where ancient river deposits are found. The light-colored areas are soft sand marking the course of White Wash out of Horse Canyon. Hikers may proceed from here (elevation 2650) up either fork of Alder, both of which involve some serious bushwhacking.

A. The North Fork departs northwest from the valley and then swings west after about a mile. It is about 5 more miles to a junction at 5600 feet with the Pacific Crest Trail on the northeast flank of Combs Peak atop Bucksnort Mountain. Typical of most mountains throughout the area, Bucksnort Mountain is cut with canyons. A heavy cover of chaparral grows over the greater part of the south side. Coulter pines grow in isolated groups in canyons and along the ridge.

B. The South Fork departs southeast from the valley, paralleling, an old jeep trail for ½ mile, and then enters dense mesquite thickets to swing southwest into the mountains. Some of this route is described as a descent route from Sage Flat below. Alder trees extend about 3 miles up canyon. The South Fork eventually meets the Pacific Crest Trail on the southeast flank of Bucksnort Mountain at about 5200 feet.

End of Side Trip

Christmas Circle	Hiway 371	Checkpoint Description
23.6	12.6	A hiking route departs west (left) into the broad mouth of Parks Canyon, named for an early-day cattleman. About 2 miles in, at the 3000-foot level, are some oak trees and seasonal springs. The canyon extends about another mile beyond these.
24.5	11.7	The "Turkey Track," where Horse Canyon joins from the north (right). Horse Canyon, together with Nance Canyon from the northwest and Tule Canyon from the west, join here to form what appears to be a giant turkey-foot track, downstream of which is Coyote Canyon proper.

Horse Canyon is negotiable by jeep for 3–4 miles, with some water and cottonwood trees to be found at trail's end. About 1 mile from the Turkey Track is a shaded area, just before the turnoff to White Wash. This was an old cattle camp, and it provides a good but waterless campsite. White Wash, to the east (right) of this camp, has large groves of tall nolina yuccas. It is possible to backpack from White Wash via Dry Wash to either the Hidden Spring trail or into Box Canyon to Lower Willows. Either way is long, rugged and waterless, but the total desert wilderness aspect of such a route may be attractive to some hardy desert backpackers. In the north end of Horse Canyon there once was a Mountain Cahuilla Indian village called Nacuta.

24.9	11.3	Junction of Tule and Nance canyons. A spring and seasonal stream are found about a mile up Nance Canyon, named for an old homesteader.

A jeep trail extends about 1¼ miles up Tule Canyon past California Department of Forestry water tanks to a cottonwood grove and spring. About another 2 miles up, at elevation 3500, is Tule Spring, reached by jeep trail from Terwilliger Valley. From Tule Spring the main canyon swings south toward its headwaters on Bucksnort Mountain, some 7 more miles up-canyon. An Indian village called Tepana was located in Tule.

The Pacific Crest Trail route runs down the length of Tule Canyon and then proceeds north over Table Mountain.

From Survey Marker 2696, marking the junction of Tule and Nance canyons, the Anza party climbed "Anza Ridge," a steep ridge separating the two canyons over virtually the same track followed by CCC road-building crews in the 1930s. This rocky, rutted, rough road today climbs 500 feet in ¾ mile in a series of switchbacks and hairpin curves. The view from the top of the ridge is superb, with Santa Rosa and Toro peaks, Coyote Canyon and its tributaries, and the dim blue of distant Borrego Valley spread before the viewer.

28.2	8.0	This small valley, part of Nance Canyon, assumes major historical significance due to the arroyo entering its northwest edge from Terwilliger Valley. This arroyo was named the Royal Pass of San Carlos by Anza and was known to later pioneers as "La Puerta," the portal, or door, to the desert. It was a place of great elation for the leaders of the Anza expedition, for they knew it to be the dividing point between the hardships and rigors of the desert crossing, now behind them, and pastoral, coastal California ahead, with its Spanish settlements and their ultimate objective, San Francisco Bay.

Christmas Circle	Hiway 371	Checkpoint Description
		Since most of this small valley and San Carlos Pass are on private property, the traveler must continue northwest on the dirt road over a final ridge and into Terwilliger Valley to where the . . .
29.9	6.3	Road turns a corner due west and becomes graded.
30.2	6.0	Private road to south (left) leads ¼ mile to the Art Carey Ranch. Because this is all private property, permission to enter must be obtained in advance. A monument on the ranch, erected by the Native Sons of the Golden West in 1924, marks "La Puerta Real de San Carlos." In rock caves nearby, and still on private property, is a valuable series of Indian pictographs. These portray, among other things, passing horsemen believed to represent Anza's mounted soldiers. Such a graphic record by native Americans, reporting initial contact between their culture and that of Europe, is a rare and priceless legacy to today's interpretive scientists.
31.6	4.6	Junction with Terwilliger Road. South (left), a dirt road leads into the middle reaches of Tule Canyon and to Tule Springs, about 5 miles south and east. The road north (right) is paved and leads through Terwilliger Valley via Wellman and Kirby roads to a . . .
36.2	0.0	Junction with Highway 371, 1.5 miles east of the small settlement of Anza (elevation 3918).

The longest year-round stream in San Diego County—Coyote Creek

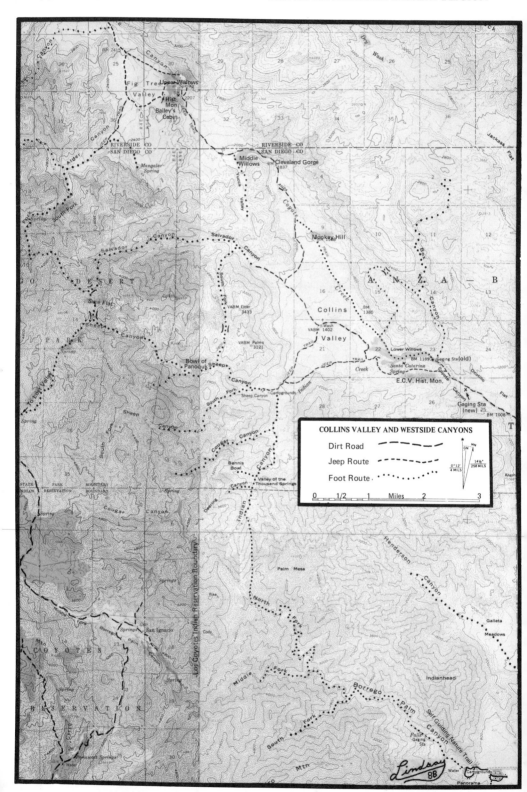

COLLINS VALLEY AND WESTSIDE CANYONS

Dirt Road

Jeep Route

Foot Route

Hiking Routes in Collins Valley's Westside Canyons

With the exception of Borrego Palm Canyon, the westside canyons of Collins Valley are the most popular hiking and backpacking areas in the Park, with good reason. Here, probably more than anywhere else in the Park, the visitor can stand amid the mystery, majesty and solitude of this desert wilderness. Mountain plateaus and peaks overlook arid bajadas and wet bottomlands in stream-laced canyon tongues. Whether by short walk, overnight hike, or challenging intercanyon traverse, these gorges beckon to all who would encounter the essential spirit of this land. Ancient granite mountains rise sharply from the channel of Coyote Canyon, where earth upheavals, faulting and erosion have left broken massifs of stone whose higher peaks and ridges are almost bare of vegetation. The broad flat of Collins Valley is a huge alluvial fan formed of debris issuing out of Indian, Sheep and Salvador canyons over many thousands of years. From any place in the Collins Valley area, the sharp peaks of the mountains cut by deep canyons form a picturesque background to the flat of the valley with its cover of desert plants.

The major canyons of the area have springs at which palm trees grow. Often, subsurface water supports palm trees high up on a canyon side, as in Salvador Canyon. The desert is still an influence up to 3000 feet elevation, where desert agave and lavender grow side by side with California juniper.

The water and the vegetation, along with the isolation, make the area attractive to bighorn sheep and a few mule deer. This is probably the western limit of the bighorn range in the Anza-Borrego area. Near palm trees and along the boulder-formed caves at the bottom of various canyons, evidence of Indian use can be found—bedrock grinding spots, shards, flaking, and fire sites.

Collins Valley's westside canyons are best explored from a base at Sheep Canyon Primitive Campground.

CAUTION: Although given mileages in these mountain-desert canyons may appear short, these are extremely rugged miles due to rapid ascents and descents, lack of defined trails, dense brush and shrubbery, repeated stream crossings, often waterless conditions, steep canyon walls, and challenging map-and-compass work. A rough guide to time planning is that these miles take three times as long as miles on trail or across open desert.

Indian Canyon

0.0	Elevation 1620. The trailhead is 0.2 mile east of Sheep Canyon Primitive Campground where an old jeep trail (now closed to vehicles) departs from the Sheep Canyon route.
0.8	Cross Cougar Canyon stream bed—access to Cougar Canyon (see below).
2.0	The draw to the west (right) leads ¼ mile into Bennis Bowl, named for Karl Bennis, an old-timer who showed early Park rangers many features of the Anza-Borrego Desert thitherto unknown to them.
2.2	Old Tin Mine tunnel on west (right) side of trail.
2.3	Elevation 2180. Deering Canyon enters from the west (right). This canyon, with its many palms hidden in its steep western wall, ascends rapidly for about a mile. It is typical of the several named and unnamed canyons that are tributary to Indian Canyon, most of which contain palm trees and seasonal streams. Although these side

canyons are rugged and remote, it is well worth the extra physical effort to enjoy the peaceful isolation among the palm fronds and the sounds of water trickling over the creek's boulders.

3.1 Elevation 2650. The canyon forks. At the confluence of the two canyons a spring supports a grove of California fan palms and several sycamore trees.

An old Indian trail turns southwest (right) and climbs steeply via switchbacks along the ridge between the canyon branches. This trail swings west, keeping south of the creek bed for about another mile to a saddle at 4160 feet on the boundary of Los Coyotes Reservation. Permission to enter must be obtained in advance from the tribal council.

The main canyon continues due south. There being no trail, the climb is very strenuous. After another 1¼ miles the canyon walls close in to become cliffs. *Experienced climbers only* may negotiate a route up the cliffs to the saddle at 4620 feet and then descend south and east into the north fork of Borrego Palm Canyon, exiting at Palm Canyon Campground (see the Borrego Palm Canyon hike).

Cougar Canyon

Cougar Canyon, actually a fork of Indian Canyon 0.8 mile south of the vehicle route, is known for its cool running stream, its massive jumble of granite boulders, its high waterfalls, its shady sycamore, cottonwood and palm trees, and its Indian *temescal,* or sweathouse, found at the north edge of the canyon's mouth. This very rugged canyon has a wide opening but it narrows suddenly and rises in a series of rock steps. A rope may be needed for security in scaling some of the near-vertical canyon walls and boulders. A waterfall cascading down a grotto system and pools deep enough to swim in await adventurous souls about 2

Temescal (sweathouse) at mouth of Cougar Canyon

miles up-canyon from Indian Canyon. About ½ mile beyond the waterfall at 3250 feet, the canyon forks, the main canyon swinging south and entering the Indian Reservation. Prior permission is required to enter. West and northwest from this fork, a small canyon runs toward a saddle on the divide between it and the south fork of Sheep Canyon. Hence a cross-country traverse can be made from Cougar canyon via this small canyon into Sheep Canyon drainage, to eventually arrive back at Sheep Canyon Primitive Campground. This traverse is *only* for experienced backpackers who are adept at cross-country route finding.

Sheep Canyon

Sheep Canyon penetrates the Anza-Borrego State Wilderness Area and is centrally located in the Coyote Canyon west-side canyon system. Sheep Canyon offers several good intercanyon traverse routes. Its stream, like those of most westside canyons, is seasonal. In late summer, it is completely dry, and only a few seeps, mudholes and small springs high up the canyon provide water for bighorn sheep and other animals. When the fall rains come, the stream starts running, and at the height of the winter rains it runs well past the campground toward Coyote Creek. As summer approaches, the stream becomes smaller, receding farther and farther up-canyon until the cycle is complete in late summer.

0.0   Elevation 1640. The trailhead is at the west end of Sheep Canyon Primitive campground.

0.2   South fork of Sheep Canyon joins from the west (left). This fork is very steep and rugged, but its palm groves are visible from camp. It runs about 4 difficult miles west into the mountains, from where a traverse south into Cougar Canyon is possible (see above).

0.5   First palm grove and spring grotto.

1.1   Elevation 2250. A small tributary canyon climbs steeply north (right) about a mile to a saddle at elevation 2900. On the other side of this saddle, the south fork of Salvador Canyon leads north to enter the main Salvador Canyon about 2 miles from the saddle (see p. 103). The main Sheep Canyon continues ascending through palm and sycamore groves within the steep canyon walls. Large boulders and dense shrubbery make passage difficult.

1.9   Elevation 2450. Past a narrow portal in the canyon between a small ridge ascending right and a steep wall to the left, the canyon opens up into a large bowl surrounded by distinct peaks. This beautiful bowl may be the place called "Panoquk" by the Cahuilla Indians and "Palm Bowl" by early cattlemen and settlers. From a vantage point on the hillside north of the brush-choked stream bed, two westward routes can be studied.

A.   Southwest of the bowl a canyon rises abruptly above a thick grove of trees. This canyon can be followed about a mile to a point from where one can climb south (left) up to the saddle west of Peak 4649. By traveling another mile over this saddle, the hiker can reach the south fork of Sheep Canyon. About 3 miles east (left) is Sheep Canyon Primitive Campground.

B.   From the bowl, Sheep Canyon proper continues northwest and requires *very* careful route selection and mapwork. From mile 1.9, just inside the bowl west of its entrance, the hiker should continue along the hillside north of the creek bed, go *through* the prominent gully that runs north (right) past Knob and Collins survey points, continue to the west edge of the bowl, and identify the point at which the canyon swings north (right) around a prominent ridgeline. This point is at about mile 2.9.

2.9   The best guide is to follow the main watercourse. Continuing to swing right as the canyon abruptly climbs, the hiker will view cliffs at the 3200-foot level. After climbing these cliffs either left or right of the stream bed, the hiker will be in a small bowl. Now keeping to the east and north (right) side of the stream bed, negotiate another set of cliffs, from atop which, at about mile 3.8, one can view the upper reaches of Sheep Canyon.

3.8   Continue from these cliff tops westward, working along the hillside just north (right) of the stream bed.

4.8   Directly north (right) of this point, at the low point of the ridge, is the saddle between Sheep and Salvador canyons and also a tributary of the south fork of Alder Canyon. Here there are two choices: (A) continue west up-canyon to the head of Sheep Canyon, or (B) ascend north (right) to the saddle for an excellent view and more route possibilities.

A.   A large grove of pine and oak trees, known as "The Grapevine," is visible about ½ mile southwest, marking a spring site (elevation 4550) near the head of Sheep Canyon. From here an old Indian trail can be followed about 2 miles southwest up-canyon and over an easy saddle at 4900 feet into Lost Valley at Shingle Spring, on the Park boundary. This Indian trail connected villages in the Warner Springs area with ones in middle and upper Coyote Canyon via Lost Valley. It may also be "The Salton Sea Trail" shown on an early (1910) survey map of the area.

B.   From mile 4.8 in Sheep Canyon, the Sheep-Salvador-Alder saddle is about ¼ mile north (right) of the stream bed and about 350 feet above it through chaparral growth. From the saddle one can see the often-snow-capped summit of Mt. San Jacinto, 35 miles north. There are three possible routes down from the saddle into Coyote Canyon: (1) northwest (left) via a tributary to the south fork of Alder Canyon; (2) north (straight ahead) via the old Indian trail; (3) northeast (right) via Salvador Canyon. Each of these three routes leaves "Sage Flat" about ½ mile north from the saddle.

The following mileages continue from 4.8 in Sheep Canyon.

Route B-1 via the south fork of Alder Canyon
5.1   Saddle at 4400 feet. Bear northwest (left) when descending through Sage Flat, into the head of a small canyon. This canyon deepens, and some rock scrambling is required.

7.2   Join the south fork of Alder Canyon near a very large alder tree, and turn north (right). Vines, down trees, stream crossings, and thorny catclaw thickets make travel difficult. A series of springs here generally provide year-round water for wildlife.

9.7   Trailhead. Enter a valley at the foot of Alder Canyon near a jeep trail. The north fork of Alder Canyon is visible, trending northwest from this valley. See p. 95 for vehicle route from here.

Route B-2 via old Indian trail and ridge
5.1   Saddle at 4400 feet. Cross Sage Flat and ascend small hill north of the flat. A trail works down the ridge to the north.

8.1   Trailhead in valley at foot of Alder Canyon.

Route B-3 via Salvador Canyon
5.1   Saddle at 4400 feet. Bear northeast (right) when descending through Sage Flat, into a small canyon. This is the head of Salvador Canyon. See below for a description of hiking up Salvador to this point.

11.0   Vehicle trail junction in Collins Valley. About 2½ miles southwest is Sheep Canyon Campground, making this Sheep-to-Salvador Canyon traverse an excellent one- or two-night backpack.

Salvador Canyon

Trail mileages are from the signpost at mile 15.1 of Trip 2 in the northwest corner of Collins Valley.

0.0   Signpost, elevation 1540.

0.3   Roadhead and vehicle turnaround.

1.2   South fork of Salvador Canyon joins from south (left) at elevation 1850. About ¼ mile up this canyon is a little palm oasis with a seasonal waterfall. About 2 miles farther is a saddle, elevation 2900. The canyon down the other side of this saddle leads about another mile into Sheep Canyon, 1.1 miles west of Sheep Canyon Campground. This gives the possibility of about an 8-mile loop trip from Sheep Canyon Campground via Salvador, South Fork, and the saddle into Sheep Canyon and back to the campground. From this point on, it becomes apparent why Salvador was once called "Thousand Palms Canyon." Although that was an exaggeration, many palms beckon the hiker to continue farther and farther up the watercourse. However, the narrow, brush-choked canyon floor, the tangle of palm fronds, the thorny mesquite, the long, reedy grasses, and the continual stream crossings combine to make passage difficult.

2.5   Canyon fork, elevation 2200. The main Salvador canyon is the northwest (right) fork. The smaller canyon straight ahead parallels the main canyon for about 1½ miles, separated from it by a long, rocky ridge. About 0.8 mile up this smaller canyon from this fork, a gully joins from the south (left). It may be possible to ascend this gully to the ridgeline, elevation 4250, just west of Collins survey station, and descend the south side into the bowl of "Panoquk" in Sheep Canyon described above.

3.2   Canyon fork, elevation 2750. Main Salvador is the southwest (left) fork.

4.4   Canyon turns decisively south and continues another mile to its headwaters.

5.0   At the top of a steep ascent, the canyon opens out somewhat. From here, go up a gully, elevation 4025, joining from the west (right) and leading toward a small peak. This will lead in 0.3 mile onto Sage Flat. Actually, any climb west (right) out of the upper reaches of Salvador will lead to Sage Flat. The low saddle at the south end of the flat, on the divide between Sheep, Alder and Salvador canyons, is described on p. 102. From here the hiker has several choices: descend the northwest tributary into the south fork of Alder Canyon, take the old Indian trail north over the ridge north of Sage Flat, descend south from the saddle into Sheep Canyon, or return via Salvador. These routes are described above.

Natural Features

The Coyote Canyon system is within the Peninsular Ranges geomorphic province of Southern California. It has been subjected to uplifting and faulting along the northwest-southeast trending San Jacinto fault zone, one of the major branches of the San Andreas fault system. The canyon's creek bed, which is on the fault line, separates two major mountain systems, the San Ysidro in the south and the Santa Rosa in the north. Because the fault zone is easily erodable fractured rock, the stream runs southeast along it after reaching the northeast sides of Collins and Fig Tree valleys. Coyote Mountain, at the mouth of Coyote Canyon, is a spur of the Santa Rosa Mountain system that has moved from the main Santa Rosa Mountain mass through fault action.

Today the land surrounding Coyote Canyon is protected through its designation as either state natural preserve or wilderness area. Legal protection extends to all features, such as rare or endangered plant and animal species and their supporting ecosystems, that are representative of plant or animal communities existing in California before the impact of civilization, and all geological and topographic features that are illustrative of representative or unique biogeographical patterns. Consequently, all vehicle entry into these protected areas is prohibited.

A trip up Coyote Canyon, from Borrego Valley at 600 feet elevation to the small settlement of Anza at 3900 feet, provides an excellent opportunity to view the gradual transistion from low-to-medium desert habitat to chaparral community.

Ocotillo, cholla, creosote, and burroweed dot the flatlands around the mouth of Coyote Canyon while beavertail, scattered fishhook, and cholla cacti are found on the rocky walls. Animals in this lower area include horned lizards, iguanas, chuckwallas, kangaroo rats, sidewinders, ringtails, coyotes and rabbits.

Beginning at Ocotillo Flat, and especially in the Collins Valley area, are fine groves of agave. Collins Valley's varied plant growth also includes large creosote, cheesebush, rabbitbrush and chuparosa bushes, palo verde trees, mistletoe, and various annual flowers. Here also are found the most fragrant flowers in the Park, including spectacle pod, mistletoe, and the purple climbing milkweed, which grows commonly on rabbitbrush. The rabbitbrush, which is very common in the valley, is also known as black-banded rabbitbrush because of a parasite that attacks the plant. The parasites may be detected by the presence of small half-inch-wide black bands around the stems of the plant.

The area around Lower Willows is the best birding spot in the park, while Middle Willows provides the best opportunity of sighting a bighorn sheep. A fairly recent sheep kill by a mountain lion in Salvador Canyon evidences the continued presence of these big cats, so prominent in early California folklore.

Beginning above Middle Willows, and especially in Yucca Valley, are healthy stands of Mojave yucca, which require both the higher elevation and the more northern latitude. This yellow-leafed yucca has its white flower cluster on a short stem. The leaves are 2 feet or more in length, and the plant itself usually attains a height of 6 feet.

Juniper trees become more apparent above Middle Willows and palm-filled canyons in Collins Valley give way to cottonwood, oak and alder groves in upstream canyons. In Alder Canyon and above Upper Willows, chamise, white sage, mangalar sumac, and scrub oak are observed, indicating the beginning of the chaparral community. Both deer and wild horses are found in the upper reaches of Coyote Canyon, and manzanita and various oak trees are common near the community of Anza.

Cultural Features

Coyote Canyon gets its name from the people who once lived within its canyon walls. They were Southern Mountain Cahuillas, a grouping of the Shoshonean linguistic family. They called themselves *wiwaiistam* (*wiwaii*—people, and *stam*—coyote), or the coyote people. Hence they were known as Los Coyotes Indians.

Their semipermanent villages were located where there was a permanent water supply, such as at Santa Catarina Spring and in Fig Tree Valley.

The earliest descriptions of these Indians were made by the diarists of the Anza expeditions. Father Pedro Font, a member of the second expedition, took a dim view of the canyon's Cahuilla Indians, describing them in the Winter of 1775–76 as "among the most unhappy people of the world." The men wore no clothing while the women wore "tattered capes" made from agave fibers. Their food was described as "tasteless" roots, grass seeds and scrubby agave, which Font considered scarce, "so their dinner is a fast." The men carried bows and a "few bad arrows." Font estimated that the Indian village at Santa Catarina had a population of about 40 Indians.

Font described the canyon itself as being "formed by various high and very rocky hills, or better, by great mountains of rocks, boulders, and smaller stones which look as it they had been brought and piled up there, like the sweepings of the world."

Anza and his party were not the first white men to penetrate Coyote Canyon, however. Pedro Fages, a Spaniard, pursued deserters from the presidio at San Diego to Borrego Valley and up through Coyote Canyon in 1772. His horse and mule tracks were discovered by Anza's first expedition two years later at Santa Catarina Spring.

Spaniards after Anza and later Mexicans used Coyote Canyon as the passage from the desert to the inland valleys of Southern California until the discovery of a better route farther south, later known as the Southern Emigrant Trail.

Despite the relatively low traffic in the canyon in the years after Anza's expeditions, the Los Coyotes Indian population began to decline seriously due to contact with whites' diseases, diet changes, and social and genetic factors. The *asistencia* (outpost) of the San Diego Mission at Santa Ysabel, just west of the park and desert, was probably an important factor in this population decline.

The Indians of Coyote Canyon remained basically peaceful until the advent of American control and taxes. In 1851, local Indians combined forces to fight the injustice of the tax, resulting in the "Garra Revolt." In this brief uprising, Indians attacked and killed some whites at Warner's Ranch as part of a plan to eventually destroy Los Angeles. Los Coyotes Indians participated in the Warner's Ranch massacre.

San Diego military headquarters sent two punitive expeditions to quell the rebellion. One expedition went to Warner's Ranch and burned the Indian village there. On December 21, 1851, the other expedition headed toward Coyote Canyon and the main Cahuilla village located in Collins Valley. After a brief skirmish in which two chiefs were killed, the Indians fled up the canyons into the mountains. The village was ransacked and burned, and prisoners were taken. In a later battle, more Indians were killed and four subchiefs were captured near Agua Caliente. On Christmas Day, as some 80 Indians watched, the rebel chiefs were executed while kneeling beside their graves.

A final blow came to the Los Coyotes village in the mid-1870s in the form of an epidemic of smallpox. The surviving Indians moved to the San Ignacio area at the head of Borrego Palm Canyon and thereafter used Coyote Canyon only as a gathering place. After 1891 the few remaining Los Coyotes Indians were confined to Los Coyotes Reservation along with other local tribes. A flash flood in Coyote Canyon in 1916 washed away the last surface remains of the old village sites.

With the Indians driven from their ancestral homes, it became easy for white cattlemen to begin using Coyote Canyon for winter grazing and for settlers to take up choice land sites there. One of the first to homestead the area around Santa Catarina Spring was Joel Reed, in the 1880s. Another was John Collins, for whom Collins Valley was named. A fight later ensued between these two men when Collins settled on land claimed by Reed. Collins attempted to grow fruits and vegetables for five years, until he and his family were driven from the property by Reed and his cattlemen friends. Reed later sold his property and moved back east. Other cattlemen used the canyon continuously from the 1880s until the 1960s, when all grazing leases in the park were terminated.

Except for development of the old De Anza Ranch at the horse camp, and the use of the Coyote Canyon creek bed as recreational thoroughfare, impact on the canyon has been light through the years, even though the threat of greater development has always seemed imminent. Borrego Valley developers have long looked to Coyote Canyon as possible route of travel to the desert resort. A long battle for a paved road through the canyon began as early as the 1940s and ended in the 1970s when conservationists scored a victory in saving this scenic, historic canyon by having it deleted from county road plans and having surrounding lands designated as state wilderness area.

AREA 3: The Borrego-Salton Seaway Corridor and the Southern Santa Rosa Mountains

(Highway S-22)

Overview and Access

The sere Santa Rosa Mountains are the loftiest and loneliest area in the entire Anza-Borrego region. From the 8700-foot summit at Toro Peak, the Santa Rosa massif runs 30 miles southeast, splitting desert from desert, until even this great range is swallowed up in its own outwash of sand flats and mud hills 200 feet below sea level in the west side of the Salton Sea basin.

The special charm and lonely allure of this area lie in the interface between mountain backbone and desert floor where precipitous canyons, hidden springs, palm oases and Indian traces are found. This is the home of the elusive desert bighorn sheep, numbering some 400 in the Santa Rosa herd.

There is little evidence of modern man in the Santa Rosas save for the Borrego-Salton Seaway, which slices across their southern flank, and its associated jeep routes, which meander along the desert floor. The presence of long-departed ones can still be sensed in burial grounds of prehistoric man, traces of ancient Indian trails and cairns of early prospectors.

Standing in the stark contrast to the Santa Rosa Mountains and its canyons are the popular, denuded, highly eroded badlands to the south and east. "Moonscape" and "fantasyland" are adjectives often used to describe this undulating landscape, which changes constantly through shadow play, lighting and actual erosion. Surrounding mineralized walls seethe with color while clay pillars seem to melt in movement. Tortuous mud washes, peculiar geological formations, thermal wells and mountains of sand combine to form a "desert meadow" of God's land made from ancient prairie lands and sea bottoms which teemed with life eons ago.

Highway S-22 from Borrego Valley east to Salton City and Highway 86 from Salton City to the Riverside/Imperial county line along the Salton Sea offer paved access to this area, and all described dirt roads, trails and hiking routes depart from them.

Trip 3: Borrego-Salton Seaway (Highway S-22) "Erosion Road"

From: Pegleg Smith Monument

To: Highway 86 junction in Salton City (21.3 miles one way; all paved road)

Via: Clark Lake/Rockhouse Canyon turnoff, Font's Point Wash turnoff, Palo Verde Wash turnoff, Borrego Badlands View, Arroyo Salado Primitive Camp turnoff, Salton View, Calcite Canyon Scenic Area turnoff, Microwave Tower and Clay Point

With Side Trips To: Palo Verde Wash, Vista del Malpais and Fault Wash via Short Wash; Rattlesnake Canyon; Villager Peak and Rabbit Peak; down Palo Verde Wash; and up Palo Verde Wash

CAUTION: All road conditions in the badlands are subject to seasonal changes. Roads can be very sandy. Check with the Visitor Center for latest road conditions.

Mileage From:

Pegleg Monument	Salton City	Checkpoint Description
0.0 [M 26]	21.3	The Pegleg Smith Monument is located at the base of the southeast tip of Coyote Mountain and at the west terminus of the Borrego-Salton Seaway, 7.0 miles east and north of Christmas Circle in Borrego Springs. The rock mound commemorates one of the greatest desert yarn-spinners that ever lived. His tales of lost gold evolved into one of the best-known legends of the Southwest. A sign at the monument reads, "Let him who seeks Pegleg Smith's gold add 10 rocks to this monument." This is the site of the annual Pegleg Smith Liar's Contest, held the first Saturday night in April.
		Coyote Mountain, a spur of the Santa Rosa Mountains that was offset through slippage along a fault, was once known as Butler Mountain, named in the 1880s for a German who claimed there was a very rich placer-gold deposit on the mountain. Like Pegleg's gold, Butler's gold mine is also lost.
		There is a steep trail up Coyote Mountain that begins near the Pegleg Smith Monument, climbs side hills and ridges, and descends into long valleys, generally following a course along the precipitous earthquake-faulted southwest face of the mountain. Vegetation is scarce—a few ocotillos, some encelia and cresote. The rocky surface of the mountain is deeply impregnated with dark red desert varnish. This trail offers an excellent view of the valley below.
0.5 [M 28]	20.8	Paved-road turnoff to the northeast (left) goes into Clark Lake and Rockhouse Canyon (see Trip 3A).
2.4	18.9	The dirt track straight ahead where the paved road angles slightly right is the old Truckhaven Trail, built in 1929 by pioneer Borrego homesteader A. A. "Doc" Beaty, using mule-drawn Fresno scrapers. The Truckhaven Trail was used by Borrego residents as a major route to the Coachella Valley until 1968, when the paved Borrego-Salton Seaway was completed. The trail was named for the Truckhaven Cafe, which was near the trail's east end at Highway 86. This segment of the Truckhaven Trail may be followed by jeep for about 5 miles, paralleling the paved road until it rejoins at the Thimble Trail turnoff.
2.8	18.5	Turnoff southeast (right) leads up Inspiration Point Wash about 3 miles to a ridge. This is the jagged west edge of the Borrego

Borrego Badlands from Fonts Point—two views

Pegleg Monument	Salton City	Checkpoint Description
		Badlands, some 1200 feet above sea level. Although not quite as high as Font's Point, the Inspiration Point area provides some excellent views of these rugged, eroded badlands.
[M 29]		A through-trip west from here to the county dump is described at the end of Trip 1C. From S-22 to the dump is about 7 miles, small OHVs only may negotiate it.
3.6	17.7	Turnoff south (right) proceeds up Font's Point Wash (signed) 4.5 miles to a spectacular overlook which isn't revealed until the visitor reaches the very edge of the rim, the high point of the badlands at elevation 1294. In recent years Font's Point Wash has been very sandy. Check at the Visitor Center for latest road condition. Font's

Pegleg Monument	Salton City	Checkpoint Description

Point, named for Father Pedro Font of the second Anza expedition, is about 800 feet above the Borrego Sink, the low point of Borrego Valley. At one time Font's Point was part of the valley bottom, but its flood plain and fresh-water lake sediments were later raised and pushed aside by the faulting along Coyote Creek Fault to their present elevation. The point offers the most scenic vista of the badlands area and is an excellent place to get an overview of Anza's Trail, which follows the San Jacinto Fault, a major branch of the San Andreas fault system. From southeast to northwest, the Anza Trail proceeds from Ocotillo Wells around the north side of Borrego Mountain, across the northeast part of Borrego Valley, along the southwest edge of Coyote Mountain and through the Coyote Canyon.

An old Indian trail ran from Font's Point north to Rattlesnake Canyon.

Side Trip Via Short Wash to Palo Verde Wash, Including Vista Del Malpais and Fault Wash (jeep route):

0.0   Font's Point turnoff, 3.6 miles east of Pegleg Smith Monument on S-22. Proceed south down a good dirt road.

2.3   Junction with Short Wash route. Turn east (left).

3.3   Junction with Thimble Trail from north (left). 2.2 miles up is Highway S-22. Route continues straight ahead, crossing a low saddle into Short Wash, a very sandy and winding route.

4.7   Vista del Malpais turnoff (signed) to south (right). Just 1.1 miles up this wash is an excellent view of the chromatic badlands. Although the viewpoint is not as high as Font's Point, the scope of its view of the badlands is much greater.

5.6   Junction to south (right) follows Fault Wash 4.4 miles to the Cut-Across Trail junction and then goes another 5 miles to Highway 78 at Ocotillo Wells. Our route continues east (straight ahead).

6.2   Palo Verde Wash. Up-wash 2.6 miles north (left) is S-22. Down-wash 3.6 miles south (right) is the Cut-Across Trail.

End of Side Trip

4.3 [M 30] 17.0   The turnout on the south side of the road is a view of Clark Dry Lake. The surface of this lake is a hard, dry clay. The rust-colored slopes of rock and gravel debris at the bases of the surrounding mountains are alluvial fans. This is Santa Rosa Overlook.

5.6 [M 31] 15.7   Turnoff south (signed) is the Thimble Trail, on which it is 2.2 miles to the Short Wash route. Sandy areas along S-22 here produce fine displays of annual wildflowers, especially sand verbena and evening primrose, after winters of sufficient rainfall.

Rattlesnake Canyon and Villager Peak/Rabbit Peak foot routes depart north from here.

Side Trip Up Rattlesnake Canyon (day hike or overnight climb):

Rattlesnake Canyon offers a fascinating day hike into its depths or a challenging overnight climb to Rattlesnake Spring. Climbers should be experienced, have a topographic map, carry a belay line and be well conditioned. Given this warning, the venture to this spring is one of the most rewarding trips in the southern Santa Rosas.

Pegleg Monument	Salton City	Checkpoint Description
		0.0 Parking turnout 5.6 miles east of Pegleg Smith Monument of S-22. Elevation 970. Commence hiking on rough surface, broken with gullies, northeastward toward the base of the ridge west of Rattlesnake Canyon.
		0.4 Lute Fault Scarp is marked by the steep ridge and the narrow gully to the west (left). One geologist has called this the largest fault scarp in the North American continent existing in unconsolidated material.
		1.4 Base of ridge. The route to Villager and Rabbit peaks climbs left up the mountain. Palo verde trees dot the route up the canyon. Proceed into the canyon.
		2.7 The arroyo joining from the northeast (right) at the 1700-foot level is the best access to the spring. (Signs of former Indians have been found west, or left, of this point about ⅛ mile up on the hill in a small flat.) Day hikers may continue north from here up the main canyon another mile to a fork at elevation 2240. Going straight ahead will take you rapidly up onto Villager Ridge. Then a sharp east (right) turn leads quickly to a large, dry waterfall and the end of the day hike. Experienced climbers may elect to negotiate this fall another half mile to a fork at elevation 2500. The main Rattlesnake Canyon leads north (left). The steep, narrow arroyo to the northeast (right) leads ¼ mile over dry falls, with great exposure, to the spring. This is the second and more difficult route than that from mile 2.7 described below.
		2.7 (Same point as noted above) Experienced climbers should rope up and ascend the ridgeline known as "The Wall" north

"Gettysburg Wash"—looking southeast from S-22 in Imperial County

Pegleg Monument	Salton City	Checkpoint Description
		(beyond) the arroyo and its difficult dry falls. Loose rock, cactus and exposure are hazards on this ascent. Re-enter the wash above the falls.
	3.2	Take the first obvious northwest (left) gully at elevation 2400. A large white boulder and white, inclined strata mark the point. Proceed north up the gully, bearing generally left and over a saddle at elevation 2970.
	3.7	Rattlesnake Spring is located in a brushy amphitheater, backdropped by white cliffs on the eastern ridgeline. Reliable water may be found in the draw below a solitary tree.

End of Side Trip

Side Trip Up Sierra Ridge to Villager Peak and Rabbit Peak (one or two night backpack)

0.0   Parking turnout 5.6 miles east of Pegleg Smith Monument. Elevation 970. Same route as described above to Rattlesnake Canyon.

3.4   This small plateau, elevation 3800, on the ridge is a good base camp. Time from here to Rabbit Peak and back to cars is about 15 hours. Route lies generally west of ridgeline past . . .

6.6   Villager Peak, elevation 5756. The route beyond is generally east of the ridgeline. Pinyon pine and juniper predominate.

10.2 Rabbit Peak, elevation 6666. (An ascent up the east ridge from the Coachella Valley is described in John Robinson's *San Bernardino Mountain Trails*.)

End of Side Trip

7.3 [M 33] 14.0   Turnoff south (signed) is Palo Verde Wash, named for the fine growth of palo verde (literally "green stick" in Spanish) trees found in this wash. The trees are leafless throughout much of the year, but put on a show of color in June or July when the bright yellow blossoms of this member of the pea family are produced.

Side Trip Down Palo Verde Wash (jeep route):

0.0   Junction of Palo Verde and S-22 at mile 7.3. Elevation 880. Turn southeast (right).

2.6   Short Wash joins from west (right). It is reported in a ranger patrolman's notes that somewhere in the badlands all the equipment for 60 men was buried by a flash flood during a government survey.

2.8   Ella Wash joins from the northeast (left).

6.4   Cut-Across Trail (four-way junction). Just 3.8 miles west and south along the Cut-Across is a junction with the San Felipe Wash route. About 4 miles east and north is the junction of the Cut-Across and the Tule Wash route near Una Palma. The side trip down Palo Verde Wash continues south (straight ahead) through the Ocotillo Wells State Vehicular Recreation Area. Off-road travel is unlimited in this designated area.

10.2 Palo Verde joins San Felipe Wash west of Squaw Peak. Two miles south is paved Highway 78 at Ocotillo Wells.

End of Side Trip

Pegleg Monument	Salton City	Checkpoint Description

Side Trip Up Palo Verde Wash (foot trail):

0.0   Junction of Palo Verde Wash and S-22 at mile 7.3. Elevation 880. Vehicles prohibited up this wash and canyon. The trail up Palo Verde Wash and canyon heads northwest (left) from the pavement, passing through some low, gray-colored hills.

0.5   The concentration of palo-verde trees is heavy here, mixed with a few smoke trees. Ocotillo grows on the edges of the wash.

1.9   Old mining campsite. A trail leads from this campsite east over a small ridge to an old molybdenum mine. One report states that this was "Molly's Mine," not a molybdenum mine. This "Moly" Mine Trail can be followed to the three Natural Rock Tanks in Smoke Tree Canyon (about a 1½ mile hike from Palo Verde Wash).

2.5   Upper Palo Verde Wash now becomes a canyon as we reach the south edge of the Santa Rosa Mountains. The trail starts up a narrow, twisting canyon, which opens up into a small valley.

3.8   The canyon leads to a steep, rock-strewn bowl, above which is Palo Verde Spring, dry in recent years (elevation 2400).

     An overnight backpack traverse to Travertine Palms is possible from Palo Verde Wash (see Trip 3E).

End of Side Trip

Jack Calvert, first full-time Supervisor of Anza-Borrego, in his "recommendation" for desert uniforms

Result of 1968 earthquake (near Clark Lake)

Pegleg Monument	Salton City	Checkpoint Description
7.6 [M 34]	13.7	Eastern forks of Palo Verde Wash north of S-22. Vehicles prohibited. The left fork is more interesting, with large smoke trees and very high, exotically eroded mud and sandstone cliffs.
9.0	12.3	The turnout to the right is a view of the Borrego Badlands, where several million years ago mammoths and primitive horses roamed along the shore of an ancient lake. The mud deposits from this lake have since been lifted up by earth movements, creating a gradient along which water from cloudbursts have carved deep, V-shaped washes. This erosion has exposed the multihued layers of these ancient mud deposits, whose appearances is ever-changing.
9.1	12.2	Smoke Tree Canyon Wash to the left. Vehicles prohibited; hiking only. Smoke trees are well represented in this wash. Like the palo-verde tree, this tree grows only in areas that are periodically visited by flash floods. The hard outer coatings of the seeds of these plants must be scratched by the action of water and sand before they will germinate. A 3-mile hike leads to the Natural Rock Tanks.
9.2	12.1	Ella Wash turnoff to the right (jeeps only). Ella Wash was named for Ella Calvert, the wife of the first Anza-Borrego Desert State Park supervisor. This wash has some interesting sandstone formations. The area around the formations is creased with deep arroyos and is suitable only for foot travel. The formations are weird and pock-marked, with many small caves. Small, marblelike concretions are numerous.
		Coachwhip Canyon to the left (jeep route). The canyon forks after ½ mile, the left fork going to the "Swiss Cheese Rocks," yellowish-red sandstone formations, pocked with holes and shaped in varied patterns. The right fork passes east of these rocks and ends 1¼ miles from S-22.
9.3 [M 35] [M 36]	12.0	Road to the southeast (right) is Arroyo Salado (signed). It is ¼ mile to the Arroyo Salado Primitive Campground. Down-wash this trail is also the old Truckhaven Trail. The route down Arroyo Salado to 17 Palms may be suitable for light autos (see Trip 3B). A one-mile hike north up Arroyo Salado leads to the fascinating Truckhaven Rocks.
10.4 [M 37]	10.9	The turnout north (left) overlooks wind caves and convoluted layers of sandstone. This is Calcite Canyon Scenic Area Overlook. The rock that forms the Santa Rosa Mountains was once a molten mass beneath the crust of the earth. It cooled, solidified and was then thrust up to its present height. A branch of the San Jacinto Fault runs along the base of the mountains. Additional evidence of earth movements can be readily noted in the low sandstone formations producing the tortured landscape along the base of the mountains. The layers have been raised, tilted and folded, and are now being eroded by wind and water. A short walk toward the mountains from this stop leads to an overlook of the north fork of Arroyo Salado Wash. This deep canyon dramatically illustrates the cutting power of flash floods. The road crosses 6 bridges in the next 2 miles.
11.4 [M 38]	9.9	Cannonball Wash bridge. A slope at the lower end of this wash is littered with hundreds of cannonball-sized sandstone concretions.
12.4	8.9	The Salton View turnout to the left overlooks the huge Salton Sea, formed in 1905–07 after poorly built irrigation headgates on the

Pegleg Monument	Salton City	Checkpoint Description
		flooding Colorado River near Yuma burst. Almost the entire flow of that mighty river was diverted into the below-sea-level Salton Basin, inundating farms, communities and the main line of the Southern Pacific Railroad. The break was sealed finally when boulder-laden boxcars were successively pushed into the torrent on a trembling trestle extending into the breach. The Salton Sea is contained in a basin which was earlier occupied by a salt-water arm of the Gulf of California and then by a great freshwater lake, Lake Cahuilla. A very short stroll toward the mountains affords one a view of Palm Wash. This is one of the main washes that drain the Santa Rosa Mountains to the Salton Basin. The microwave relay tower, located on the east boundary of Anza-Borrego Desert State Park and the San Diego/Imperial county line, is virtually the only man-made object to mar the otherwise unspoiled view of thousands of acres of desert wilderness.
12.6	8.7	Jeep roads depart on both sides (signed). The route southwest is the Truckhaven Trail, which can be followed 2.7 miles into Arroyo Salado. The route north leads 1.9 miles to Calcite Canyon Scenic Area and Palm Wash (see Trip 3C).
13.3	8.0	Microwave Tower, Park boundary and county line. The highway now proceeds east on the old Truckhaven Trail.
17.2	4.1	The route of the old Truckhaven Trail is straight ahead along the ridgeline toward Salton City. Only 0.1 mile east is a rutted road dropping off to the north (left). This leads to Four Palms Spring, a good campsite. The highway drops south off the bench onto the flatlands. Coves west of here provide excellent, windsheltered campsites.
18.2	3.1	The dirt road to the south (right) leads about 1 mile to Oh My God Hot Springs (actually a thermal well), surrounded by tamarisk trees. This is a popular area that has been built up through the years by desert visitors. Although it is located on private land, it has been open to the public. Visitors have built a series of connecting shallow pools each with a different degree of warmth.
19.9	1.4	Clay Point is north (left) of the road. This is the pointed lower end of the outwash slope from the Santa Rosa Mountains.
21.3	0.0	Junction with Highway 86 in Salton City. Motels, restaurant, gas stations, stores. A loop trip back to Borrego Valley may be made by following Highway 86 south 12.6 miles to Highway 78, and then going west 29 miles to Borrego Springs. Or one may proceed north 12 miles to Travertine Rock, visiting some of the Salton Sea marinas and sea-front resorts en route (see Trip 3D).

Trip 3A: Clark Valley and Rockhouse Canyon

From: Highway S-22 near Pegleg Smith Monument

To: Rockhouse Valley and Old Santa Rosa Indian Village

Via: Clark Dry Lake (dirt road), Rockhouse Wash (jeep route, then foot trail), Hidden Spring and Rockhouse Valley

Mileage From:

S-22	Checkpoint Description
0.0	The paved-road turnoff to the north around Coyote Mountain spur into Clark Valley is ½ mile east of Pegleg Smith Monument on S-22.
1.6	Pavement ends. Bear left from junction along west side of Clark Dry Lake. Prior permission is required to take the road to the right which goes about 1½ miles to the University of Maryland's Clark Lake Radio Observatory. (This is a $1 million scientific station that has one of the largest radio antennas on earth. The facility detects radio noises and energy emitted from more than 400 galaxies, some as far as 2 billion light years away. At least a dozen of the galaxies were undiscovered before the completion of the observatory in 1961.)

This observatory road also leads to Clark Well, approximately 3 miles from the junction. This well, the first permanent well in the Borrego area, was dug in 1906 by Fred and Frank Clark, pioneer cattlemen of the area. Reportedly they began digging at 10 a.m. and by late evening were watering their horses with water found 15 feet down.

Directly across from Clark Lake, about 2 miles east, is Little Clark Lake. The cover around the lake is predominately salt bush, mesquite and galleta grass.

Avoid driving over Clark Lake in wet weather, when it turns into a quaking mass of mud.

The road running along the west side of Clark Dry Lake, along the edge of the Coyote Mountain fan, was built by the Army during the early 1940s when it used the area for desert maneuvers. Clark Lake and Clark Valley once supported

Clark Dry Lake and Santa Rosa Mountains

S-22	Checkpoint Description

a number of homesteaders. The remnants of cabins can be found on the north and south sides of the lake and in the sandy, creosote-covered valley west of the playa. Straggling rows of tamarisk, brown and stunted from lack of water, old fences and wells, broken glass and rusted automobiles, tin cans and weathered boards can be seen. One might say that Clark Valley has had four stages: Indian, homesteader, military, and now scientific and recreational.

5.7   Survey station Noll. On the hillside to the left is a seismographic sensing instrument that faces Toro Peak and relays information via a station on the peak. On the right is the classic desert scene of alluvial fans leading down from steep canyons to a dry lake bed. One can also trace the line of a branch of the San Jacinto Fault along the Santa Rosas. The Cahuilla Indians had a winter camp in the low but sheltering sand dunes on the north side of the dry lake. Near survey station Corp, Indian petroglyphs may be found at the base of a red-varnished-granite wash spur.

7.9   Beginning here are the best areas for pencil cholla.

8.7   Alcoholic Pass Trail coming down from Coyote Mountain joins Rockhouse Canyon on the left. This old Indian foot trail is a short cut to Coyote Canyon from Clark Valley. The Clark Valley side slopes gently up the fan of Coyote Mountain; the trail is very sandy. A trail threads through these rocks into the pass, a small, rolling flat between two prominent rock peaks. At the crest, the ground drops away suddenly at the San Jacinto fault line to the wide bottom of Coyote Creek, and the trail emerges near Desert Gardens (see Trip 2).

9.6   Junction with Butler Canyon to the left (signed). Our route turns sharply right up onto the stream bank, and continues northwest up Rockhouse Canyon Wash. Jeeps can proceed up Butler Canyon for about 0.7 mile, and hikers can then continue northwest to Jackass Flat.

10.2   This is a very rugged, boulder-strewn canyon for 2 miles beginning here, reminiscent of Middle Willows in Coyote Canyon. These large boulders and the walls of exposed sediment in the wash attest to the force of flash floods in this canyon.

12.9   A sign says no vehicles are allowed beyond this point. You can hike up-wash to Hidden Spring, Rockhouse ruins and Old Santa Rosa ruins, following an old Indian trail. A large palo-verde tree grows in the wash bottom about ¼ mile south of Hidden Spring.

14.1   Hidden Spring (signed) is at the entrance to Rockhouse Canyon narrows. This spring, always containing some water except during the heat of summer, is on the north bank below the large bench that leads to Jackass Flat. A deeply worn switchbacking trail rises up the steep bank from the spring to the flat, where a large Indian village was once located on the west side above the spring. Mortar holes dot most of the large boulders. The Nicolas Swartz mine is about 4 miles west of here across Jackass Flat. Hikers can climb onto the flat and cross it westward (left) to the 9.6-mile junction mentioned above for an alternate return trip from Hidden Spring. This return mileage is about 6 miles.

The route up Rockhouse Canyon to Rockhouse Valley is about 3½ miles long, winding around the southeast end of Buck Ridge. This is a narrow, winding canyon with near-vertical walls. Vegetation along the route includes ocotillo, creosote, indigo, joint fir, rabbitbrush, desert lavender, bladderpod, encelia, desert willow and buckhorn, barrel and fishhook cactus.

Somewhere in this canyon is supposed to be the remains of an ancient emerald mine that was worked from the earliest times by desert Indians who traded the gems as far south as Mexico and beyond. It is said that Indian spirits watch over the mine and protect it from encroachment. Marshal South, a desert writer who once lived on Ghost Mountain above Blair Valley, reported that he,

Checkpoint Description

Robert Thompson, a mining engineer, and Pablo Martinez, a descendent of one of the old Indians who used to work in the emerald mine, went into Rockhouse Canyon to find the mine site. Martinez did lead them to the site that his great-grandfather had described in repeated stories, but they found that an earthquake of "Indian spirits" had covered the primitive diggings with tons of rock. They did manage to find one small and perfect emerald, South reported, but that was all that was left of the mine.

14.9   Just below the Riverside County line, vertical fault lines and dikes are visible on the granite and gneiss rock walls. A dry waterfall is here. Once a jeep club forced its way through by building a road over the wall to the left and winching up.

16.1   An open valley (Mojave Valley, or Flat of Yucca) with an unnamed fork leading northeast into the Santa Rosas, where the remains of an Indian village can be found.

17.5   Entrance to broad, juniper-covered Rockhouse Valley at the foot of Toro Peak. An old Indian trail above the wash to the right can be followed to the rockhouse ruins. Vegetation in the area includes juniper, Mojave yucca and rabbitbrush. Directly across the valley to the northeast is Nicholias Canyon, with Toro Peak jutting above it. The radio tower on the peak is visible from here. According to old-time cattleman Lester Reed, Nicholias Canyon was named for the last Indian to live in the canyon, Nicholas Gauche. Another souce says the canyon was named for Nicholas Swartz, who prospected in the area. The canyon leads to the Santa Rosa Indian Reservation, from which Toro Peak can be reached. There is water in springs along the canyon where alder trees grow. In a small flat area on the west bank of the canyon are metates in some of the granite rocks. The ruins of Gauche's rockhouse are found on a ridge just east of the canyon near one of the springs. A row of cottonwoods are found in a basin to the north and east of the site of the rockhouse. Another old Indian trail led from Alder Canyon to the Santa Rosa Indian Reservation.

18.1   Three rockhouse ruins are found on a ledge just northeast (right) of the main wash. The walls remaining on the ruins are about 2–3 feet high. Lester Reed reported that one of the houses belonged to the Manuel Torte family. Torte, one of the last chiefs of the Rockhouse Valley Indians, was born at Old Santa Rosa. His son, Calistro, was born in a village at Jackass Flat. Another house belonged to the Andreas family. They obtained their water by digging a shallow hole in the desert surface about ½ mile east of the Torte rockhouse. After much rainfall, native animals will also dig in this area for water. Reed reported that the Tortes and Andreases moved to the Santa Rosa Indian Reservation when too many white men began interfering in the Indian way of life in the valley. Another inhabitant of these rockhouses is mentioned in Jack Welch's Anza-Borrego ranger patrol notes. Welch reported that in 1906 miner Nicholas Swartz built and lived in the third rockhouse in this valley. He was the miner reputed to have taken $18,000 worth of gold nuggets out of his mine before leaving for Chicago, where he later died.

The locale of Old Santa Rosa is on the north side of the valley, in the low point across from the valley entrance where a reddish brown hill is seen. It is about a 2-hour hike from the valley entrance to the Old Santa Rosa ruins, following an Indian trail across the valley through small washes. There are about 5 sites in the ruins. A BLM sign is posted at the largest ruin, which is circular with a diameter of about 17 feet. The sign reads: *Ancient Indian ruins and artifacts in the vicinity of this notice are fragile and irreplaceable. The Antiquities Act of 1906 protects them for the benefit of all Americans. Enjoy But Do Not Destroy Your American Heritage.* A dry seep is found behind the large ruin on the hillside, where slick mortars are also visible.

An old Indian trail from Rockhouse Valley leads toward Martinez Canyon to the east and eventually to Highway 86. Lester Reed reports that this used to be a main trail but "no doubt this trail would be found very rough at the present time, for it is seldom used any more."

J.W. Robinson, in *San Bernardino Mountain Trails,* reports that an old Indian trail proceeded from this Indian village up the mountainside to Alta Seca bench and thence on to Horsethief Canyon. The route is very difficult and dangerous to follow, suitable only for experienced mountaineers, and requires an overnight bivouac and a vehicle pickup arrangement at the selected northern roadhead.

Trip 3B: 17 Palms Section of Borrego Badlands

From: Highway S-22 at Arroyo Salado Campground

To: Highway 86 near Salton City (16.8 miles one way; light auto to 17 Palms, then jeep)

Via: Arroyo Salado, 17 Palms, Five Palms, Tule Wash, Pumpkin Patch, Giant Sand Dune, Tule Spring

With Side Trips To: Truckhaven Trail, Cannonball Wash, North Fork Arroyo Salado (jeep route)

CAUTION: All road conditions in the badlands are subject to seasonal changes. Roads can become very sandy. Check with the Visitor Center for latest road conditions.

Mileage From:

Arr. Sal. Junction	Hiway 86	Checkpoint Description
0.0	16.8	Turnoff to Arroyo Salado Primitive Campground (signed), 9 miles east of Pegleg Smith Monument and 12 miles west of Salton City.
2.2	14.6	Junction from northeast (left) with old Truckhaven Trail (signed). Main route continues southeast (straight) down Arroyo Salado. The side trip mileages from this junction describe some of the easterly track of the old Truckhaven Trail, on which the off-road explorer can relive the early-day challenges of desert travel by Model A's and such.

Side Trip Truckhaven Trail

0.0	Arroyo Salado/Truckhaven junction at "Beaty's Icebox," a former small mud cave at the foot of the grade in which construction crews stowed perishable foodstuffs. It was here that "Doc" Beaty made a permanent camp for himself and the men who constructed the Truckhaven Trail. The cave has since collapsed but the hill still carries the original name. Climb northeast through a narrow wash out of Arroyo Salado and into the north fork of Arroyo Salado. A sharp turn downwash leads to ...
1.2	A junction from which Truckhaven climbs steeply northeast (left) up and over another ridge. Down-wash one may travel about 8 miles to a confluence with the main Arroyo Salado at sea level, just north of which is Oh My God Hot Springs (see p. 115).
1.6	The Truckhaven Trail now traverses Cannonball Wash, so named because of its concretion formations similar to those

A windy day at 17 Palms

Desert post office at 17 Palms

Arr. Sal. Junction	Hiway 86	Checkpoint Description
		at the Pumpkin Patch. Cannonball Wash may be traveled 0.7 mile down-wash to the north fork of Arroyo Salado. The Truckhaven Trail climbs northeast (left) out of Cannonball.
	2.7	The trail joins S-22, 0.7 mile west of a Microwave Tower. **End of Side Trip**
3.6	13.2	Seventeen Palms turnoff (signed) to the west (right). The main route continues down-wash. Two-tenths of a mile west from the turnoff lies this well-known watering place of the Borrego Badlands (elevation 410). The oasis gets its name from the 17 palms that originally stood there. Many are the legends and superstitions surrounding the area, and the tales of lost mines and prospectors. Here a spring, a grove of palm trees, and a visitor's register consisting of a wooden keg full of notes lodged in the palm fronds of two adjoining palm trees welcome the modern-day traveler. This desert post office was begun by early-day travelers and prospectors, who also used to leave a fresh-water supply for those who followed. In extreme emergencies, the saline water of this oasis would be drinkable, although it is highly laxative. Wild animals in this area are extremely dependent on this water, it being the only year-round drinking hole for many miles. Because most animals come at night to drink, no overnight camping is allowed near the oasis. During the year over 100 species of birds stop to rest and refresh themselves here.
3.9	12.9	Junction with Arroyo Salado east-bound route (signed). The main route continues south (right), climbing out of Arroyo Salado toward Five Palms. Arroyo Salado may be followed down-wash east to Lone Palm about 8 miles from this junction, and thence to Highway 86 about 4 miles farther at Bridge no. 58-13.
4.3	12.5	Five Palms Spring. Only two of the palms remain standing, the others having been either vandalized or used for target practice by military aircraft during World War II.
5.2	11.6	Enter Tule Wash and join Cut-Across Trail from the west (right). The Cut-Across Trail may be followed upwash 1.4 miles to Una Palma, which is about ¼ mile north of the wash. Except for some mesquite near this lonely palm tree, the area appears void of any vegetation and closely resembles a moonscape. From Una Palma the Cut-Across Trail trends southwest toward Borrego Mountain (see Trip 1C). It also intersects Palo Verde and Fault washes for a possible loop trip back north to Arroyo Salado Primitive Campground and Highway S-22. The main route continues southeast (left) down Tule Wash.
6.1	10.7	Basin Wash joins from west (right). It can be followed 2.3 miles west (left) to join the Cut-Across Trail.
6.4	10.4	Park boundary sign. Entering Bureau of Land Management (BLM) areas interspersed with private holdings.
7.3	9.5	Pumpkin Patch turnoff to south (right) on west side of a mud outcropping on the south bank. About 0.3 mile along this turnoff is an interesting geologic feature, a field of concretions that covers an area the size of a city block. One theory is that each concretion is a clump of sandstone that was encased underground in a resistant crust of cementing chemicals such as calcium carbonate or hydrous calcium sulfate

Arr. Sal. Junction	Hiway 86	Checkpoint Description
		(gypsum). Water from torrential rainstorms dissolved these chemicals at the surface and carried them down through cracks a few feet into the ground, at which depth the chemicals precipitated out and solidified around the more resistant clumps of sandstone. This process repeated itself countless times over the millenia until the chemicals had built up quite a thick crust—a hardpan—on each clump of sandstone. Erosion eventually stripped off the overlying material, exposing the field of concretions we see today. The shapes of the concretions are highly varied, reflecting the varied texture of the original sandstone before it became encrusted. Although the Pumpkin Patch area has been highly vandalized, you'll still see a few cannonballs, barbells, marbles, plates, breadsticks and long cylinders. Pumpkin Patch is a particularly fragile area that deserves protection. Please do not deviate from the clearly marked route of travel or disturb any of the rare concretion specimens.
13.0	3.8	Former Giant Sand Dune (site). A huge moving sand dune once stood prominently alone here and was visible from miles away at several points. One ranger wrote that it reminded him of "a giant manta ray inching its way across the desert, probing and feeling a tentative course across the gullied plain with its two feeler-like horns."
14.3	2.5	Tule Spring, year-round source of brackish water. A white alkaline moat surrounds the spring. Old-timers call this McCain Spring after Jimmy McCain, an old eccentric who used to travel the desert in two wagons joined together and pulled by six burros. The actual McCain Spring is 2 miles south of here in the San Felipe Hills.
14.4	2.4	South Fork of Tule Wash joins from the southwest (right).
16.8	0.0	Highway 86 near Salton City at Bridge no. 58-14 (stores, gas, restaurant, motels and casinos).

Una Palma near 17 Palms

Co-author Lowell Lindsay in the Pumpkin Patch

Trip 3C: Calcite Canyon Scenic Area and Palm Wash

From: Highway S-22 near Microwave Tower

To: Salton City/Highway 86 (9.4 miles one way; jeep route)

Via: Palm Wash

With Side Trips To: Calcite Mine, Sheep Tanks

Mileage From:

S-22	Hiway 86	Checkpoint Description
0.0	9.4	Calcite Jeep Road (signed) departs Highway S-22 12.4 miles east of Pegleg Smith Monument and 8.9 miles west of Highway 86 just west of Microwave Tower. The road drops steeply down into . . .
0.1	9.3	South Fork of Palm Wash. Up-wash (left) can be driven for about ½ mile, and down-wash (right) can be driven 2.3 miles to join the main Palm Wash and go on to Salton City. Our route climbs steeply up the north bank onto a small mesa and then back down.
0.8	8.6	Junction of Calcite Mine Road (straight ahead) and Palm Wash route east (right).

Side Trip to Calcite Mine

The road to the mine continues along the south lip of the main Palm Wash, winding in and out above a chasm with perpendicular sandstone walls. The road descends gingerly into this wash and then abruptly rises through broken fields of tilted, pockmarked sandstone strata to the mine. All along the road one may see the long, narrow slots where the calcite was mined.

S-22   Hiway 86   Checkpoint Description

At the end of the road, 1.9 miles from S-22, there was once a sturdy little shack perched high on the hills, but it is long gone. The view from the mine is magnificent, and the twisted, gnarled formations all around this mine site would arouse even the most blasé person. Directly northeast behind the mine is Locomotive Rock, a huge length of tilted white sandstone strata, pocked with wind caves, and resembling a modern streamliner forging its way up a steep hill. The mine area has been honeycombed with many large slots cut into the tops and sides of the hills for removal of the calcite pockets.

This mine site provides a splendid view of the east part of the park and of the washes running to the Salton Sea. One can see Seventeen Palms and most of the palms growing in Palm Wash. The hills on which the claim is located are of sandstone, eroded into fantastic shapes. The mine dates from World War II, the calcite having been used for bombsites due to its excellent double-refraction property. Calcite is a carbonate, one of the commonest of minerals, and is found in many kinds of rocks.

Hikers may descend into and up the narrow cleft northeast of the mine, climbing over steep, dry waterfalls. About 1½ miles northeast over the mesa beyond Locomotive Rock are the Sheep Tanks.

End of Side Trip

Route departs Mine Road east (right) into Palm Wash's main fork. An old miner's camp was in the wash. Hikers can proceed up-wash north to the mine area, about 1.8 miles.

Indian trail between Sheep Tanks and Calcite Mine

S-22	Hiway 86	Checkpoint Description
1.9	7.5	The north fork of Palm Wash joins from northwest (left) at the county line and state park boundary (signed).

Side Trip to Sheep Tanks

Proceed northwest (left) up the north fork. This deep, winding, colorful wash has been called the most striking canyon in the Calcite region. About 1.7 miles up-wash are the Sheep Tanks. The limit of vehicle travel will vary with the latest storm conditions. The Sheep Tanks are in a small arroyo entering from the west (left) into a small circular bay in the wash just beyond a fairly deep sandstone cut. About 100 yards beyond the boulder-choked entrance is the first of three tanks, sparkling like a deep green jewel under the 50-foot cliffs. Access to view the other two tanks is by scaling the almost vertical south wall onto a wide sandstone shelf. They lie in the bottom of a deep cleft, precluding immediate access. The capacity of the three tanks is about 20,000 gallons! These are all typical *tenajas,* desert basins that collect and hold rain water, which animals use.

End of Side Trip

Our route continues down Palm Wash.

S-22	Hiway 86	Checkpoint Description
2.7	6.7	The south fork of Palm Wash enters from the southwest (right). 1.6 miles up this wash is Calcite Mine Road. Between this point and Highway 86 are some 29 native palms, standing forlornly in the badlands of the Palm Wash drainage system. They are like sentinels guarding the decimated remains of a once-flourishing race—burned by fire, tattered by wind and rain, and wasted by vandals, yet proud and erect among the bits of petrified wood from their predecessors.
4.8	4.6	One Palm.
5.5	3.9	Two Palms.
6.3	3.1	Survey station Tipy, elevation 137. A burnt palm trunk and some vegetation mark the site of a former spring. About ½ mile south beyond a low ridge is Four Palms Spring, a good campsite in a badlands cove. The spring lies in a small ravine at the base of three palm trees.
9.4	0.0	Highway 86 north of Salton City at Bridge no. 58–46.

Trip 3D: Salton City to Travertine Rock

From: Junction of S-22 and Highway 86

To: Riverside/Imperial county line

Via: Highway 86 (11.7 miles one way, paved road)

With Side Trips To: Wonderstone Wash (jeep route, foot route)

Mileage From:

S-22/86 Junction	County Line	Checkpoint Description
0.0	11.7	Junction in Salton City, of Highway S-22 and Highway 86. Proceed northwest on Highway 86.
1.2	10.5	The old Truckhaven Cafe site on the east side is marked by tamarisk trees around a concrete slab. The old Truckhaven Trail joins 0.1 mile farther north.

S-22/86 Junction	County Line	Checkpoint Description
1.5	10.2	Bridge no. 58–45 across Anza Ditch. A profuse stand of large smoke trees is found in this wide, shallow, sandy but smooth wash. Just 3.8 miles west is Four Palms Spring.
1.9	9.8	Palm Wash at Bridge no. 58–46 is negotiable by jeep 9.4 miles to Microwave Tower on S-22.
2.8	8.9	Coral Wash at Bridge no. 58–47 may be traveled by jeep about 3 miles to its head in the badlands near survey station Dusty (elevation 314).
3.4	8.3	Grave Wash at Bridge no. 58–48 is named for a grave, long since washed away, that was marked by a pile of stones on the side of the wash.
4.2	7.5	Big Wash at Bridge 58–50 is a huge, rough wash which ends in a group of mud hills 7.3 miles from Highway 86. Smoke trees are the predominant growth, together with cheesebush, indigo, ocotillo, tamarisk, galleta grass, catclaw, burroweed and desert aster. Up Big Wash you pass three picturesquely named survey stations—Hot (469 feet), Cool (857 feet) and High (1833 feet)—on the way to its source on the flank of Pyramid Peak.
4.6	7.1	Gravel Wash, with gravel pit on south bank.
5.9	5.8	Unnamed wash, negotiable westward for about 5 miles, to a point where there is a group of many large palo-verde trees. Jeep travel is impossible beyond this point.
7.5	4.2	Paved road east to Salton Sea Beach Marina and Helen's Harbor. To the west is a trail leading toward Wonderstone Wash and Rainbow Rock quarry, visible as orange and red formations on a mountainside.

Side Trip Up Wonderstone Wash

After about 1.5 miles, the trail turns south (left), crosses under a powerline, turns west (right) and enters Wonderstone Wash. Approximately 1.5 miles farther up-wash is the Rainbow Rock quarry on the hillside to the north (right). This may be explored afoot. Early Indians (San Dieguito Indians, circa 9,000 or 10,000 B.C.) used the Wonderstone from this 80-acre quarry site to make stone implements. This is one of the largest and oldest quarry sites in the United States. Do not disturb anything in this area; most of it lies within the Torres Martinez Indian Reservation, and it is a valuable archeological site. Wonderstone is a cream-colored rock interlaced with dark red bands. One ranger has described it as looking like strawberry juice poured into thick cream. It polishes well. One theory about the creation of the Wonderstone deposit states that when Travertine Spur moved eastward to its present position, it ground against the parent Santa Rosa block in passing, and the friction of the two blocks grinding together created the Wonderstone. Growth in the wash is predominately palo verde.

Hikers can proceed up Wonderstone Wash about 7 more miles, crossing the state park boundary some 5 miles from the Helen's Harbor/Highway 86 junction. The route passes through narrow canyon defiles and around dry waterfalls onto a dissected bench on the southeast flank of the Santa Rosas at about the 2400-foot level. This area is described

S-22/86 Junction	County Line	Checkpoint Description
		below in Trip 3E, the Travertine Palms to Palo Verde Canyon backpack traverse. **End of Side Trip**
8.9	2.8	The original route of Highway 86 (then Highway 99), via the defunct Coolidge Springs service station, diverges slightly left to rejoin Highway 86 about 2.3 miles farther north. The ancient shoreline of freshwater Lake Cahuilla is clearly visible along the base of the Santa Rosas to the west, forming a band along the foot of the hills.
11.4	0.3	Travertine Rock. These rocks mark the easternmost point of the Santa Rosa Mountains. The point received its name before scientists had an opportunity to critically examine the deposits there. True travertine is a solid deposit, but the material found here is calcareous tufa—a porous, lightweight variety of travertine. It originally was calcium carbonate in solution, deposited by the lapping waters of the old lake. The parent limestone from which it came is much in evidence in this area. Ancient Indian inscriptions are visible at Travertine Point in the calcareous tufa along the old shoreline, amidst graffiti of contemporary vandals.
11.7	0.0	Riverside/Imperial county line. Just north of the county line a dirt road departs west (left) along a powerline. One mile away is the roadhead to commence hiking toward Travertine Palms, some 2½ miles farther southwest along Travertine Palms Wash toward the third bay extending into the base of the mountains. An alternate hiking route is via the first wash crossed by the dirt road, 0.4 mile from Highway 86. This is Garnet Wash, so named for the garnet fragments that make this sandy wash pink. About one mile southwest up Garnet Wash is the beginning of an old Indian trail that crosses two low saddles to arrive at the palm oasis. The first

Travertine Rock

saddle, or low hill, has marine deposits from the Pliocene epoch (Palm Springs formation), when this region is believed to have been the floor of an ancient sea several million years before Lake Cahuilla or the Salton Sea was formed. It is another 2 miles to Travertine Palms from this saddle. The old Indian trail was probably used by the Cahuillas to secure salt from the dry basin where the Salton Sea was later formed. Travertine Palms was used as a watering spot by these Indians before climbing to the higher elevations of the Santa Rosas. An excellent view of the Salton Sea, about 4 miles away, is obtained from the small cove in which the palms are located. There are about 70 trees in the grove, the tallest being about 30 feet high. Originally this oasis was called Stein's (Steen's) Rest, for John Stein (Steen), who was credited with planting palm seeds around the spring in 1903. Fig Tree John, a Cahuilla Indian recluse who is alleged to have had a gold mine in the area, was said to have obtained water from the spring at Travertine Palms while working his mine. Immediately west of the palms on the far side of the hills is a very high cliff of red clay and gray mudstone. There is a small cave under the cliff and mortar holes in the rocks nearby. It was no doubt an old Indian shelter, for the roof is blackened with the smoke of campfires. Farther south in this same wash is a deep arroyo.

Travertine Palms (Salton Sea in distance). Note the exotic Arabian date palm in foreground, not native to the area.

Trip 3E: Travertine Palms to Palo Verde Canyon (foot route, backpack traverse)

This rugged, waterless, lonely two-day traverse across the southeastern Santa Rosas offers the backpacker a challenging and intimate desert wilderness experience. Other than the Indian trails along the route, there is virtually no evidence of man's presence to mar the awesome stillness and desolate grandeur of this remote desert mountain fastness. These canyons and slopes, lonely but far from lifeless, are the haunt of the desert bighorn sheep and numerous smaller denizens, while typical desert and arid-area vegetation abounds—palo verde and creosote at lower elevations, agave, ocotillo and some juniper in the higher reaches.

This route, only for experienced desert backpackers, requires careful cross-country map-and-compass techniques and an ample supply of water—at least 2 gallons per person. There are two key landmarks: the pinyon-covered peak called Rosa (survey station at 5038 feet) on the topographic map and an unknown peak called Pyramid (3460 feet) in this book (see foldout map). Pyramid Peak is clearly visible from Highway 86 at the Riverside/Imperial county line, looking like a pyramid on the southwest horizon atop the main ridgeline.

Mileage From:

County Line/
Hiway 86

Junction	Checkpoint Description
0.0	Proceed west about 1 mile along a good dirt road. Park and hike southwest along Travertine Palms Wash and across a rocky bajada toward Travertine Palms (described above in Trip 3D). Elevation 40 feet.
3.0	Entrance to Travertine Palms bay. The palms are about ½ mile in. Continue southwest in the wash around the north side of the ridgeline, always toward Pyramid Peak on the horizon.
5.2	Enter a narrow gully where walls squeeze in to shoulder width in some places, blocking out the sky overhead. At about mile 5.5 bypass a wash entering from the west. Continue southwest up-wash. A gully opens up at about mile 5.7.
6.2	Another wash enters from the west at the center of the west boundary of Section 23. Bear south, toward Pyramid, keeping Rosa on the right side.
7.4	Depart Travertine Wash, which turns west up onto Rosa mountain. Proceed southwest up a small arroyo. A small Indian sleeping circle or agave cook ring on the right bank marks the entrance to this arroyo.
7.9	Cross a saddle at the head of the arroyo (elevation 2000) and enter Wonderstone Wash drainage area. Contour southwest (left) across a relatively flat but broken bench, crossing three arroyos and heading for a saddle just northwest of Pyramid. At approximately mile 8.9 atop a small knoll are ruins of a stone structure, 10 feet square, with walls 1–2 feet high and a door opening to the southsouthwest.
10.5	Cross a saddle (elevation 3200) northwest of Pyramid into Smoke Tree Canyon drainage. A lone juniper amid ocotillo and agave marks the saddle. Contour west (right) above arroyos at the head of Smoke Tree Canyon, crossing a divide to the west and descending northwest to . . .
11.7	Palo Verde Canyon. Proceed down-wash to . . .
12.4	The great dry waterfall just above Palo Verde spring (dry), dropping hundreds of feet to the canyon floor. Don't try it. Backtrack several hundred yards up-wash to the most feasible looking gully joining from the west. Ascend this gully to the ridgeline just west of Palo Verde canyon and descend the ridgeline until its slopes become gentler, permitting entry onto the Palo Verde Wash floor. continue down-wash to . . .
15.7	Junction with paved Highway S-22.

Natural Features

The Santa Rosa Mountains and the Borrego Badlands are the main geographic features of this area. The Santa Rosa Mountains, as part of the Peninsular Range province, are usually described as fault-block mountains which have been uplifted on their east side and tilted westward, creating a distinct eastern escarpment. The abrupt descent to the fairly level desert floor east of them can be seen from the Salton Sea facing these mountains. The crest of these mountains angles down gradually southeast from Toro Peak, following the San Jacinto fault line, until it merges into the Borrego Badlands on the south.

All this mountainous area and the canyons leading into it within the boundaries of Anza-Borrego Desert State Park are part of a state wilderness area, and hence all features in it are fully protected and man is only a visitor. This is a rough, rocky, little-visited wilderness where one of the largest herds of desert bighorn sheep still survives. The desert slopes, dotted with ocotillo, cholla, yucca and barrel cactus, give way to juniper and pinyon pine at higher elevations.

The Borrego Badlands, in contrast to the Santa Rosa Mountains, consist of fairly recent stream, lake and plain deposits that were uplifted through fault action and then carved and eroded by running water and wind.

This vast, undulating badlands area is rich in Pliocene and Pleistocene fossils which show that mastodons, camels, sabertooth cats, horses and even a spectacular condorlike vulture with a wing span of 17 feet lived in this area some 1–2 million years ago. The entire area of the badlands was once part of a grassland with wooded areas and streams.

Technically a badlands is an intricately sculptured landscape that is the result of flash-flood erosion in weak rock. Fast-running flood water has carved a labyrinth of V-shaped gorges within these clay hills. In the east part of the badlands, erosion has exposed layer upon layer of mud deposits laid down in an ancient lake several million years ago. Iron deposits within the badlands give the landscape a colorful display of pink, red, yellow and green hues. The pink, red and yellow rocks were oxidized; the green ones were reduced and have sulfur mixed into them.

The badlands washes have a variety of plants and animals, but these become sparse on the east edge of the badlands, where the mud hills are found. Sand absorbs water and consequently can hold more moisture for plants, whereas mud is almost impermeable to water. In general there are both more sand and more water in the west part of the badlands. The water of the area is very alkaline, and plants and animals have had to adapt to this condition and to the limited supply of water along with the extreme summer heat.

Common sandy-wash plants include smoke trees, palo-verde trees, desert willows, creosote, burroweed, brittle bush, indigo bush, galleta, cheesebush, desert lavender, locoweed, desert aster and various annual flowers including verbena, dune and desert primrose, spectacle pod, sand lupine, bladder pod and desert lily.

Animals common to the Borrego Badlands' sandy washes include the kit fox, gray fox, antelope ground squirrel, desert iguana, sidewinder, zebra-tail lizard and coyote. A free park brochure available at the Visitor Center entitled "Seventeen Palms" explains how these animals have adapted to the harsh living conditions of the desert. The antelope ground squirrel, for example, can allow its body temperature to reach 108°F without any ill effect. It is able to conserve on valuable water because it doesn't have to cool its body so much. The zebra-tail, or gridiron, lizard reacts to the heat by arching its black-and-white-barred tail high over its head like a scorpion, to provide increased air exposure, which maintains a cooler body temperature. Some mice and kangaroo rats have also evolved a method of adapting to the heat and to the scarcity of water. They don't drink water, but through a special metabolic process they can produce as much as 0.7 gram of water from one gram of "dry" seeds.

Most of the desert creatures spend the hottest part of the day underground, which saves a substantial amount of water since their tunnels remain much cooler than the outside air.

Cultural Features

According to Cahuilla Indian legend, all the land in the north half of Anza-Borrego Desert State Park and the Santa Rosa Mountain area, and the ancient people who inhabited it and called it home, were created by Mukat.

In the beginning, says the legend, there was only darkness. Then lightning occurred three times. The third time, two forms appeared, which became eggs and hatched, and two fully grown men emerged, Mukat and Tamaioit (or Temaiyauit). Together they made the earth and the sky. Each created his own people, but Tamaioit's people were ugly— they were alike in front and back, and had webbed feet. The two argued about whose people were better, whether or not there should be death, and who was the older of the two. Finally Tamaioit became so angry that he decided to leave and go below ground, taking his creations with him.

Mukat lived with his people until they became disenchanted with him after three incidents. In the first incident the people loved a funny man among them named To, but Mukat gave the rattlesnake fangs and poison and had it bite and kill To. The second incident involved Moon Maid, whom the people loved and who taught them ceremonies, stories and ways of doing things. When Moon Maid discovered that Mukat desired her, she left the people and rose up to the sky. In the final incident Mukat turned some of the people into animals and trees and caused them to speak different languages. He taught the ones who still had a human form to make bows and arrows and told them to shoot one another. He said the arrows would not harm them—but he lied, and many of them died.

After these deceptions, the people no longer wanted Mukat, and they caused him to become ill and die. As Mukat's body burned on his funeral pyre, Coyote stole his heart and ran away with it, later consuming it. A year after Mukat's death, the people held a mourning ceremony for him. The place where they had burned Mukat's body later grew things that the people needed to eat such as beans, melons and corn. Thus, according to Cahuilla legend, all things both bad and good were Mukat's creations.

In time, some of Mukat's people became oriented toward Santa Rosa and what is now known as the Cahuilla Reservation. They became what we call Northern Mountain Cahuillas, and their villages were found in Rockhouse Valley, Horse Canyon and Terwilliger Flats. A Southern Mountain Cahuilla group became

**Jimson weed (Datura).
Used by Mountain Cahuillas
in Toloache ceremony.**

oriented toward Coyote Canyon. A third group, the desert Cahuillas, lived in the area of today's Torres Martinez Indian Reservation, just north and east of Travertine Rock and the Santa Rosa Mountains.

The Cahuillas lived in small family groups, moving from high camps to low camps and back during the yearly gathering cycle. There was frequent communication among all of Mukat's people, and their various Indian trails and campsites are still visible today in the Santa Rosa Mountains area.

As much a part of the area as Indian myths are the lost-gold-mine stories. In fact, the most famous lost-mine legend of the Southwest, next to that of the lost Dutchman mine of Arizona, is that of the lost Pegleg Smith gold mine. The story has as many variations about the dubious activities of Pegleg as there are those who tell it.

There was an authentic Pegleg, whose real name was Thomas Long Smith. He was a mountain man, Indian fighter, horse thief, trader, adventurer and grand prevaricator. He lost his leg as a result of an Indian fight in 1827 and thereafter used a pegleg. It was during a trapping expedition in 1828 that Pegleg crossed the desert in order to sell his furs in Los Angeles. A few black pebbles which were later discovered in Los Angeles to be almost pure gold he claimed to have found on one of three buttes in the Anza-Borrego area. But evidently Pegleg was not interested in gold at that time, because it was not until the 1850s that he began to talk about his gold, in trade for a few brews. He led some expeditions to the alleged site, and spent his remaining years drinking and spinning yarns of his fabulous lost gold mine.

After his death in 1866, the legend of this gold mushroomed. New Peglegs were created, and legends of lost Indian gold were intertwined with the story of Pegleg's gold. Adding fuel to the various stories were the claims of some prospectors of having seen the gold or having come close to it.

The most recent claim of having found the gold, which caused the biggest excitement in recent years, was made in *Desert Magazine* in March 1965 by a man who called himself "the man who found Pegleg's black gold." He wrote to the editor, enclosing a sample of his gold nuggets and stating that he had discovered Pegleg's gold 10 years earlier by accident and had since marketed $314,650 worth of nuggets by removing the black covering and selling them in Alaska and Canada. Over the next several years, this man sent letters to *Desert Magazine* answering questions asked by the readers, each time enclosing a small gold nugget with his letter. All the nuggets, some with the original black coating and others that had been cleaned and polished, were on display at *Desert Magazine's* office in Palm Desert prior to the untimely end of that excellent publication.

Also helping to perpetuate the Pegleg legend is an annual Pegleg Liar's Contest held the first Saturday night of April at the Pegleg Smith Monument. That particular weekend also celebrates the birthday of Harry Oliver, an early homesteader of Borrego Valley and a former Hollywood art director who was the greatest promoter ever of the Pegleg legend. One time he salted old prospector's diggings, coyote holes and desert caves with 200 wooden peglegs, all weathered to look old. According to Oliver, prospectors "seem to figure it's easier to find a mine someone else has lost than to find one no one ever found, so most of them are huntin' for the mysterious lost ones that's been talked about so much."

Oliver was responsible for forming the first Pegleg Smith Club, in 1916, and was later instrumental in beginning the first Lost Pegleg Mine Trek, in 1948. He went out to his old homestead in advance of the date, drew a circle on the ground and left signs which read: "Let him who seeks Pegleg Smith's gold add ten rocks to this monument," and "The bigger the rocks, the better luck you'll have." Thus the Pegleg Smith Monument was born.

The yearly campfire get-togethers, which are a revival of those begun by Oliver, feature an informal liar's contest open to all who have a tale about Pegleg's lost gold. There is also usually a cake to wish Harry Oliver a happy birthday.

Thirteen miles east of the Pegleg Smith Monument and the locale of this annual liar's contest is the calcite-mine area. Here was a mineral that proved to be more than mythical, and mining it proved more successful than early attempts to find gold, uranium and oil in this area.

Famed desert artist John Hilton first heard of the calcite deposit from a prospector who was looking for Pegleg's gold. Hilton took out a claim on the deposit, and then sought a market for it. But it was not until several years later, when World War II began, that a market did open up, whereupon Hilton, and a friend, Ralph Willard, had to re-establish the claim.

Calcite was sought during the war years because of its quality of double refraction, which was a requirement of polarized gunsights. The war closed the doors to foreign suppliers of calcite, and the deposits in the Borrego Badlands became the most important in the Western Hemisphere.

Hilton and Willard extracted the calcite as quickly as they could, but without financial backing and proper equipment they were not able to turn a profit on their mining venture. They eventually sold their claim to a mining company, which was able to construct a road to the area and bring in proper machinery. As the war progressed, so did the mining operation, until the camp looked like a small town. The success of the mining operation was short-lived, however, because laboratory experts soon developed a synthetic crystal that could take the place of optical calcite in gunsights.

Today the calcite area is much the same as when Hilton first saw it, and, like the Indian myths and the gold legends, the calcite-mine story has now become another tale told about this desert area.

AREA 4: Southern Anza-Borrego and the Yuha Desert along the Pioneer Corridor

(Highways S-2 and 98)

Overview and Access

In the 19th century thousands of emigrants crossed the Yuha and southern Anza-Borrego desert along the Pioneer Corridor en route to California and the gold fields. They followed the emigrant trail—the only all-weather overland trail to California and the route selected for the first mail and stage line linking California to the East. And yet, hardly any emigrants realized the variety and richness of the land beyond the hot, dusty road.

The Civil War, combined with the opening of less rugged and/or more direct routes to California, caused the virtual abandonment of the Southern Emigrant Trail as a major thoroughfare. It was left to those in recent times who either were looking for a short cut between El Centro and Los Angeles or wanted to explore virtually an unknown land. Even the state park system remained unaware of what the southern half of the Anza-Borrego region contained until, beginning in the winter of 1952–53, they began regular patrols of this area. And until very recently only 4-wheel-drive vehicles could make the trip down the Pioneer Corridor without mishap.

This, the least trafficked area of the Anza-Borrego, contains much to attract the hiker and road explorer alike. In addition to the historically significant points of interest along the corridor, there are literally scores of palm-filled canyons, piney woodlands rich in gold diggings, winding and twisting mud hills abundant in Pleistocene fossils, volcanic hills that show patterns of lava flow, and mountains capped with ancient coral and oyster reefs. Also, archeological evidence indicates that some 3000 or more years ago, Yuha man made this desert his home.

Beginning from Scissors Crossing at the junction of Highways 78 and S-2, the Pioneer Corridor extends some 60 miles, following the path of the old emigrant trail through Box Canyon, Mason Valley and Vallecito to the turnoff to Palm Spring and the Carrizo Badlands, where the emigrant trail continues on and enters the Carrizo Impact Area, a closed area formerly used as a Navy bombing range. From the emigrant trail turnoff, the Pioneer Corridor continues south over Sweeney Pass to Ocotillo and the BLM lands in the Yuha Desert. All trips within this area originate from the paved S-2 corridor.

NOTE: All animals, vegetation and natural features are fully protected within the boundaries of the state park. No collecting is allowed. Hunting and collecting are generally allowed in adjacent BLM-controlled lands in accordance with pertinent state and federal laws. Collection of desert native plants is generally prohibited. Check with the BLM area office in El Centro for latest information on particular species and the specific areas of interest.

Trip 4: The Imperial Highway (S-2)

From: Scissors Crossing (Junction of S-2 and 78)

To: Ocotillo (Junction of Highways S-2 and I-8, 48 miles one way, all paved road)

Via: Earthquake (Shelter) Valley, Blair Valley, Vallecito, Agua Caliente Hot Springs, Bow Willow area and Carrizo Badlands

With Side Trips To: Moonlight Canyon and Inner Pasture (hike), Indian Gorge (light auto), Bow Willow Canyon (hike), and Carrizo Canyon (hike)

Mileage From:

Scissors Crossing	Ocotillo	Checkpoint Description
0.0 [M 17]	48.0	The trip begins at Scissors Crossing at the roadside monument commemorating the Butterfield Overland Mail. A few hundred yards north is the site of the San Felipe Stage Station, the last stop in desert country for westbound traffic, Warner's Ranch being 17 miles west in the rolling hill country just beyond the San Felipe
[M 19]		Valley. Earthquake Valley and San Felipe Valley join at Scissors Crossing, and their waters flow out through a gap in the mountains to the northeast called Sentenac Canyon.
4.0	44.0	NACO WEST (private membership only RV park, but store is open to the public) in Earthquake Valley. Stewart Hathaway, an early cattle rancher from Julian and a landowner in the valley, reported there was once a large natural lake in the valley, but the effects of an earthquake in 1905 drained it. Today there is only a depression in the south end of the valley. The valley was made available to homesteading around 1900, two of the first homesteaders being Louis and Elsie Bushore, who claimed 640 acres of land at the north end of Earthquake Valley and soon began dry farming. The biggest landowner in the valley today is Jack Napierskie, who first arrived here in 1950 and now owns about 70 per cent of the valley. Many of the residents and real-estate interests do not like the graphic name Earthquake Valley, preferring to call it "Shelter Valley." Granite Mountain to the west stands alone, detached from the Oriflamme Range of which it is a part. It rises abruptly from the floor of Earthquake Valley at elevation 2200 to the peak at 5600 feet and is pierced by scores of old mine shafts and tunnels. Several canyons cut the faces of Granite Mountain, exposing rocks of various colors and creating shadows that highlight the scene.
4.4 [M 22]	43.6	Park boundary and Pinyon Mountain turnoff east (left, signed). The dirt road forks after 0.1 mile. The northeast (left) fork leads some 3 miles into the North Pinyon Mountain area, a little visited but attractive section of the park. The east (right) fork is the beginning of the Pinyon Mountain Road (see Trip 4A).

Scissors Crossing	Ocotillo	Checkpoint Description
5.3	42.7	The dirt road turnoff southeast (left, signed) leads toward Little Blair Valley over the tracks of the old overland stage trail (see Trip 4B). The paved road continues south over Little Pass into . . .
6.0 [M 23]	42.0	Blair Valley. The turnoff southeast (left, signed) leads 0.5 mile to Little Pass Primitive Campground and the Foot and Walker Pass Monument on the old stage route. On this steep pass separating Blair and Earthquake valleys, passengers on the overland stage had to walk and even push the coaches over the rocky ridge. Note the deeply worn and rutted tracks of the coaches, which are well preserved on this portion of the overland trail (for a further description of Blair Valley, Ghost Mountain, Little Blair Valley and the Smuggler Canyon hike, see Trip 4B).
7.1 [M 24] [M 25]	40.9	This is the junction of S-2 and the California Riding and Hiking Trail entering Box Canyon.
8.7	39.3	Box Canyon Monument is on the south (left) side of the road. It was here that Lt. Col. Phillip St. George Cooke and his Mormon Battalion widened the narrow chasm with hand tools in 1847, during the Mexican War, to allow wagons to pass freely, thus creating the first wagon road on the southern route to California. Even after the trail through the canyon was widened for the larger coaches of the Butterfield line in 1858, the hubs of the wheels would often scrape the solid rock walls. Two dim roads are visible from the Box Canyon Overlook on the opposite wall of the canyon. Both roads had to be routed up and around to avoid a 30-foot dry waterfall. The upper road is the older Mormon route.
[M 26] 10.0 [M 27]	38.0	Exit Box Canyon. The dirt road turnoff west (right, signed) is the Oriflamme Canyon route of the San Antonio-San Diego Mail, or

Box Canyon

Scissors Crossing	Ocotillo	Checkpoint Description
		"Jackass Mail," as it was called because the mountain crossing to San Diego was made on mules. The Oriflamme Canyon route is also the short cut from San Diego to the desert first used by Pedro Fages in 1772. As the mail route it was first used by Joseph Swycaffer and Sam Warnock, who in 1854 established a biweekly mail service between San Diego and Yuma. Later in 1857 US Postmaster General Aaron V. Brown awarded an interim contract to James Birch of California to carry the overland mail on the Southern Emigrant Trail between San Antonio, Texas, and San Diego, California, an estimated 1476 miles in 30 days' travel time, on a bimonthly basis with stagecoaches leaving each terminus simultaneously. The regular contract was later awarded to John Butterfield to set up the exact route and stations, except that instead of going to San Diego, the Butterfield route went on to Los Angeles and then to San Francisco. For a description of the Oriflamme route, see Trip 4C. From here the California Riding and Hiking Trail (Desert Section) goes up Oriflamme Canyon into the high mountains along the Sunrise Highway.
		S-2 now proceeds through Mason Valley, named for James E. Mason, who was the first patentee of the old Vallecito station in 1878 or 1879 after its abandonment in 1877. Mason was also the stagecoach driver who took the first westbound overland mails on the initial run of Birch's Jackass Mail. Mason later acquired patent, in 1891, to 160 acres in the valley that now bears his name. Note the white dumps of an old tourmaline mine across Mason Valley on the slope near the base of the Laguna Mountains. The mine has not been worked since 1914.
		A rugged old wagon road from Mason Valley up Salt Creek into the Laguna Mountains brought hay and wild oats for animals and wood for cooking and heat to the Vallecito, Palm Spring and Carrizo stage stations.
12.2 [M 29]	35.8	Butterfield Ranch is a private campground for mobile homes, tents and recreational vehicles, with gas, supplies, cafe, swimming pools and jacuzzi pools. Many residents stay year-round in this beautiful, tree-shaded, well-watered mobile-home community. For reservations write Butterfield Ranch, Star Route, Julian CA 92036.
[M 30] 13.4	34.6	Viewpoint on the Campbell Grade, named for Everett Campbell, who constructed the road in the 1930s with an easier grade than the Butterfield route, which lies 100 yards north over the boulder-studded Vallecito hill. From this grade Vallecito Valley is seen spread out below, with the old stage and wagon ruts along the overland trail clearly visible crossing the plain in the foreground.
[M 34] 17.8 [M 35]	30.2	The Vallecito Stage Station County Park and Campground (piped water, flush toilets, tables) is shaded by large mesquite trees. Group campsites are available. For years the adobe station at Vallecito was the best-known watering spot between Los Angeles and San Antonio. It was the first really restful westbound stop after crossing 100 miles of grim desert between Yuma and Vallecito. The first permanent sod building was erected by the military in 1852 as a subdepot for Army Supplies. A Lt. Murray even had a showerbath constructed. The small building was later incorporated into the larger salt-grass sod structure erected by the Butterfield Overland Mail in 1858. The station stood on a knoll beside the salt-grass

Vallecitos Stage Station

Scissors Crossing	Ocotillo	Checkpoint Description
		swamp from which the house itself was contructed. A barn crammed with hay for the horses stood not far from the house.
		Through the years, the Vallecito station was occupied by one tenant after another. James R. Lassitor was the stationmaster throughout the days of the Butterfield Mail and later until his death in 1863. John Hart next took up residence in the old sod house, staying until his death in 1867. Other residents followed, but it was not until James E. Mason that the lonely valley had a legal owner. Both Hart and Mason were buried in the Vallecito cemetery near the old station. Another owner, C.F. Holland of Los Angeles, later gave San Diego County the land upon which the crumbling ruins of the stage station stood, and in 1934 Dr. and Mrs. Louis Strahlmann of San Diego began the process of restoring the old station to its original condition. Today only one room and its roof are parts of original structure. The original roof was made from hand-hewn beams, pegged and tied in place with rawhide, then covered with willow poles and tules before a final topping of sod. A bronze plaque dedicated to James E. Birch, "the man who put an empire on wheels," is mounted on the south side of the restored station. Note the thick adobe walls, which provided excellent insulation from the heat and cold.
18.8	29.2	Park boundary.
19.2	28.8 [M 36]	Smuggler Canyon joins from the north (left). See Trip 4B for a description of the hiking route in Smuggler Canyon.
19.4	28.6	A small wash on the south (right) side of the road leads up into the Sawtooth Mountains. It offers a good route to hike over to Agua Caliente Hot Springs, about 2.5 miles away. Where the main wash

Scissors Crossing	Ocotillo	Checkpoint Description
		turns abruptly southwest (right) 0.7 mile from the road, take care to bear southeast (left) up a tributary wash and over a small saddle. After descending from the saddle and before reaching Agua Caliente, the hiker will enter a palm-tree oasis.
20.0	28.0	Bisnaga Alta Wash is north (left, signed, hike only). The route goes about 2.5 miles to the base of the Vallecito Mountains, passing through excellent displays of its scientific namesake, the barrel cactus, with cholla, other succulents, ocotillo and chuparosa. Some elephant trees are found at trail's end.
[M 38]		
21.7	26.3	Turnoff south (right, paved) goes to mesquite-shaded Agua Caliente County Park and campground (tent and trailer camping facilities—piped water, flush toilets, hookups, tables, fireplaces and ramadas). For years there have been legends about the curative powers of the 98° mineral waters for those suffering from arthritis and rheumatism. Special features of the campground include indoor jacuzzi pools, mineral baths and an outdoor wading pool. Agua Caliente Springs Store, 0.4 mile from the campground, sells gasoline and supplies. This park is well tended, with a ranger always available. There is a fee for camping. See page 37 for more information.

Hiking Route to Moonlight Canyon and Inner Pasture

The Moonlight Canyon Trail is an easy 1.5 mile loop, with an option to climb to Inner Pasture. The trail departs from the campground at campsite 82, ascends 350 feet south over a saddle, and leads back down into Moonlight Canyon. A left turn at the saddle will take the hiker back to the campground past some water seeps at the canyon base.

A right turn up Moonlight Canyon will take the hiker about 1.5 miles farther, over a low pass, into Inner Pasture. This isolated and picturesque desert valley in the Sawtooth Mountains was a favored cattle-grazing area in earlier days. Although it is traversed by a jeep route from Canebrake Canyon, public vehicle access is prohibited over the private property in Canebrake.

From Inner Pasture the hiker may return via the same route down Moonlight Canyon. An alternate return route is to follow the wash northeast through a narrow, winding canyon to intersect Highway S-2. The distance form Agua Caliente campground via Moonlight Canyon and Inner Pasture through this northeast canyon to S-2 is about 6 miles. It is another 3 miles northwest along the highway back to the campground. Take care not to leave Inner Pasture via the private dirt road southeast into Canebrake Canyon.

24.9	23.1	The June Wash turnoff is north (left, jeep route, signed). This can be followed about 4.5 miles north toward the southeast flank of Whale Peak. A ½-mile hike up the ridgeline just east of the vehicle deadend yields a view of the upper reaches of Sandstone Canyon directly below, with the vast Fish Creek drainage spread out to the east. This ridgeline at the headwaters of Arroyo Tapiado, Arroyo Seco del Diablo and Sandstone Canyon is a divide between the Carrizo watershed of the southern Anza-Borrego region and the San Felipe watershed of the northern region. It is a geographical anomaly that such a divide could occur on the south side of the mile-high barrier of the Vallecito Mountains. The explanation is that Fish Creek cut

Scissors Crossing	Ocotillo	Checkpoint Description

through the Vallecito Mountains at Split Mountain to join the San Felipe wash system to the north. Fish Creek, as an antecedent or pre-existing stream, was able to maintain its course by cutting downward faster than the Vallecitos were being uplifted.

26.1   21.9 The Canebrake Canyon turnoff is southwest (private, no entry without permission).

26.4 [M 43] 21.6 Turnoff northeast (left, dirt road, signed), following Vallecito Creek down-wash, leads to Palm Spring oasis and stage station site, 1.7 miles from S-2. This was the probable site of the first palm-tree oasis to be described in California. In 1782 Pedro Fages was on his way to San Diego after delivering messages in Yuma when he stopped at Palm Spring to rest, finding "a small spring of good water, near which there were three or four very tall palm trees." Water has existed at this mesquite-surrounded watering spot since Indian times, as is shown by the scattering of shards and the remains of cooking fires and camp middens. This became a very important watering stop on the Emigrant Trail midway between the water at Carrizo Cienega and that at Vallecito. When Butterfield Stage stations were erected at Carrizo and Vallecito, a relay station was established at Palm Spring. The small adobe building and corrals have long since disappeared, leaving the oasis again quiet for the desert wildlife. A monument marks the site of the way station. The palm trees found here are not the original palms. Emigrants in the 1850s cut down the original palms and used them as firewood. Park personnel planted the trees found today.

Trip 4D describes the route farther down Vallecito Creek Wash to Arroyo Tapiado, Arroyo Seco del Diablo, Dropoff and the site of the Carrizo Stage Station.

[M 45]
29.0   19.0 Well of the Eight Echoes is on the north (left) side of the road. The heavy, reverberating echoes of a yell down this 15-inch-diameter, 20-foot-deep iron pipe give a clue to the origin of its name. These wells may have been drilled in the hope of finding oil or possibly, as **[M 46]** some claim, for the purpose of irrigating cotton.

29.6   18.4 The Indian Gorge turnoff is to the southwest (right, jeep road, signed).

Side Trip Up Indian Gorge

0.0 Junction at S-2. Proceed southwest along a sandy road to . . .

0.8 Entrance to Indian Gorge, a narrow canyon with a scattering of boulders and smoke trees.

1.8 Torote Canyon joins from the northwest (right). This rocky wash can be hiked one-mile to a large bowl. *Torote* is the Spanish word for elephant tree. Dozens of these trees are found along the slopes of this canyon wash. The hiker can bear south (left) another 3 miles to cross a ridge into North Fork Indian Canyon and the roadhead noted below.

Beyond Torote Canyon, Indian Gorge widens into Indian Valley.

2.0 To the southeast (left) a low saddle borders the arroyo. At the near (west) end of this saddle is the beginning of an old Indian trail that leads south over the saddle to Palm Bowl. A small rock monument marks the beginning of this trail, which is at

Scissors Crossing	Ocotillo	Checkpoint Description
		first very faint. Bits of broken pottery are scattered along this route. After about ½ mile the trail descends sharply into Palm Bowl. More than 100 Washingtonia palms are found in this natural amphitheater.
	2.7	Fork of North Indian Valley (right) and South Indian Valley (left). The North Indian Valley road is negotiable by jeep for nearly 3 miles, ending at the mouth of a narrow canyon guarded by native palms. Near the trees is a silted-in rock tank inscribed with the name "McCain"—an early-day cattle and pioneering family. The Salton Sea and the Chocolate Mountains are visible to the east.

The South Indian Valley road is also negotiable for about 3 miles, ending at a rugged canyon. There are more palms in this south fork than there are in the north fork. Up this road 0.2 mile from the fork is a huge granite boulder a few hundred feet to the left, on the rear side of which is a smoke-blackened cave that was used as an Indian shelter. Bedrock morteros are found behind the boulder.

[M 46] **End of Side Trip**

29.8	18.2	Road forks. Paved road turns south (right). A good dirt road (the old county road) continues straight ahead 1.4 miles to enter Bow Willow Creek Wash. The old Carrizo Stage Station is another 6.3 miles east along the Carrizo Creek wash bed—jeep only (see Trip 4D).
[M 47]		
30.6	17.4	The turnoff west (right, dirt road, signed) leads to Mountain Palm Springs and a primitive campground. The campground 0.6 mile in has chemical toilets but no water. There are five main palm groves and about 400 palm trees in this area. Mountain Palm Springs Canyon has two forks branching from the campground.

A. The North Fork of Mountain Palm Springs Canyon leads approximately ½ mile from the campground up a rocky arroyo to North Grove, which is visible from the campground. Northwest of North Grove, about ¼ mile, is Mary's Bowl Grove, where some elephant trees may be found in addition to palm trees. About ½ mile due west of North Grove is Surprise Canyon, which may initially appear drab and uninteresting. However, it is worthy of its name. Palm trees are scattered along the sandy floor, and approximately ¼ mile farther up, Surprise Canyon suddenly opens into a magnificent amphitheater called Palm Bowl, where more than 100 palms fringe the back edge of the bowl. A tiny spring is found at the rear of the oasis. An old Indian trail leads north from the southeast side of the bowl over a ridge ½ mile into Indian Gorge.

B. The South Fork of Mountain Palm Springs Canyon has two palm groves, about ½ mile apart. The lower grove is called Pygmy Grove. Palm trees here are stunted, the trees being about half the size of normal Washingtonia palms. There are about 50 palms in this group. The upper oasis, called Southwest Grove, has slightly more trees than the lower grove. A sign at Southwest Grove points the way to Torote Bowl, about another ½ mile up canyon, where some elephant trees

Scissors Crossing	Ocotillo	Checkpoint Description
		may be found. It is approximately 1.5 miles back down the canyon from Torote Bowl to the campground.
31.9 [M 48]	16.1	Turnoff west (right, dirt road, signed) leads south around Egg Mountain to Bow Willow Canyon and campground. The willows

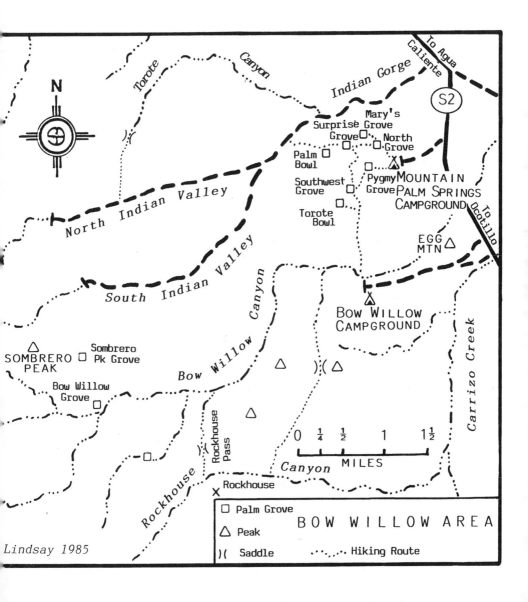

Lindsay 1985

Scissors Crossing	Ocotillo	Checkpoint Description

growing in this canyon wash are among the largest in the Park. The canyon possibly gets its name from the desert willows in the canyon, which were cut by the native Indians for their bows. There are many palm groves in Bow Willow's secluded side canyons. Some elephant trees also grow in the area.

Side Trip Up Bow Willow Canyon

0.0 Junction on S-2

1.6 Bow Willow maintenance area at the beginning of Bow Willow campground. The campground (elevation 950) was the site of an ancient Indian village. One can see morteros in the granite boulders and broken pottery strewn over a wide area. There will be 15 developed sites with tables, shade ramadas, limited water and chemical toilets. The campground will accommodate tents, trailers and pickup campers. A flood in 1984 destroyed the original campsites. New sites are being developed and should be available in 1985. Vehicles are not permitted beyond the campground. This canyon affords entry to an excellent hiking area with the possibility of loop day hikes or an overnighter.

2.0 Just west of the first ridge from the campsites, a trail leads south up an arroyo and over the ridge approximately 2.5 miles to Rockhouse Canyon via Single Palm. A hike may be made by following Rockhouse Canyon west about 1 mile to a stone cabin (the rockhouse) and then going directly north over a saddle called "Saddleback Ridge" approximately 1½ miles into Bow Willow Canyon. Down-canyon east to the starting point at mile 2.0 is 2.5 miles. Total loop hike is about 7 miles.

4.5 A huge and beautiful bowl. Beyond this point the main canyon becomes steep, with many boulders and a delightful seasonal stream. Palm groves dot the canyon floor.

5.5 A climb up the steep canyon to the northwest (right) leads to Sombrero Peak Palm Grove, clearly visible from a distance on the side of Sombrero Peak at 2500 feet elevation. There are about 90 tall, slender Washingtonia palms in this grove.

5.7 The main canyon forks and turns south at the base of Sombrero Peak. Hikers may climb past another palm grove into McCain Valley and its jeep trails. Bow Willow Creek begins high beyond in the In-Ko-Pah Mountains.

End of Side Trip

32.1	15.9	Turnoff southwest (right, hiking route) in the middle of Carrizo Creek leads up Carrizo Canyon. *Carrizo* means reed grass in Spanish, and the name refers to the tall, bamboolike plant found growing along moist arroyos, in cienegas and at springs and waterholes. Carrizo grows in the manner of desert palms—"feet in the water and head in the sun." Carrizo Wash begins in the Jacumba and In-Ko-Pah Mountains amid tumbled boulders near Jacumba and drains northward through Carrizo Gorge and Carrizo Canyon, reaching the desert floor near Bow Willow. The gorge drops in elevation from 2800 feet to the desert floor at 950 feet. Due to this great range of elevation, there is a variety of plant life from chaparral in the upper gorge to lower Sonoran plants in the canyon.

| Scissors Crossing | Ocotillo | Checkpoint Description |

Despite the roughness of Carrizo Canyon, it was selected as the route of the San Diego and Arizona Eastern Railroad. The building of the railroad is considered an engineering feat. Construction crews dug 21 tunnels through portions of the granite mountain and erected several wooden trestles across the chasm. Seventeen of the 21 tunnels on the SD&AE are in Carrizo. From the desert floor at Bow Willow, Carrizo Creek leads east to the Carrizo Stage Station site and through the slot between the Coyote and Fish Creek mountains. It then veers north again as Carrizo Wash, joining the San Felipe Wash near Harpers Well.

Side Trip Up Carrizo Canyon (hikers only)

0.0 Junction with S-2. The entrance to Carrizo Canyon is a wide, sandy arroyo. The sandy floor of the canyon is covered with a forest of smoke trees and desert willows.

2.5 Rockhouse Canyon Wash to the west (right) has a wide, sandy entrance. An old cattlemen's line shack constructed of stone is found 3.3 miles in on a bench on the south side of the canyon. The bowl-shaped head of this canyon is surrounded by rocky hillsides. Up the west (right) tributary canyon from this bowl-shaped valley are three aged palms. If one crosses the saddle

Trestle in Carrizo Gorge

Scissors Crossing	Ocotillo	Checkpoint Description

directly north from the stone cabin, it will lead about 1 mile to Bow Willow Canyon. (See hikes described above.)

4.0 Tributary canyons are to the east (right) and west (left). There are several palm trees up the west-side canyon. A hike up the east fork will lead to Carrizo Palms, below the railbed of the San Diego and Arizona Eastern Railroad. The 170 palms found here, between tunnels 20 and 21 of the railroad, may also be reached from Indian Hill in the Dos Cabezas area of the park. When construction crews were blasting tunnels for the railroad, between 1912 and 1919, the water in these palm oases became crucial to the working crews, who installed a pump to boost this water to their camp 400 feet up the mountainside above the oasis.

Bighorn sheep and mule deer live in the upper reaches of this rough terrain. The canyon becomes steeper and rockier farther south.

End of Side Trip

| 32.2 [M 49] | 15.8 | Turnoff east (left, jeep route) is another alternate route to the Carrizo stage site. |

The road now enters Sweeney Canyon and starts up the steep grades of Sweeney Pass. This climb had long been a barrier to most vehicles trying to follow the rough Imperial Highway route in the 1930s and 1940s. In 1952, county engineers constucted a sinuous route snaking along the hillsides which finally enabled conventional vehicles to negotiate Sweeney Pass with ease. By the early 1960s the entire Imperial Highway had been paved.

| [M 51] 34.7 | 13.3 | Turnoff northeast (left, signed, jeep route) drops off the plateau into Canyon Sin Nombre ("Canyon Without Name"). Eroding floods have cut deeply through the gravel-covered Sweeney Pass area to form Canyon Sin Nombre. The high, sheer canyon walls are composed of rock of many shades of red and brown. This canyon winds 4 sinuous miles between igneous-rock walls which give way to mudstone and sandstone layers before it joins the Carrizo Wash route. The route is narrow and boulder-choked in places. |

| 35.1 [M 53] | 12.9 | Turnoff on the north (left) side of the road goes to Carrizo Badlands Overlook and rejoins the pavement after 0.2 mile. |
| 36.8 | 11.2 | Turnoff southwest (right, jeep route, signed) is Jojoba Wash, named for the abundant jojoba shrubs found here. The jojoba, or goatnut, is undergoing intensive experimentation and cultivation in the arid Southwest as a high-quality specialty lube-oil substitute. In particular it is felt that jojoba may replace whale oil, and thus reduce the commercial hunting of these endangered mammals. |

The Jojoba jeep route penetrates the Volcanic Hills for about 5.5 extremely rough miles and then joins the Dos Cabezas road near the old railroad station (see Trip 4E). Masses of black and dark-red lavalike rock seem to flow in among the granite Volcanic Hills. Overlying a good portion of the base of the hills is an extension of the Imperial Formation containing fossil marine shells. There is also evidence of Indian use in the flat areas and among the boulder-formed caves. Trails wind through the several passes to the north and west.

Old Sweeney Grade about 1940   **Canyon Sin Nombre**

Scissors Crossing	Ocotillo	Checkpoint Description
36.8	11.2	Turnoff northeast (left, jeep route, signed) leads 1.6 miles around a ridge to the Dolomite Mine, clearly visible on the slope of the Coyote Mountains. The mine, now abandoned, once yielded dolomite marble, which was trucked 8 miles south to the rail siding at Dos Cabezas station. The mine ruins offer an excellent vantage point from which to study the Dos Cabezas/Mortero Wash area at the base of the Jacumba Mountains, with the broad, barren desert valley of Palm Canyon Wash stretching to the south and east.
39.2 [M 55]	8.8	The road passes through a gap lined by dark-colored rocks. These rocks and the black and red hills to the west are the best examples of volcanic activity in the Anza-Borrego region. Some petrified wood can be found in the hills west of the road. Just look—do not collect specimens in the Park.
39.5 [M 56]	8.5	A dirt road crosses the highway. The southwest branch (right, signed) leads through Mortero Canyon 4 miles to the Dos Cabezas station (see Trip 4E). The northeast road (left, signed) is another Dolomite Mine road, which crosses North Mortero Wash and then proceeds northwest to the quarry.
		The highway crosses Lava Flow Wash to . . .
39.8	8.2	The Imperial Highway monument at the county line and the Park's east boundary. The Boyce Aten post of the El Centro American Legion built this monument in 1933 when their dream of a "First class roadway from El Segundo on the coast to El Centro" was in fact nothing more than a set of meandering, sand-bound tracks, passable to little more than animal-drawn vehicles.
		The highway continues across the desert plain, with numerous tracks departing northeast toward old mining prospects on the

Scissors Crossing	Ocotillo	Checkpoint Description
		southwest flank of the Coyote Mountains. These mountains are interesting geologically. The San Diego Natural History Museum says that the Coyote Mountains were an island of granitic and metamorphic rocks at the time of deposition of Miocene-Pliocene sediments. The deposition was accompanied in its early stages by some volcanism which laid down a sheet of lava over much of the surrounding area. Geologists call the flow Alverson Andesite. One of the most striking features seen as the mountain is approached is the manner in which all strata dip away from the center in every direction. Erosion has cut away many of soft clay layers and left hard sandstone or oyster reefs projecting as isolated hills in badlands areas. Many of the reefs are composed almost entirely of organic calcite, chiefly oysters, firmly consolidated. In other places there are large areas completely covered with fossil oyster shells, pectens and barnacles. These are weathered out free, and except for etching by the windblown desert sand, are in a perfect state of preservation.
44.0	4.0	Turnoff south (right, dirt road, signed) leads to Dos Cabezas and Mortero Palms area (see Trip 4E).
46.7	1.3	The crossroad is Shell Canyon Road, offering access to Fossil (Alverson or Shell) Canyon to the north (left). To enter the canyon, follow the road north past a quarry and on into the gorge. At the lower (south) end of the canyon are fossil coral reefs which rise atop the narrow sandstone and mudstone walls. The coral dates back 3–5 million years. Farther up-canyon, extensive beds of oyster shells which overlie the coral reefs await the visitor. The canyon bluffs and ridges, which in some places tower 150 feet above the canyon floor, are excellent for sample fossil and rock-collecting. There are also some good rillensteine specimens.
48.0	0.0	Junction with Interstate 8 and old Highway 80 in the small town of Ocotillo (gas, supplies, restaurants, sheriff's office).

Fossil (Alverson) Canyon

Trip 4A: Pinyon Mountain

From: Highway S-2 in Earthquake Valley

To: Ocotillo Wells (Highway 78, 38.6 miles one way, dirt road first few miles, one-way jeep route thereafter to Olla Wash, then two-way jeep route, dirt road and paved road into Ocotillo Wells)

Via: Pinyon Mountain Valley, Harper Flat, Hapaha Flat, Fish Creek Wash and Split Mountain

Mileage From:

Hiway S-2	Checkpoint Description
0.0	Signed turnoff for Pinyon Mountain Road at Park boundary, 4.4 miles southeast of Scissors Crossing. Proceed east along the dirt road, climbing through increasingly luxuriant stands of Mojave yucca, nolina and agave into the pinyon-juniper belt.
4.0	A low saddle marks the entrance into Pinyon Mountain Valley. The road crosses several more washes into this beautiful and secluded mountain vale with an average elevation of 3800 feet. Numerous excellent campsites nestled among the pines are available just off the road.
5.7	This is the high point of the route at 3950 feet. Just beyond, on the north side of the road, is a huge, lone pinyon which may be the largest in the Park. Pinyon nuts were a staple of the Indians. This piney mountain island in the desert sky was a favored retreat of earlier inhabitants. A walk up the gentle slope on the north side of the road will yield superb vistas of Borrego Valley and Borrego Badlands, with the Santa Rosas etched against the sky on the far horizon.
6.4	This is a departure point, at elevation 3850, for a hike up Whale Peak to the south (right). This hike goes about 3 miles through a narrow rocky wash, across open meadows and up brushy slopes to the summit at elevation 5349. A cairn with a visitor's register marks Whale Peak as one of the Sierra Club's 100 notable Desert Peaks in Southern California. Whale Peak has some of the finest displays of flora in the Anza-Borrego area. Lack of a major fire in the area has allowed all plant life to grow into large, well-developed specimens. The nolina and Mojave yucca have trunks 10–12 feet tall. The single-leaf pinyon pines and California junipers are large and abundant. Other plants include typical chaparral and cacti of the 4000-foot elevation.
7.4	The Squeeze, or Fat Man's Misery. The route passes between two rocks just over 6 feet apart, marking the end of travel for fat vehicles. Imprudent drivers will leave paint behind as their price of passage through upper Pinyon Wash.
8.0	The main route makes a sharp right turn up a rocky path in a small wash. (One can continue down this wash about ½ mile to a deadend at a 35-foot dry water chute.) The main route tops a small ridge, just beyond which is ...
8.3	The Pinyon Mountain Dropoff, also known as "Heart Attack Hill." Of the several dropoffs in the Anza-Borrego region, this is probably the most hazardous. Put the vehicle in lowest gear. Keep headed downhill and don't apply brakes until the bottom. A fishtail action or sideways slide might result in turning over. It is wise to let passengers walk down this one. From here the route works back into Pinyon Wash over a series of smaller ridges and gullies.
9.0	Re-enter Pinyon Wash. One can hike up-wash west a short distance from here to the ruins of an outpost constructed by Julius and Amby Harper and Julius's son Akim around 1921. The cabin ruins are about 500 yards up-wash in a narrow side draw entering the wash on the south (left) side. It was a one-room structure measuring about 12 x 25 feet, with the back and ends quarried out of the rock. Agave stalks formed the studs and rafters for the roof, and the front and the roof were made from corrugated sheet iron. Old-time desert explorer Karl Bennis

Hiway S-2	Checkpoint Description

reported to Ranger Jack Welch in 1956 that one of the Harper brothers and his wife spent their honeymoon in this remote cabin. About 200 yards farther west up the main wash are two old concrete dams built by the Harpers between 1918 and 1922 which are now filled with sand to form two smooth, giant steps on the canyon floor.

9.2 The route touches Harper Flat and turns sharply right. This huge, gently sloping, bowl-shaped valley in the heart of the Vallecito Mountains was a favored cattle-grazing area. It is now absolutely closed to vehicular traffic. Hikers may exit the flat to the north down either Pinyon Canyon to Highway 78 or down Harper Canyon to the old Kane Springs Road (see Trip 1). Harper Flat was the site of one of the largest Indian camps in the Anza-Borrego area. A complex of Indian trails radiates from the area. Also found in this area are cupule petroglyphs, which are pock-marked rocks, the pocks resembling little mortero holes with diameters up to 3 inches. They are considered one of the oldest styles of petroglyphs. What makes these in Harper Flat unusual is that there is a definite pattern to them. The holes are in a straight line, with several holes in a ball at one end of the line.

The route departs Harper Flat to the south up another wash and over a ridge into the Fish Creek drainage at the head of . . .

10.2 Hapaha Flat, which lies ahead at an average elevation of 2500 feet in the path of frequent floods. The resulting abundant vegetation and the remoteness of the area make it a favorite grazing and hunting area for bighorn sheep, deer, rabbits and associated predators. The desert plants are typical of this elevation: Mojave yucca, Whipple yucca, agave, indigo bush, desert lavender and California juniper. Looking southeast from the higher part of the north end of Hapaha Flat, one's gaze extends across the Vallecito Badlands and the Yuha Desert. At numerous locations bedrock morteros and metates, roasting pits and pottery fragments indicate heavy Indian use.

10.6 Split rock bears pictographs of colored lines as well as petroglyphs. This is an old Indian campsite and is a good one for today's campers. Mortero holes are found on the boulders on the surrounding mountainside.

12.8 Dave McCain Spring turnoff north (left). McCain, an early-day cattleman, piped water from a spring down to his cattle at the head of Fish Creek. The spring has been dry for several years.

13.6 There are traces of a large Indian camp along the base of the mountains to the northeast (left). This south end of Hapaha Flat now narrows into a wash.

17.3 Olla Wash joins from the west (right). This is the end of the one-way Pinyon Mountain Road. The route continues east down Fish Creek Wash, through Split Mountain past the primitive campground on the hill to . . .

30.5 The pavement. (See Trip 1D for details of the trip through Fish Creek and Split Mountain.)

38.6 Ocotillo Wells at the junction with Highway 78.

Split Rock in Hapaha Flat

Trip 4B: Blair Valley, Little Blair Valley and Smuggler Canyon

From: Blair Valley

To: Earthquake Valley (dirt road, 7.9 miles one way)

With Side Trip To: Indian Pictographs and Smuggler Canyon (dirt road and hiking trail)

Mileage From:

Blair V. Turnoff	L. Blair V. T'off	Checkpoint Description
0.0	7.9	Turnoff east (left) from S-2 is 6.0 miles southeast of Scissors Crossing at Little Pass. Proceed around the north end of Blair Dry Lake to the popular Little Pass Primitive Campground. This large camping area will accommodate tents, trailers, pickup campers and groups of all sizes. Blair Valley, Little Blair Valley and Earthquake Valley would form a 10-mile-long trough west of the Pinyon Mountains if it were not for a semicircular upthrust of granite that separates the three into distinct areas. The granite is laced with pegmatite dikes that have long been the subject of prospecting. Runoff from heavy rains floods the low part of Blair Valley and remains for several weeks.
0.5	7.4	Fork to Foot and Walker Pass (vehicles prohibited). Just north of this fork the deep ruts of stage and wagon traffic over a 100 years old are marked by a monument. Here passengers had to dismount and help push coaches up the steep incline and over the granite ridge separating Blair Valley from Earthquake Valley. This is one of the best preserved portions of the old Emigrant Trail.
		The dirt road continues around the northeast edge of the dry lake and south up the valley to . . .
2.7	5.2	A fork. The southwest fork (right, signed) is a dirt road which leads ¼ mile to the trailhead for Ghost Mountain. This trail climbs steeply south and east 0.7 mile to the ruins of Yaquitepec, the 1930s and 1940s home of the Marshal South family. After the Depression had cut off South's income as a writer, he and his poetess wife, Tanya, turned to primitive natural living. They hand-built an adobe home, and cisterns to catch and store rain water. They lived much like the early Indians, gaining sustenance from the desert and wearing little

The South family's home at Yaquitepec on Ghost Mountain

Blair V. Turnoff	L. Blair V. T'off	Checkpoint Description
		clothing. Three children were born to them during their sojourn on Ghost Mountain. South became a regular contributor to *Desert Magazine,* writing monthly about their experiment in primitive living until the mid-Forties.
		The east fork (left) continues over a small pass into Little Blair Valley to a . . .
3.5	4.4	Trailhead (signed). The southeast trail (right) leads ¼ mile to an excellent site of numerous Indian bedrock morteros—deep grinding holes in the granite boulders. The Indians would collect seeds from the desert plants, grind them down for storage in baskets or clay pots (ollas) and use them later.
		The road (straight ahead) continues east to . . .
3.6	4.3	Fork (signed).

Side Trip to Indian Pictographs and Smuggler Canyon (dirt road, hiking route)

0.0		The northeast (right) fork leads to . . .
1.5		A roadhead. The hiking route commences here, leading over a small pass into the upper reaches of Smuggler Canyon. This is one possible route to climb Whale Peak. To do so, bear left (north) up Smuggler Canyon and then northeast to the summit.

The hiking route to the pictographs leads southwest (right) down Smuggler Canyon to . . .

2.5   A very prominent boulder on the west side of the stream bed on which the pictographs are well displayed. This Indian rock art has been painted on rather than etched into the rock (petroglyphs) by early day Kumeyaay Indians. The pictographs are unusual for their well-executed yellow and red designs consisting of interlaced elements in a diamond-chain motif. The diamond chains and chevrons are typical of Luiseño rock art and show the influence this Indian group had on the neighboring Kumeyaay. Pictographs were commonly done by shamans—priests or medicine men. Continue downstream . . .

2.9   Past another boulder with bedrock morteros to a superb overlook into the great Carrizo Valley, backdropped by the rugged peaks of the Tierra Blanca, Jacumba and Coyote mountains. Hikers may backtrack here or continue down a steep, winding pitch into the flatlands at . . .

6.4   The mouth of Smuggler Canyon on Highway S-2, just east of Vallecito Stage Station for a pre-arranged pickup.

End of Side Trip

The route of Trip 4B continues north (straight) into Little Blair Valley and around the west and north sides of another dry lake. Cross a low divide and bear west (left) along the hillside to . . .

| 6.9 | 1.0 | The north side of Foot and Walker Pass. Turn north along the tracks of the old stage route to . . . |
| 7.9 | 0.0 | Join S-2. |

Trip 4C: Oriflamme and Chariot Canyons

From: Highway S-2 in Mason Valley

To: Highway 78 at Banner Store (generally jeep only, 11.4 miles one way, a mountain bicycle route)

With Side Trips To: Rodriquez Canyon (dirt road) and Sunrise Highway (dirt road, then hike via the Pacific Crest Trail/California Riding and Hiking Trail)

Note: There are several gates along these routes. They MUST be closed after passage.

Mileage From:

Mason Valley	Banner Store	Checkpoint Description
0.0	11.4	Depart Highway S-2 west at southwest end of Box Canyon (signed). This is the route followed by the short-lived San Antonio-San Diego Mail line, which left the Emigrant Trail and turned up Oriflamme Canyon and headed toward San Diego. Because the mountain crossing was not suitable for regular stagecoaches, passengers transferred at Vallecito from coaches to mules. Hence the line was dubbed the "Jackass Mail." Although the importance of this mail line declined with the opening of the Butterfield Mail in 1858, it was still used for several years. The route follows the Anza-Borrego Desert Section of the California Riding and Hiking Trail into the mountains.
0.3	11.1	The route enters Vallecito Wash, which is sandy and may be very soft for the next mile.
2.1	9.3	Junction of Rodriguez and Oriflamme canyons. The main route bears west (left).

Side Trip Up Rodriguez Canyon (this offers an alternate parallel route to Banner Store.)

0.0 Junction. Bear northwest (right) up-canyon.

0.3 The rutted trail to the north (right) leads 1.5 miles to an old mining prospect and cabin ruins on the southeast flank of Granite Mountain. This is a good point from which to climb this barren, rocky massif.

The road enters a narrow canyon and climbs onto a broad flat to . . .

2.5 The Guy Urquhart turkey ranch. Ruins of the ranch buildings east of the road may be explored. Catalpa, sugar bush and screwbean mesquite predominate here.

3.8 Summit

5.0 The road intersects the Pacific Crest Trail (signed). The trail turns north (right) and follows the old Ranchita Mine road past the ruins of a large five-stamp mill.

5.2 The California Riding and Hiking Trail (signed) departs north (right) down the hillside.

Both trails now lead along the road to . . .

5.8 Junction of Chariot Canyon and Rodriquez Canyon roads. Trails turn south (left) up-canyon. North (right) leads to . . .

7.3 The Banner Store on Highway 78.

End of Side Trip

Mason Valley	Banner Store	Checkpoint Description
2.1	9.3	Junction of Rodriquez and Oriflamme canyons. Bear west (left).
2.9	8.5	The site of state-operated Camp Carlton is among the alders and sycamores along the stream. Crews based here in the 1930s hacked out the Mason Valley Truck Trail with little more than rudimentary hand tools. The route now pitches sharply upward along this trail as it clings precariously to the mountainside. Far below in the bottom of the canyon are stock trails where the Daley ranchers on horseback still herd cattle from high mountain meadow to desert plain and back again as the seasons dictate.
5.8	5.6	This is the Chariot Canyon/Mason Valley Truck Trail junction at the divide of the San Felipe and Carrizo drainages. The main route continues northwest (straight) down into Chariot Canyon.

Side Trip Along the Riding and Hiking Trail to Sunrise Highway

0.0   Junction. Proceed southwest (left).

0.7   The old Lassitor hay road cuts steeply up through thick chaparral to the southwest (it is impassable to vehicles and crosses private property). From 1857 to 1861 James R. Lassitor used this and the Salt Creek route to the south to freight hay, wild oats and firewood from his ranch in the Cuyamaca Mountains down to the major transcontinental stage station at Vallecito. Over 100 years later the process is still the same, only the product has changed. Today, trucks roar down the Banner grade just a few miles north carrying fuel to service stations, which feed thirsty cars along the old Butterfield Trail.

2.0   This is a major trail junction and the end of travel for vehicles. At this point, marked by a water tank south of the road, the Desert Section of the California Riding and Hiking Trail joins the main trail, which here coincides with the Pacific Crest Trail. Hikers have two choices from here: 1) descend north (right) 1.3 miles into Chariot Canyon and on to the San Felipe Valley 5 miles farther, or 2) proceed west (straight ahead) through a locked gate, then south (left) through another locked gate and a shallow valley to . . .

3.4   The Sunrise Highway (S-1) near the Fages Monument, 1 mile east of the junction of the Sunrise Highway and Highway 79. The Oriflamme Canyon route to the desert is known as the Pedro Fages Trail. The text on the monument on the east side of S-1, states that

> On October 29, 1772, Colonel Pedro Fages headed east from San Diego searching for army deserters. It was the first entry by Europeans into Oriflamme Canyon. From there, Fages and his men traveled through Cajon Pass, around the Mojave and the Central Valley, and eventually reached Mission San Luis Obispo. As a result, he discovered the Colorado Desert and the San Joaquin Valley. Two years later Juan Bautista de Anza followed a portion of the trail blazed by Fages from San Sebastian through Coyote Canyon.

The Pacific Crest Trail and the California Riding and Hiking Trail cross the highway to the west toward Cuyamaca Lake,

Mason Valley	Banner Store	Checkpoint Description
		then divide to lead through different parts of Cuyamaca Rancho State Park.
		End of Side Trip
5.8	5.6	Junction of Chariot Canyon and Mason Valley Truck Trail.
6.3	5.1	A road (locked gate) joins from the southwest in the bottom of the canyon. The Pacific Crest Trail and the California Riding and Hiking Trail come down this grade from Sunrise Highway and continue north along Chariot Canyon road. Sycamore and cottonwood trees along a small stream coupled with lavish spring wildflower displays make this one of the most inviting canyons in the entire area.
7.0	4.4	The exit from the park through a gate marks the beginning of the famed Chariot Canyon gold diggings of the 1870s, which were part of the Julian-Banner gold rush. Gold was first discovered in the San Diego hills on Coleman Creek in late 1869, and with the discovery of the Washington Mine, which was staked out on George Washington's birthday in 1870, a full-scale rush to the Julian area was on. The town of Julian was laid out, and prospectors began searching the hills and canyons surrounding the town. In the Fall of 1870 George V. King was searching for gold down the hill from Julian along the Banner Grade and up Chariot Canyon. He passed the Ready Relief and Redmon diggings, and climbed upward out of the densely wooded canyon to the mountainside covered with scrub oak and manzanita, where he noticed a large white quartz boulder. There he discovered one of the richest veins in the Banner area, and named it the Golden Chariot Mine. About $2 million worth of bullion was eventually taken from the mine. Other mines in Chariot Canyon included the Cold Beef, Chariot, Lucky Strike, Golden Sugar and Golden Ella. Today abandoned shacks, stamp mills and empty tunnels remain along much of the length of this once-booming canyon. In recent years, however, the Golden Chariot, Cold Beef and Golden Ella have been reopened and are being worked again. The mines are on private property and visitors are not welcome.
9.9	1.5	This is the junction with Rodriguez Canyon road to the northeast (left). The Pacific Crest Trail and the California Riding and Hiking Trail turn here to cross Highway 78, 2.2 miles northeast.
11.3	0.1	Junction with Highway 78. Turn east (right) to . . .
11.4	0.0	The Banner Store and Recreation Ranch (gas, supplies, private campground open to the public). This was once a center of activity during the Julian-Banner gold rush days of the 1870s and 1880s. Just to the east of the store is the former Banner Queen Guest Ranch, near the site of the old Banner Queen gold mine.

Trip 4D: Carrizo Wash to Stage Station Site

From: Highway S-2

To: Carrizo Stage Station Site (11.0 miles one way; dirt road to Palm Spring, then jeep road)

With Side Trips To: Arroyo Tapiado (jeep route) and Arroyo Seco del Diablo (jeep route)

Mileage From:
S-2 at Palm
Spring Turnoff   Checkpoint Description

0.0	Proceed east from S-2 at Palm Spring turnoff (signed), 4.7 miles south of Agua Caliente.
0.4	Turnoff north (left) is to View of the Badlands Point, 1.7 miles up-wash. From here one can see miles of the twisting Carrizo Badlands. The main route proceeds southeast down Vallecito Wash.
1.0	Turnoff north (left) is to Mesquite Oasis and Palm Spring, 0.6 mile up-wash. The historic description of Palm Spring is found in Trip 4. This was the site of the Palm Spring Station, a stop on the Butterfield Overland Mail.
2.4	Turnoff north (left) is to Arroyo Hueso (Bone Wash). This wash is a bowl-shaped valley surrounded by badlands and dotted with mesquite and smoke trees. It is named for vertebrate fossils that have been found here.
2.6	The prominent mud hummock just northeast (left) of the wash is the site of one of Jasper's water signs, which is responsible for the name of this locale. James A. Jasper, a San Diego County supervisor, was responsible for guide signs being place a mile apart along several of the dim and dusty trails threading the San Diego backcountry in 1895. The old emigrant trail from San Felipe Pass southeast to Carrizo gap was marked in such a manner by Jasper's iron signs. Directions painted on the signs gave distances to settlements and waterholes. In later years someone painted the words "Hollywood and Vine" on the two metal plates of the sign here, and the name has stuck.
4.6	Turnoff north (left) leads to Arroyo Tapiado. This and Arroyo Seco del Diablo are the two most visited washes in this area. Arroyo Tapiado is a typical badlands wash with sparse vegetation. Of particular interest are the towering, eroded mud walls, which have developed numerous caves through the action of running water eating away at the walls. These caves are dangerous to enter because the mud walls could easily collapse. Also interesting are the sandstone concretions found in the upper reaches of the wash.

Side Trip Up Arroyo Tapiado

0.0	Turnoff into Rainbow Basin.
3.1	The Big Mud Cave runs for several hundred feet into the mudhills.
6.3	The turnoff east (right) up onto West Mesa leads 2.2 miles over to Arroyo Seco del Diablo, providing a round-trip possibility. Note the sandstone concretions in the upper reaches of the wash.

End of Side Trip

5.4	Little Devil Wash joins from the north (left). For hikers only, it can be followed about 2 miles up onto West Mesa, from which there is a good view of the surrounding badlands.
6.1	Turnoff north (left) leads up Arroyo Seco del Diablo (signed). This is the longest wash in the Carrizo Badlands. Like those of Arroyo Tapiado, the walls show variegated stratification. In some places the sediments have been folded into synclines and anticlines.

S-2 at Palm Spring Turnoff	Checkpoint Description

Side Trip Up Arroyo Seco del Diablo (Devil's Dry Wash)

0.0   Turnoff.

1.0   There is a seep here which makes the name of the wash a misnomer.

5.7   Turnoff northeast onto Middle Mesa. The road follows a generally northern course across the mesa 1.5 miles to a steep bank which is Diablo Dropoff. From here the road plunges down a sandy hill, winds across a little flat and then disappears into a deep wash (Dropoff Wash), which leads down to the Fish Creek watershed. The distance from Diablo Dropoff to Fish Creek Wash is about 1 mile. This is a one-way-only road; the hill between the top of the mesa and Fish Creek should not be climbed.

5.8   Cut-Across Trail to Arroyo Tapiado (2.2 miles west) is on the west (left).

End of Side Trip

7.4   Confluence of Carrizo Creek and Vallecito Creek. A hard right (west) turn here leads about 4 miles back to Highway S-2 via any one of three routes, as follows:

    0.1   Canyon Sin Nombre departs south (left) through a superb smoke-tree forest and climbs steeply to gain the summit of Sweeney Pass on S-2 near Mileage Marker 51 at the Carrizo Badlands Overlook (Trip 4).

    0.2   South Carrizo Creek road turns southwest (left), passing through lush green mesquite thickets and past an old homestead to reach S-2 near Mileage Marker 49.

    0.3   Bow Willow Creek swings northwest (right), past the old Bow Willow Ranger Station site to reach S-2 near Mileage Marker 46. This is the Old County Road and the easiest route out of the Carrizo Badlands.

    The route down Carrizo Creek continues straight ahead (east) through heavy tamarisk growth in the running stream.

9.5   Exit creekbed left (northeast) at Carrizo Creek signpost.

10.1   Fork. Right (southeast) branch goes to the Graves cabin on private property at the edge of the marsh. Bear left (northeast), over a low ridge to . . .

10.6   end of eastbound route at the beginning of the Carrizo Impact Area, a 27,000-acre no-man's land which has been closed to the public since 1942 except for a few years between 1959 and 1962. The Army leased the land from the state for use as a bombing range beginning in 1942. The Army then leased the area to the Navy, which also used it as a bombing range until 1959. In that year the Navy sent in special teams to remove any dangerous explosives and then returned the land to the state. The area was again opened to the public. Soon afterwards, however, park visitors began finding live bombs, and in 1962 a man was injured in an explosion while trying to remove some scrap materials from the area. The range was then closed and has remained so since then.

    Turn south (right) 0.3 mile and park to commence exploration of the fascinating marsh area around the old Carrizo Stage Station site. The station probably nestled up to the low ridge to the right (west). The melting adobe walls below a Jasper waterhole marker on the ridge are pictured in a 1935 photo in Parker's classic *Anza-Borrego Desert Guide Book*.

11.0   This was an important stop for emigrants and later those riding on the overland stages because it was the first station reached after crossing the hardest and driest part of the Colorado Desert. It was also the first desert stop where something green was growing. A few hundred feet west of the old station site are a few boulders on the bank of Carrizo Creek marking the site of an old grave. The grave belongs to Joe (some sources say Frank) Fox, who was killed by a deputy sheriff about March 1, 1886, when he ran after being accused of horse thievery in Arizona. The Fox brothers had joined a cattle drive from near Tucson, Arizona, to Warner's Ranch. The sheriff had trailed them from Arizona, finally catching them with the cattle drive at Carrizo Creek.

Trip 4E: Dos Cabezas/Mortero Palms

From: Highway S-2

To: Dos Cabezas Primitive Campground (7.7 miles one way, jeep only)

Via: Mortero Wash, Dos Cabezas Station

With Side Trips To: Indian Hill, Hayden Spring and Devils Canyon

Note: Routes in this area are particularly subject to heavy damage due to severe flash-flooding. Be alert to possible re-routing in washes and canyons. Cross-check map and landmarks often. Old roads crisscross this area and can be confusing.

Mileage From:

S-2	Checkpoint Description
0.0	Begin trip at Highway S-2/Mortero Road junction (signed), 8.2 miles west of Ocotillo. Proceed south along edge of Volcanic Hills.
1.6	Cross Mortero Canyon Wash and climb out opposite (south) side.
3.1	Turnoff to the quarry is northwest (right).
3.9	Turnoff northwest (right) leads to the Indian Hill area.

Side Trip to Indian Hill

0.0	Turnoff
0.1	Dos Cabezas Mine (abandoned) is north (right) of the road. Limestone used for roofing materials was quarried here.
0.5	This is the first of several turnoffs in the next mile north (right) to the Jojoba Wash route. This route may be followed about 5 miles north across a large flat, and into Jojoba Wash to join Highway S-2. It is extremely rugged and absolutely jeep-only. It is also called the Old Freight Road and is reported to have run to some lost mines.
1.3	Indian Hill (hiking only) is 1 mile west (left) across the abandoned railroad tracks. The hill, actually a large rock outcrop, stands prominently in the southern part of this large flat. Northwest of the hill are the circa-1910 remains of the main railroad construction camps for crews working the lower end of the Carrizo Gorge route. Farther northwest below the railroad bed, about 1.5 miles from the hill, is the East Fork of Carrizo Canyon with its numerous palm trees (see Trip 4). The huge granite boulders of Indian Hill have tumbled together to form usable caves, which made the area attractive to Indians. Numerous pictographs, smoke-blackened caves, pottery fragments and flakings attest to the heavy Indian use of this area. This area also has the distinction of being one of the oldest Indian-occupied areas in Anza-Borrego Desert State Park. Pinto Basin Indians used a rock shelter at Indian Hill about 3000 B.C. These early Indians used darts but lacked the bows and arrows of later Indians. They also lacked pottery. This Indian Hill area is a fascinating area for the hiker to explore.
2.0	**End of Side Trip at the end of the road.**

4.1	The water tower and loading ramp are opposite the ruins of Dos Cabezas Station. The ghosts of the San Diego and Arizona Eastern Railroad hover over this lonely and forlorn scene. Here one can conjure up an image of thundering steam engines, double-headed on the point of hundred-car freight trains, pounding through this valley from the awesome chasm of Carrizo Gorge. After 12 years of heartbreaking setbacks and near superhuman labor, the first through-train, "The Golden Spike Limited," rolled through Carrizo on November 15, 1919. San Diego magnate John D. Spreckels' line traversed 147 miles of sparkling

Dos Cabezas Station on the old SD&AE Railroad (looking north)

seacoast, snowbound mountains, treacherous canyons and blazing desert, dipping even into Mexico, to freight the great agricultural wealth of the Imperial Valley west to tidewater.

Although passenger service ended on January 11, 1951, the railroad continued as a vital freight artery until September 10, 1976. On that day Tropical Storm Kathleen slammed into the desert mountains to deal a nearly final blow to dozens of trestles and bridges and end the half-century contest between railroad men and mother nature. Although the line was reopened briefly in 1981, recurrent storms closed it quickly. While new owners labor yet again to rebuild, it would seem that nature's intent is clear. The line and the land will revert to bighorn sheep domain, where man afoot is only a visitor. Neither he nor his machines are to remain. Today only ghostly whistles of long-gone locomotives echo in the Carrizo Gorge between crags and peaks which continue to bear the fanciful survey names of Grunt, Gasp, Moan, Groan, Puff and Windy. They still sing the saga of "the impossible line."

5.5   The crossover to the south (right) leads toward Dos Cabezas Spring.

          The road ahead generally parallels the railroad and then swings north to a junction with Highway S-2, 6.0 miles farther.

5.6   The turnoff northwest (right) parallels the railroad on the southwest side to the vicinity of Piedras Grandes (Large Rocks), a jumble of huge boulders great for rock-climbing practice near Dos Cabezas station.

S-2	Checkpoint Description

6.8   Here is another turnoff northwest (right) to Piedras Grandes, 1.6 miles away.

7.0   The rocky outcropping southeast of the road harbors a line shack, built in 1920 by Robert McCain as an outpost for tending sheep. The green palm fronds of the Mortero Palms may be seen from here in a little canyon off to the southwest.

7.3   Turnoff west (right) leads 0.3 mile into Palm Canyon and the Mortero Palms. Harry Cross of El Centro built two cabins at the base of the boulder-strewn ridge which served as his bee camp beginning in the 1920s. For years afterward he would come up to these cabins whenever there was a good flowering season. A steep trail leads to the palms, which are tucked away in a canyon bowl rimmed with brown and white granite. Over 100 palms stand closely grouped together. There is an intermittent small waterfall at the end of the grove. The bedrock mortar holes, which are the namesake of this canyon, are found about 300 feet downslope from the palms.

7.4   Turnoff southeast (left) leads to Cyd Hayden Spring.

Side Trip to Hayden Spring and Devils Canyon

0.0   Turnoff. Proceed southeast.

0.9   The remains of a cabin are 0.3 mile south (right) in a cove in the hills.

1.6   Cyd Hayden Spring is 0.7 mile south (right) up an arroyo.

3.8   The road has passed over a low saddle and into the bottom of Devils Canyon. This was the original route of the Mountain Springs cutoff from the Southern Emigrant Trail in the Yuha Desert over the mountains west to San Diego. Hikers may follow the old route up-canyon to the south and west (right) and under a bridge carrying Interstate 8 traffic westbound. The old cutoff trail climbed 1000 feet in 3.8 miles to Mountain Springs. The Stage Station Historical Marker is nearby.

        The jeep route turns northeast (left) down-canyon toward Sugarloaf Mountain and then north across the tracks to . . .

8.6   A junction with highway S-2 at Dos Cabezas Road.

End of Side Trip

7.7   Dos Cabezas Spring is located in a cove surrounded by fractured and decomposed old granites of the Jacumba Mountains which are covered with desert varnish and jumbled in piles along the mountainside. The area is reminiscent of Joshua Tree National Monument. From a distance two rock masses can be distinguished against the skyline above the spring. These distinct rock groupings account for the name of this area—Dos Cabezas, or Two Heads. Another set of "two heads" can be seen directly above the spring on the skyline as two huge, smooth brown boulders. The one on the right has an amazing profile, clearly showing a forehead, nose, mouth and chin, while the one on the left, though smooth and having no profile, is shaped well enough to be called a head. As one leaves the spring, it is apparent that these two rocks are but parts of a larger rock mass on the ridge crest. The climb up the steep slope to the top of the ridge where the Cabezas are located is strenuous, but the view is well worth it. The protection offered by the surrounding mountains and more ample underground water have produced a better-than-average stand of typical desert plants in this area. Desert willow is the predominant tree in this cove, while mesquite and sugarbush are also found. Both cholla and ocotillo literally cover the desert floor in this area. Dos Cabezas Primitive Campground will accommodate tents and pickup campers more readily than trailers. The campground has no toilets, no trash cans and no camping fee.

Trip 4F: Yuha Desert (Bureau of Land Management area) loop trip starting and
    ending at Ocotillo (32 miles one way; paved and dirt roads)

With Side Trips To: Davies Valley and Painted Gorge

Mileage from Ocotillo along:

Hiway 98	Hiway S-80	Checkpoint Description
0.0	32.0	Junction of Highway S-80 (old US Highway 80) and S-2 in Ocotillo. Proceed south under Interstate 8. Cross the abandoned San Diego and Arizona Eastern Railroad tracks to . . .
0.7	31.3	End of S-2, junction with Highway 98, the Yuha cutoff road. Turn east (left).
2.1	29.9	Clark Road.

Side Trip into Davies Valley (jeep road)

0.0   Turnoff from Highway 98, Proceed southwest (right) on Clark Road to . . .

1.6   Fork. The south (left) road enters Davies Canyon and leads to some mining prospects, but this is not the route into the valley. The west (right) road leads around a buttress and angles left into a broad canyon mouth which leads into . . .

4.4   Davies Valley. This is a picturesque valley in the rugged Jacumba Mountains. It is a good rockhounding area, with agate, petrified wood and garnet in relative abundance. Though not of gem quality, most specimens are polishable. This is a heavily used OHV area. OHVs are required to stay on existing roads. Lack of water limits backpacking, although it is a fairly popular day-hiking area. A distinct geologic formation in the valley area is an ancient volcano. The area contains a large variety of plant life and archeological evidence of recreational interest. Adjacent areas such as Pinto Canyon, Myer Valley and Skull Valley provide good opportunities for backcountry camping, exploring and other wildland experiences. Pinto Canyon has the only known petroglyphs in the Yuha area.

End of Side Trip

| 6.5 | 25.5 | Turnoff north (left) is Hocker Drive, or Anza Trail Road, to Vista de Anza and Yuha Basin. The loop trip turns north here. |

    Two miles farther east on the paved road is Coyote Road "B" and the Crucifixion Thorns area. This unique stand of this plant, located in a natural depression, is surrounded by a barbed-wire fence with a walkway entry on the northeast side. This site has probably the largest concentration of the crucifixion thorn plants in southern California. The plant (*Holacantha emoryi*) is relatively common in the desert basins of Arizona and Sonora and is found only in the deserts of North America. It is similar to the biblical "Crown of Thorns," hence its common name.

| 7.4 | 24.6 | Fork. The northeast (right) fork goes another 0.8 mile to Vista de Anza and an inoperative microwave-relay station one mile beyond, near the highpoint (elevation 531) of the Yuha Badlands. The microwave station is a prominent checkpoint visible from throughout the Yuha Basin. Vista de Anza historical monument is on the edge of the bluff overlooking the formidable Yuha Basin. Juan |

Hiway 98	Hiway S-80	Checkpoint Description

Bautista de Anza is believed to have passed over this spot during his first expedition from Sonora to California in 1774.

The bluff is a good place to orient oneself to the Yuha Basin. The basin is made up of low hills, intricately eroded alluvial badlands, and flat gravel terraces. The Yuha Intaglios and the Yuha Man site are both located on the gravel terraces along the western rim of the Yuha Basin. Yuha Well is located in the sand hummock on the north side of Yuha Wash, in the lower part of the basin. From this bluff the extensive oyster-shell beds of the Yuha Basin can be seen. These shells and other marine fossils were left behind by a sea that once covered the entire area. The Yuha Basin area is a popular area for collecting calcite and petrified shells. Specimens of limonite can be collected on the windblown surfaces of Yuha Wash. The road continues past Vista de Anza and the microwave relay station to rejoin Highway 98 4.6 miles from where it left that highway at mile 6.5 above.

The north fork (straight ahead) continues bearing right around the rim of the Yuha Basin past the Intaglio area. Intaglios are giant line drawings etched into the desert pavement by aboriginal Indians. They are the rarest type of prehistoric art created by native peoples of the California desert. Intaglios are also found along the Colorado River near Blythe and in four other sites in the Borrego area. Unfortunately, intaglios are most vulnerable to vehicle damage. In 1975 a section of the Yuha Intaglios was greatly damaged by one or more motorcycles running over it repeatedly in circular patterns. Portions of a metal fence surrounding the figure had been torn down and removed. This destruction was not a casual act of vandalism but a deliberate act of destruction according to a BLM official. REMINDER—vehicle travel on the rim of the Yuha Basin is permitted *only* on designated roads.

The loop route drops off the rim, now leading east to . . .

| 12.1 | 19.9 | Intersect another dirt road at the head of a valley which runs |

Intersect another dirt road at the head of a valley which runs northeast between the Yuha Buttes (vehicle travel prohibited in this valley). The Yuha Buttes contain a core of early Pliocene marine sediments surrounded by extensive deposits of Pliocene non-marine sands and outwash gravels. The shell beds to the east of Yuha Buttes are abundant with fossil marine oysters and other mollusk shells from the Pliocene epoch, dated about 3–5 million years ago in this area. These are reminders of the time when the Gulf of California inundated this area prior to the delta dam built by the Colorado River. The Yuha oysters (*Ostea heermanni*) and oyster reefs can also be found on the Coyote Mountains, Superstition Mountain and Signal Mountain.

One mile southwest (right) along this road is Yuha Well, where Anza camped in 1774 and again in 1776. The exact location of the six wells opened by Anza is unknown. The present well site is located north of the wash. It was near here on Dec. 9, 1776, that Father Pedro Font of the second Anza expedition pondered the many oyster shells found in the area.

I have come to surmise that in olden times the sea spread over all the land, and that in some of the great recessions which histories tell us about, it left these salty and sandy wastes uncovered . . . Indeed . . .

Hiway 98	Hiway S-80	Checkpoint Description
		one finds on the way many piles of oyster shells, mixed with the earth and half buried, and other shells and maritime signs. It is not possible that people should have made such mountains of shells by carrying them from the sea so great a distance merely to bury them in piles.

In 1901 San Diegans organized the Yuha Well Oil Co., installed a drilling rig and spudded in a well. Charles H. Swallow, then a San Diego County supervisor, was superintendent and general manager. After a year's prospecting they found no oil, and the project was abandoned. Ralph Jasper, who signed all waterholes around the turn of the century, was not able to find out the meaning of the term "Yuha" or who first applied it to the waterhole. In 1905 a pump and trough were installed for cattle.

The loop route turns north (left), climbing over the ridgeline of the Yuha Buttes and bearing northeast past several crossing routes to join . . .

14.6	17.4	The old San Diego Stage route. This was an alternate route branching from the emigrant trail for stagecoaches to San Diego by way of Mountain Springs. Turn east (right) to an . . .
18.3	13.7	Overpass over Interstate 8 at Dunaway Road.
19.8	12.2	Intersect Highway S-80 (old US 80), the Evan Hewes Highway. Turn west (left) along a paved road to . . .
23.0	9.0	Plaster City. The narrow-gauge Gypsum Mining Railroad interchanges with the truncated San Diego and Arizona Eastern Railroad here. The area north of Plaster City to the Naval Reservation boundary and west to the Coyote Mountains is designated "open" by BLM, allowing unrestricted OHV travel *except* along the Southern Emigrant Trail and the Butterfield Overland Mail route. The Plaster City area contains some collectible material from an ancient coral reef and fossil wood, but variety and desirability are lacking.
27.8	4.2	Turnoff north (right, dirt road, signed) leads to the popular Painted Gorge area on the southeast slope of the Coyote Mountains, which receives a significant amount of recreational use. This extraordinary canyon, with its brilliantly colored rock formations and narrow canyon walls, is used as a staging area for trips into the Plaster City Open Area by OHVs. For collectors, good rillensteine specimens can be found near the old marble quarry off Painted Gorge Road. This "worm-eaten" limestone is found in various shades of pink, yellow and lavender, and the supply is almost inexhaustible.

Side Trip into Painted Gorge

0.0   Turnoff on S-80, 4.8 miles west of Plaster City and 4.2 miles past several gravel pits and quarries.

5.3   Fork. The north fork (straight ahead, jeep route) leads about 5 miles to join the old Butterfield Overland stage route at the Naval Reservation Boundary. The stage route can be followed about 9 miles southeast to Plaster City.

The west fork (left, dirt road) leads into Painted Gorge to . . .

7.4   End of vehicle travel. Hikers can explore the fascinating canyons and cliffs beyond.

End of Side Trip

Hiway 98	Hiway S-80	Checkpoint Description
28.5	3.5	This highway bridge was washed out by Hurricane Kathleen in 1976, and it was not restored for more than a year. This point is the confluence of Palm Canyon Wash, which drains the Dos Cabezas/Mortero Canyon area, and Coyote Wash, which drains the In-Ko-Pah Gorge/Myer Valley/Davies Valley/Ocotillo area. Hurricane floods from the latter drainage in both 1976 and 1977 severed Interstate 8 in several places, interrupting travel on this vital artery between Imperial Valley and San Diego. Three drownings in the Ocotillo area in 1976 were attributed to Kathleen's torrential waters. These again are a tragic reminder to the desert explorer of the very real hazards of flash floods in the desert.
29.0	3.0	View of the abandoned San Diego and Arizona Eastern Railroad. The tracks here were suspended in midair where the Coyote Wash trestle was washed out in 1976.
32.0	0.0	Junction of S-2 and S-80 in Ocotillo.

SD&AE Railroad tracks washed out by Hurricane Kathleen in 1976

Natural Features

The oldest rock bodies found in the region are metasediments dating from the early Paleozoic Era, about 500 million years ago. They are exposed in the Coyote Mountains in the southern end of the park.

Volcanic eruptions occurred in the Miocene Epoch, laying down a sheet of lava in the Dos Cabezas, Jacumba Valley and Carrizo Impact areas. This is recorded in a rock layer called Alverson andesite, which has been dated as 20.4 million years old. Remnants of the lava flow are particularly striking in the red and black rocks of the Volcanic Hills in Jojoba Wash and just west of the Imperial Highway monument.

Fossil sites within the Vallecito, Fish Creek and Carrizo badlands areas are particularly outstanding. Theodore Downs, curator of vertebrate paleontology at the Los Angeles County Museum, has called these sites "one of the most remarkably complete sequences of animal life to be found anywhere in the world." What makes the area so outstanding is the way in which the sedimentary layers have been tilted and eroded, revealing an orderly progression of fossil remains in a 10-mile segment from Split Mountain (the oldest and lowest layer) southwest to Canebrake Canyon (most recent).

The oldest exposed rocks in the Split Mountain area are found in the Anza Formation. This is an alluvial-fan deposit consisting of red, coarse-grained sandstone-and-boulder conglomerate. It underlies the Split Mountain Formation and is middle Miocene in age, over 12 million years old. The Split Mountain Formation is dated late Miocene to early Pliocene. It consists of four distinct layers. From bottom (oldest) to top (youngest) they are: (1) localized deposits of conglomerate

Fish Creek Badlands—dark cappings on hills at upper left and center right are fossil oyster-shell reefs

(bouldery stream sediments), (2) gypsum beds (these mark the area's first marine deposition; a shallow sea formed, then later evaporated, leaving gypsum deposits), (3) sandstone—a marine turbidite (underwater "landslide") bed with a few marine trace fossils in it, and (4) additional, localized turbidite deposits.

The Imperial Formation (Pliocene, 4–5 million years old) contains marine claystone and sandstone, oyster-shell reefs, mollusks and some corrals, which are located south of Split Mountain and in the Coyote Mountains.

The Palm Spring Formation (late Pliocene, 3–4 million years ago, through early Pleistocene, 1½–2 million years ago) contains terrestrial sandstones and claystone with fragments of silicified wood. This formation is found in upper Fish Creek, Arroyo Seco del Diablo, Arroyo Tapiado, Deguynos Canyon, east of Canyon Sin Nombre and south of the Mud Hills.

The Canebrake Conglomerate (middle Pleistocene, 700,000 to 2 million years ago) consists of a conglomerate of granitic and metamorphic debris, which is a coarse form of the Palm Spring Formation. It is found on the southeast slope of the Vallecito Mountains, at Vallecito Creek and in the west end of the Coyote Mountains.

An abundance of terrestrial fossils from the Pleistocene Epoch found in both the Palm Spring Formation and the Canebrake Conglomerate indicate that a grassland with wooded areas and streams once existed in this region. Camels, mastodons, sabertooth cats, musk oxen, ground sloths and horses roamed in this area while various birds roosted and nested in the trees. Among the most spectacular birds was the *Teratornis incredibilis,* a condorlike vulture with a wing span of 17 feet. Over 100 species of fossil mammals, birds, reptiles, amphibians and invertebrates have been recorded in this region.

During the same (Pleistocene) epoch from which many of the vertebrate fossils date, active faults in the area began breaking up the Peninsular Ranges into their present form. The Elsinore Fault created a natural path from Rodriguez Canyon, through Mason Valley, Vallecito Valley, and Mountain Palm Springs to the Coyote Mountains, which became the route of the overland trail. A spur of the Elsinore Fault runs to Agua Caliente Hot Springs, where it has allowed the hot springs to surface. Another fault in the area is the Earthquake Valley Fault through Harper and Hapaha Flats, which is the path followed by the popular Pinyon Mountain Road. Yet another major fault created Carrizo Canyon, the route of the San Diego and Arizona Eastern Railroad.

Cultural Features

There's a valley I know in the wastelands
 Where, down through the greasewood and sage,
Like a dim, ghostly thread from the years that have fled,
 Stretch the tracks of the Overland Stage.

Lone, ghostly and dim in the starlight;
 Grey, desolate and pale in the dawn,
Blurred by heat-waves at noon—still o'er mesa and dune
 Wind the tracks of the wheels that have gone.

Old coaches whose wheels long have mouldered,
  Old stage-teams whose hoofs long are dust;
Still, faint and age-greyed, wind the old wheel-ruts made
  By tires long since crumbled to rust.
And down where the silence lies deepest—
  Like a lone, crumbling bead on a thread—
In the mesquite-grown sands the old stage-station stands,
  Hushed with memories—and ghosts of the dead.
The desert rays wake not its brooding.
  But oft 'neath the star-powered sky,
Round the walls on dark nights there move dim, ghostly lights,
  As once more the old stages sweep by.
And again, across dune, wash and mesa,
  As the dead years turn back on their page,
Pass the dim, racing teams from a ghost-world of dreams,
  Down the tracks of the Overland Stage.

Thus wrote Marshal South, itinerant poet and writer who for many years lived with his family in Indian primitiveness atop Ghost Mountain overlooking the tracks of the Southern Emigrant Trail and the Butterfield Overland Mail route. Although it has been over 100 years since the last stage rolled along this once-major thoroughfare, still the drama and excitement of the period of history remain alive in this desert where little of the surrounding landscape has changed.

It was not until the Mexican War that the loneliness and isolation along Vallecito and Carrizo creeks was broken. Although a few Spaniards and Mexicans had crossed this desert before, their impact had been negligible. Then the silent peacefulness was permanently shattered beginning with Gen. Stephen Watts Kearny and his Army of the West. In November 1846 guide Kit Carson led them from New Mexico to California through the Carrizo Corridor and along Vallecito Creek to Mason Valley, Box Canyon and San Felipe Valley. Several weeks later Kearny was followed by Lt. Col. Philip St. George Cooke and his Mormon Battalion, whose primary objective was to blaze a wagon road to California from Council Bluffs, Iowa, via Santa Fe, New Mexico. In doing this they became the first group to make a passage by wagon across the southern desert to California.

Like Kearny, Cooke's battalion of men found the journey across the Colorado Desert very difficult, well earning the name of *Jornada del muerto* (journey of death). Diaries describe the desert crossing as littered with the carcasses of dead animals that dropped from exhaustion and thirst.

The most crucial part of the journey came when the battalion reached the rocky chasm of Box Canyon on Jan. 19, 1847. The passage was too narrow for the wagons, and the battalion had lost all its picks, shovels, and spades while crossing the Colorado River. The men were exhausted—many of them were even shoeless, having worn out their shoes crossing the desert. With no other choice, the men began hacking away at rocky walls with only hand axes. The first wagon had to be completely disassembled and carried through the chasm. The second one was carried through, and after more hours of work the remaining wagons were rolled through with their loads undisturbed. The battalion continued on to San Felipe and joined Gen. Kearny's forces in San Diego 10 days later.

Soon after the discovery of gold in California in 1848, Cooke's wagon road became known as the Southern Emigrant Trail. Over the next several years literally thousands of people flocked to California along this all-weather route.

In November and December of 1853, the Southern Pacific Railway Survey, headed by Lt. R.S. Williamson, surveyed the Southern Emigrant Trail and surrounding areas for a proposed Southern Pacific railroad. But after a thorough investigation they found the route too impracticable for a railroad and recommended San Gorgonio Pass to the north as a better route. There were other plans for the Southern Emigrant Trail.

In 1856 Congress passed a bill creating the first overland mail and passenger service between California and the East, linking San Francisco with St. Louis. On June 22, 1857, the US Postmaster awarded a contract to James E. Birch for his San Antonio to San Diego Overland Mail line, a carrier that covered 1476 miles in 30 days between San Antonio, Texas, and San Diego, California, via the Carrizo Corridor and over the Cuyamaca Mountains by way of Oriflamme Canyon.

The service was superseded in 1858 by the inauguration of the Butterfield Overland Mail, which was designed to carry mail and passengers from Missouri to San Francisco. The route followed by the Butterfield stages was also through the Carrizo Corridor and Vallecito, but instead of going over the Cuyamaca Mountains to San Diego, the stages proceeded through the San Felipe Valley to Warner's Ranch and Temecula and then on to Los Angeles.

In 1858 the major desert stations in the lower Colorado Desert included Fort Yuma, Pilot Knob, Cooke's Well, Alamo Mocho, Indian Wells and Carrizo. The last few miles to Carrizo were the hardest. A special postal inspector who rode over the route in 1858 made note of the great numbers of abandoned wagons, carcasses and whitening bones near Carrizo Creek which had been left by emigrants in preceding years. Carrizo was the first stop where a traveler could see something green growing in the desert. It was an important change station, located at a tule marsh which was a major surfacing pool for the underground waters flowing down from the mountains to the west. The marsh was choked with bayonetlike tules and ringed with creosote bush, burroweed and mesquite.

The mail road continued west up Carrizo Creek for about 2½ miles, following a fairly straight course. When it met the Vallecito drainage coming in from the northwest, the ruts turned up this sandy wash to reach the Palm Spring Oasis.

The Palm Spring station was built beside an all-year fresh-water spring on the edge of the badlands halfway between Carrizo and Vallecito. Before the station was built, a grove of tall palms grew around the spring and the oasis was a favorite resting place for soldiers, emigrants and mountain men. But by the time the station was built in 1858, all the palms had been chopped down to feed traveler's campfires.

The next station, which has been restored and is now a San Diego County Park, was Vallecito, located in a fairly long and narrow valley couched between the rocky buttresses of the Pinyon, Vallecito and Tierra Blanca ranges. The station was located near the rim of a marsh on a little rise of land. Water in this marsh under the white foothills of the Tierra Blancas has always been abundant, rising in small pools among the clumps of long marsh grass, disappearing in summer but always near enough to the surface to be obtained with a little digging. Vallecito was the last outpost of civilization, the jumping-off point for those going east.

After leaving Vallecito, west-bound stages wound up and over the small pass between Vallecito and Mason Valley and went up the valley to enter the narrow opening of Box Canyon, which led up to Blair Valley. The road continued across the white playa over a little pass to Earthquake Valley and to the San Felipe station in San Felipe Valley, 18 miles northwest of Vallecito. From here it was a straight, gentle climb to Oak Grove and Warner's Ranch along the route now followed by the Pacific Crest Trail.

The overland mail ceased running along the southern route in 1861 due to the beginning of the Civil War, and with the coming of the railroad the old emigrant road and Butterfield Overland Mail route became virtually a ghost trail.

And ghosts this trail does have.

There is a phantom stage that is reportedly seen on occasion on the old Butterfield route between Carrizo and Vallecito, as well as a white horse and a lady in white who roam the desert around the old Vallecito stage station.

According to legend, the stagecoach was robbed and the driver killed, yet it still tried to make its way to Vallecito. In the story of the white horse, four bandits robbed the Butterfield stage of $65,000 and then road toward Vallecito. Two of the bandits were shot and killed. The remaining two bandits buried the money before reaching Vallecito. There they quarrelled, and finally shot and killed each other. Since then, whenever someone gets near the buried treasure, the ghost of the leader's white horse is said to appear, gallop across the sand, and then disappear as it gets near. Once the horse appears, legend has it, it is futile to look for the treasure because the phantom has erased all traces of the cache.

The apparition of the lady in white at Vallecito is said to be the ghost of a young woman who had been riding the stage from somewhere in the East en route to Sacramento. She arrived at Vallecito ill and weak from the rigors of the trip, and her condition worsened and she died. When her baggage was opened, a white dress, which was to have been her wedding gown, was found. She was dressed in the gown and buried near the station. It is said that she frequently arises from her grave to wander restlessly about the station.

To walk the old emigrant trail or the Butterfield road today or to visit the restored Vallecito Station is to capture a little of the past, where even the ghosts may be real.

Bibliography

General

Anza-Borrego Desert State Park. Collection of information sheets, correspondence and miscellaneous material. Park Archives in Visitor Center

Borrego Sun. 1949–1985.

Bureau of Land Management, Yuha Desert Unit. Collection of information sheets and miscellaneous material. El Centro office.

Fairchild, Frank, and Merle E. Beckman. "Unit History, Anza-Borrego Desert State Park." Compiled by Merle E. Beckman. ABDSP headquarters.

Lindsay, Diana E. "Anza-Borrego Desert: The Story of the Nation's Largest State Park." Unpublished master's thesis, California State University, San Diego, 1973.

——. *Our Historic Desert: The Story of the Anza-Borrego Desert.* San Diego: Copley Books, 1973.

——, and Lowell E. Lindsay. Collection of correspondence, ranger patrol reports, miscellaneous material and interviews. Authors' files.

Welch, Jack P. Ranger Patrol Reports. Authors' files.

Outdoor Skill

Adolph, E.F., and Associates. *Physiology of Man in the Desert.* New York: Interscience Publishers, 1947.

Cepek, Dick, and Walt Wheelock. *Rough Riding.* Glendale: La Siesta Press, 1968.

Nelson, Dick, and Sharon Nelson. *Desert Survival.* Glenwood, Arizona: Tecolote Press, 1977.

Olsen, Larry Dean. *Outdoor Survival Skills.* Provo: Brigham Young University Press, 1967.

Mandolf, Henry I., ed. *Basic Mountaineering.* San Diego: San Diego Chapter of the Sierra Club, 1970.

Winnett, Thomas. *Backpacking Basics.* Berkeley: Wilderness Press, 1988.

Trail Guides and Area Descriptions

California, Department of Parks and Recreation, Resources Agency. "Borrego Palm Canyon Nature Trail Guide." November 1977.

——. "Elephant Trees Discovery Trail." April 1982.

——. "Erosion Road." February 1976.

——. "Narrows Earth Trail." March 1975.

——. "Riding Trails of Coyote Canyon." n.d.

——. "Seventeen Palms." n.d.

——. "Southern Emigrant Trail." December 1970.

Chase, J. Smeaton. *California Desert Trails.* New York: Houghton Mifflin Co., 1919.

Cowan, Ernie. "Anza-Borrego's Forbidden Canyons." *Desert Magazine,* XXXIV (April 1971) 12–14.

——. "Anza-Borrego's Scrapbook Trail." *Desert Magazine,* XXXVI (August 1973), 15–17, 40–41.

Ford, Walter. "San Felipe Hills." *Desert Magazine,* XXXIII (April 1970), 23–25.

Henderson, Randall. *On Desert Trails Today and Yesterday.* Los Angeles: Westernlore Press, 1961.

——. "Palm Oasis in Mortero Canyon." *Desert Magazine,* IV (November 1940), 17–20.

——. "Palms of the Carrizo Country." *Desert Magazine,* X (April 1947), 19–22.

——. "Vanishing Oasis of Palm Wash." *Desert Magazine,* VIII (August 1945), 9–12.

——. "Where Anza Blazed the First Trail." *Desert Magazine,* II (April 1939), 18–23.

——. "Wild Palms of the San Ysidros." *Desert Magazine,* VIII (July 1945), 17–22.

Leetch, George. "A Trip to Indian Country." *Borrego Sun* (March 18, 1976), 15.

——. "Desert Adventure with 4-Wheel Drive." *Borrego Sun* (January 8, 1976), 10–11.

——. "Gold-Rush Ghosts Ride Chariot Canyon." *Borrego Sun* (May 19, 1973), 13.

——. "Jasper Trail Artifacts Take You Back 5,000 Years." *Borrego Sun* (December 30, 1972), 10.

——. "Pinyon Area Trip Divides Men, Boys at Big 'Drop-Off'" *Borrego Sun* (February 24, 1973), 6.

——. "Sandstone: Queen of the Desert Washes." *Borrego Sun* (March 31, 1977), 7, 10.

Livesay, Harry D. *Horseman's Guide to California Trail Riding.* Norco: BanCog Publications, 1983.

Parker, Horace. *Anza-Borrego Desert Guide Book.* Edited by George and Jean Leetch. Revised edition. Borrego Springs: Anza-Borrego Desert Natural History Association, 1979.

Robinson, John W. *San Bernardino Mountain Trails.* Fourth edition. Berkeley: Wilderness Press, 1986.

Schaffer, Jeffrey P. et al. *The Pacific Crest Trail, Volume I: California.* Fourth edition. Berkeley: Wilderness Press, 1989.

Schad, Jerry. *Afoot and Afield in San Diego County.* Berkeley: Wilderness Press, 1986.

Natural History

Anza-Borrego Desert Natural History Association. "Birds in the Anza-Borrego Desert State Park." November 1983.

——. "Mammals of Anza-Borrego Desert State Park." 1980.

——. "Reptiles of Anza-Borrego Desert State Park." 1980.

Bean, Lowell John, and Katherine Siva Saubel. *Temalpakh: Cahuilla Indian Knowledge and Usage of Plants.* Morongo Indian Reservation: Malki Museum Press, 1972.

Blackwelder, Eliot. "Geomorphic Processes in the Desert." *Geology of Southern California.* Edited by Richard H. Jahns. California Division of Mines, Bulletin No. 170. San Francisco: California Division of Mines, 1954.

Bowers, Stephen. *Reconnaissance of the Colorado Desert Mining District.* California State Mining Bureau. Sacramento: A.J. Johnston, Superintendent State Printing, 1901.

California. Department of Parks and Recreation. Resources Agency. "Anza-Borrego Desert State Park Mammals, Reptiles and Amphibians." Compiled by Ernest Brown. Revised January 1969.

——. "Flowers, Trees, and Ferns of Anza-Borrego Desert State Park." Compiled by Dalton E. Merkel. May 1965.

Collection of miscellaneous educational materials on desert flora, fauna and geology. San Diego Museum of Natural History. Education Department.

Cornett, Jim. *Wildlife of the Southwest Deserts*. Desert Hot Springs, California: Nature Trails Press, 1975.

Dibblee, Jr., T.W. "Geology of the Imperial Valley Region, California." *Geology of Southern California*. Edited by Richard H. Jahns. California Division of Mines. Bulletin No. 170. San Francisco: California Division of Mir es, 1954.

Downs, Theodore. *Fossil Vertebrates of Southern California*. Berkeley: University of California Press, 1968.

——, and John A. White. "A Vertebrate Faunal Succession in Superposed Sediments from Late Pliocene to Middle Pleistocene in California." *Report of the 23rd International Geological Congress*. Edited by Miroslav Malkovsky. X. Prague, Czechoslovakia: published by the Congress, 1968.

Durham, J. Wyatt. "The Marine Cenozoic of Southen California." *Geology of Southern California*. Edited by Richard H. Jahns. California Division of Mines, Bulletin No. 170. San Francisco: California Division of Mines, 1954.

Hilton, John. "Mining for Gunsights." *Desert Magazine,* XIII (October, 1950), 5–8.

Hinds, Norman E. A. *Evolution of the California Landscape*. California Division of Mines, Bulletin No. 158. San Francisco: California Division of Mines, 1952.

Jaeger, Edmund C. *Denizens of the Desert, A Book of Southwestern Mammals, Birds, and Reptiles*. New York: Houghton Mifflin Co., 1922.

—— . *Desert Wild Flowers*. Stanford: Stanford University Press, 1941.

—— . *The California Deserts*. 3rd ed. Stanford: Stanford University Press, 1955.

Jahns, Richard H. "Investigations and Problems of Southern California Geology." *Geology of Southern California*. Edited by Richard H. Jahns. California Division of Mines, Bulletin No. 170, San Francisco: California Division of Mines, 1954.

Laudermilk, J.D. "The Rillensteine Case." *Desert Magazine,* IV (December 1940), 10–12.

Lindsay, Diana E. "Elephants of Anza-Borrego." *Desert Magazine,* XXXVII (January 1974), 8–11.

Munz, Philip A. *California Desert Wildflowers*. Berkeley: University of California Press, 1969.

Sharp, Robert P. *Geology: Field Guide to Southern California*. Dubuque: Wm. C. Brown Co., 1972.

Stewart, Richard M. "Geology and Mineral Resources of Anza-Borrego Desert State Park." Division of Mines. San Francisco: October, 1956.

Went, Frits W. "The Ecology of Desert Plants." *Scientific American,* CXCII (April 1955), 20, 68–75.

Woodard, Geoffrey D. "Geologic Notes." *American Association of Petroleum Geologists Bulletin,* LVIII, 3 (March, 1974), 521–539.

Cultural History

Bailey, Philip A. *Golden Mirages*. New York: The Macmillan Co., 1949.

Bean, Lowell John. *Mukat's People: The Cahuilla Indians of Southern California*. Berkeley: University of California Press, 1972.

Bolton, Herbert Eugene, trans. and ed. *Anza's California Expeditions*. 5 vols. Berkeley: University of California Press, 1930.

Botts, Myrtle. *History of Julian.* Julian, California: Julian Historical Society, 1964.

Childers, W.M. "Preliminary Report on the Yuha Burial, California." *Anthropological Journal of Canada,* XII, 1 (1974), 2–9.

Conkling, Roscoe P. and Margaret B. *The Butterfield Overland Mail 1857–1869, Its organization and operation over the Southern Route to 1861; subsequently over the Central Route to 1866; and under Wells, Fargo and Company in 1869.* 3 vols. Glendale: The Arthur H. Clark Co., 1947.

Cooke, Philip St. George. *The Conquest of New Mexico and California: An Historical and Personal Narrative.* New York: G.P. Putnam's Sons, 1878.

Fages, Pedro. "The Colorado River Campaign, 1781–1782." Edited by Herbert Ingram Priestly. *Publications* (Academy of Pacific Coast History), III (May, 1913), 133–233.

Gifford, Edward Winslow. *Clans and Moieties of Southern California.* Publications in American Archaeology and Ethnology, Vol XIV. Berkeley: University of California Press, 1918.

——. *The Kamia of Imperial Valley.* U.S. Bureau of American Ethnology. Bulletin No. 97. Washington, D.C.: Government Printing Office, 1931.

Heizer, R.F., and M.A. Whipple. *The California Indians, A Source Book.* Second edition. Los Angeles: University of California Press, 1971.

Humphreys, Alfred Glen. "Thomas L. (Peg-leg) Smith." *The Mountain Men and the Fur Trade of the Far West: Biographical Sketches of the Participants by Scholars of the Subject.* Edited by Leroy R. Hafen. 8 vols. Glendale: The Arthur H. Clark Co., 1966.

James, George Wharton, *The Wonders of the Colorado Desert.* 2 vols. Boston: Little Brown, and Co., 1906.

Kroeber, A.L. *Handbook of the Indians of California.* U.S. Bureau of American Ethnology. Bulletin No. 78. Washington, D.C.: Government Printing Office, 1925.

Moriarty, James Robert III. "The San Dieguito Complex: Suggested Environmental and Cultural Relationships." *Anthropological Journal of Canada,* VII, 3 (1969), 1–16.

Pourade, Richard F. *Ancient Hunters of the Far West.* San Diego: The Union-Tribune Publishing Co., 1966.

Reed, Lester. *Old Time Cattlemen and Other Pioneers of the Anza-Borrego Area.* Hemet: Hungry Eye Books, 1980.

Rensch, Hero Eugene. "Fages' Crossing of the Cuyamacas." *California Historical Society Quarterly,* XXXIV (March 1955), 193–208.

——. "Woods' Shorter Mountain Trail to San Diego." *California Historical Society Quarterly,* XXXVI (June 1957), 117–132.

South, Marshal. "Tracks of the Overland Stage." *Desert Magazine,* XI (November, 1947), 11.

Spier, Leslie. *Southern Diegueño Customs.* Publications in American Archaeology and Ethnology, Vol. XX. Berkeley: University of California Press, 1923.

Strong, William Duncan. *Aboriginal Society in Southern California.* Publications of American Archaeology and Ethnology, Vol. XXVI. Berkeley: University of California Press, 1929.

Templeton, Sardis W. *The Lame Captain: The Life and Adventures of Pegleg Smith.* Los Angeles: Westernlore Press, 1965.

Treganza, Adan E. "Possibilities of an Aboriginal Practice of Agriculture Among the Southern Diegueño." *American Antiquity,* XII (January 1947), 169–173.

U.S., Department of Interior, Bureau of Land Management. California Desert Planning Program. *Background to Prehistory of the Yuha Desert Region,* by Margaret L. Weide and James P. Barker. Contract No. 52500-CT4-296(N). June 30, 1974.

Wallace, William J. and Edith S. Taylor. "The Surface Archeology of Indian Hill, Anza-Borrego Desert State Park, California." *The Masterkey,* XXXIV (January-March 1960), 4–18.

Welch, Jack P. "The Butterfield Overland Mail." *News and Views,* XX (June 1963), 1a–24a.

Williams, Brad, and Choral Pepper. *Lost Legends of the West.* New York: Holt, Rinehart and Winston, 1970.

Woodward, Arthur. "Oasis at Vallecito." *Desert Magazine,* V (March 1942) 22–26.

Mountain Palm Springs